Oklahoma Legal Research

Carolina Academic Press
Legal Research Series

Suzanne E. Rowe, Series Editor

Arizona, Second Edition — Tamara S. Herrera

Arkansas — Coleen M. Barger

California, Second Edition — Hether C. Macfarlane, Aimee Dudovitz & Suzanne E. Rowe

Colorado — Robert Michael Linz

Connecticut — Jessica G. Hynes

Federal — Mary Garvey Algero, Spencer L. Simons, Suzanne E. Rowe, Scott Childs & Sarah E. Ricks

Florida, Third Edition, Revised Printing — Barbara J. Busharis & Suzanne E. Rowe

Georgia — Nancy P. Johnson, Elizabeth G. Adelman & Nancy J. Adams

Idaho — Tenielle Fordyce-Ruff & Suzanne E. Rowe

Illinois, Second Edition — Mark E. Wojcik

Iowa — John D. Edwards, M. Sara Lowe, Karen L. Wallace & Melissa H. Weresh

Kansas — Joseph A. Custer & Christopher L. Steadham

Kentucky — William A. Hilyerd, Kurt X. Metzmeier & David J. Ensign

Louisiana, Second Edition — Mary Garvey Algero

Massachusetts — E. Joan Blum

Michigan, Second Edition — Pamela Lysaght & Cristina D. Lockwood

Minnesota — Suzanne Thorpe

Missouri, Second Edition — Wanda M. Temm & Julie M. Cheslik

New York, Second Edition — Elizabeth G. Adelman, Theodora Belniak & Suzanne E. Rowe

North Carolina — Scott Childs

Ohio — Katherine L. Hall & Sara Sampson

Oklahoma — Darin K. Fox, Darla W. Jackson & Courtney L. Selby

Oregon, Second Edition, Revised Printing — Suzanne E. Rowe

Pennsylvania — Barbara J. Busharis & Bonny L. Tavares

Tennessee — Sibyl Marshall & Carol McCrehan Parker

Texas, Revised Printing — Spencer L. Simons

Washington, Second Edition — Julie Heintz-Cho, Tom Cobb & Mary A. Hotchkiss

West Virginia — Hollee Schwartz Temple

Wisconsin — Patricia Cervenka & Leslie Behroozi

Wyoming — Debora Person & Tawnya Plumb

Oklahoma Legal Research

Darin K. Fox
Darla W. Jackson
Courtney L. Selby

Suzanne E. Rowe, Series Editor

Carolina Academic Press
Durham, North Carolina

Library of Congress Cataloging-in-Publication Data

Fox, Darin K.
Oklahoma legal research / Darin K. Fox, Darla Jackson, Courtney Selby.
pages cm. -- (Legal research series)
Includes bibliographical references and index.
ISBN 978-1-61163-134-0 (alk. paper)
1. Legal research--Oklahoma. I. Jackson, Darla. II. Selby, Courtney. III. Title.

KFO1275.F69 2013
340.072'0766--dc23

2013014907

CAROLINA ACADEMIC PRESS
700 Kent Street
Durham, North Carolina 27701
Telephone (919) 489-7486
Fax (919) 493-5668
www.cap-press.com

Printed in the United States of America.

Dedicated

to Albert O. Brecht,
my mentor and friend.
—D.K.F.

and to Richard E. Ducey,
with gratitude and love.
—C.L.S.

and to family
(Nathan, Jacob, and Scott),
my inspiration and support.
—D.W.J.

Summary of Contents

Contents

List of Tables and Figures

Tables

Figures

Series Note

The Legal Research Series published by Carolina Academic Press includes titles from states around the country as well as a separate text on federal legal research. The goal of each book is to provide law students, practitioners, paralegals, college students, laypeople, and librarians with the essential elements of legal research in each jurisdiction. Unlike more bibliographic texts, the Legal Research Series books seek to explain concisely both the sources of state law research and the process for conducting legal research effectively.

Preface and Acknowledgments

This book is the first publication to explore comprehensively both the sources of Oklahoma and tribal law and the best strategies to employ when researching that law. It will be valuable to a wide range of audiences, from novices to seasoned legal researchers.

Writing the book was a collaborative effort, although each author took a leading role in various chapters. Darin Fox was the primary author for the chapters dealing with online legal research, secondary sources, researching judicial opinions, and legal citation. Darla Jackson was the primary author for the chapters on judicial opinions, statutory research, legislative process and history, administrative law, and tribal law. Courtney Selby was the primary author for the chapters on research process and legal analysis, the Oklahoma constitution, citators, and research strategies and organization.

Many people contributed to the development and completion of this book and we gratefully acknowledge their contributions. For substantive and editorial review of the text, we thank Suzanne Rowe. For guidance and shared expertise in some of the details and nuances of Oklahoma legal research, we appreciate Melanie Nelson, Lee Peoples, Joel Wegemer, and Jennifer Gerrish. For proofreading and offering continuing support of our efforts, we are grateful to Jill Markman, Elaine Bradshaw, Katie Brown, Marilyn Nicely, and Jennifer Prilliman. Finally, we would like to thank the entire staffs of the University of Oklahoma Law Library, the Oklahoma City University Law Library, and the University of Tulsa Mabee Legal Information Center for their support.

We recognize Bloomberg Law, Fastcase, W.S. Hein & Co., LexisNexis, the Oklahoma State Court Network, and Thomson Reuters for permission to reproduce portions of their online and print products in this work. Due to the small size of this book, some screens have been cropped and some page excerpts slightly modified. Please note that further reproduction is prohibited.

Darin K. Fox
Darla W. Jackson
Courtney L. Selby
July 2013

Oklahoma Legal Research

Chapter 1

The Research Process and Legal Analysis

I. Oklahoma Legal Research

While the fundamentals of legal research are similar in any American jurisdiction, it is the savvy researcher's intimate knowledge of the unique nature of the law and legal resources in the relevant jurisdiction that will truly set her apart from her peers. Thus, this book focuses both on critical legal analysis skills as well as on the specialized knowledge required to conduct exceptional legal research in Oklahoma. This book is designed for use by seasoned attorneys revisiting less familiar areas of Oklahoma law, as well as those who are brand new to Oklahoma law and legal research.

II. The Intersection of Legal Research and Legal Analysis

Mastery of legal research and legal analysis are inextricably linked, and exceptional lawyering requires that both of these arts be practiced with diligence, care, and attention to detail. Thus, while this book focuses on the process of conducting legal research in Oklahoma, it necessarily includes critically important discussions of the legal analysis required to move through the research process successfully.

To better understand the phrase "legal analysis," consider some of the questions that may arise as lawyers use this important skill in research. After learning the facts of any problem that requires legal research, a lawyer begins the research process by analyzing the facts to identify the questions presented in the problem. Engaging in this legal analysis requires that the lawyer make informed decisions about the types of authorities to consult and the format in which to consult them. After choosing a legal authority, the lawyer will search in an index or the full text of documents for specific terms; which terms he uses and how he searches will be informed by the way in which he analyzed the problem and articulated the research questions. Determining which of the search results speak most directly to the questions presented is also a product of legal analysis. Thus, while the focus of this book is the process of legal research, the companion skill of legal analysis will necessarily be included in the discussion.

III. Types of Legal Authority

The fundamental goal of every legal research project is to discover controlling authority in the appropriate jurisdiction that will aid in determining how the legal questions at issue should be resolved. The best way to achieve this aim is first to know which authorities are controlling given the problem you seek to resolve, and then to determine if those authorities are relevant to the issues at hand.

The authorities that have the power to control the outcome of a legal dispute are called primary authorities. Simply stated, primary authority is the law itself. Primary authorities include constitutions, statutes, regulations, case law, administrative decisions, and rules of evidence and procedure. Primary authorities are "created by a branch of the government acting in its lawmaking capacity," be they judicial decisions, legislative enactments, or administrative rules or decisions.[1]

In contrast to primary authorities, secondary sources consist of commentary about the law. However, secondary sources never have the power to control the outcome of a legal dispute. They can be

1. Christina L. Kunz et al., *The Process of Legal Research* 7 (7th ed. 2008).

more or less persuasive, but they are never controlling. Secondary sources include law review articles, American Law Reports annotations, treatises, legal encyclopedias, Restatements, looseleaf services, and other forms of explanatory work about the law. Secondary sources serve to help a researcher understand and interpret principles of law, find citations to primary authorities, and gather practical advice about handling particular types of legal matters. Secondary sources are considered by many to be some of the most valuable and underutilized resources in legal research.

In addition to understanding the distinction between primary and secondary authorities, a researcher must understand whether these authorities are mandatory or persuasive. "Mandatory authority, which can also be called binding authority, refers to authority that the court is obligated to follow."[2] It is critical to remember that only primary authorities can be mandatory. In contrast, persuasive authorities are those that may influence or persuade the court, but by which the court is not bound. Both primary and secondary authorities can be persuasive.

In order to determine whether a particular authority is mandatory or persuasive, the savvy researcher will undertake a straightforward analysis. The first part of a mandatory/persuasive analysis consists of determining whether a particular resource is primary or secondary. As noted, only primary authorities can be mandatory. Thus, if the source in hand is secondary, it is necessarily a persuasive authority. If the source in question is a primary authority, an additional layer of analysis is required. Only authorities that are binding on the court that has jurisdiction over the dispute will be mandatory. In all matters of Oklahoma law, the Oklahoma Constitution, Oklahoma state statutes, and Oklahoma administrative regulations are binding. Oklahoma's judicial decisions require a slightly more careful review because of the unique court structure of the state, and the analysis will be slightly different depending on whether the nature of the case is civil or criminal.[3]

2. Amy E. Sloan, *Basic Legal Research: Tools and Strategies* 5 (5th ed. 2012).

3. Melanie Nelson, *Oklahoma Court Opinions and Their Precedential Value* (unpublished guide, 2011) (copy on file with the Law Library at the Maurice A. Deane School of Law at Hofstra University).

Supreme Court opinions designated for publication as formal opinions have precedential value and are mandatory authority. Those opinions issued by the Court of Civil Appeals that are approved for publication by the Supreme Court have the same precedential value as a Supreme Court opinion.[4] Opinions that issue from the Court of Civil Appeals designated as "Released for Publication by Order of the Court of Civil Appeals" have only persuasive value unless approved for publication by the Supreme Court.[5] Opinions designated "Released for Publication by Order of the Court of Civil Appeals" are persuasive evidence of the way the appellate courts will interpret the law on a given issue. Thus, their strong persuasive value is recognized not only by the Oklahoma Supreme Court, but also by the Tenth Circuit Court of Appeals in cases where state law controls the issue.[6]

Opinions from Court of Civil Appeals that are not designated as "Released for Publication by Order of the Court of Civil Appeals" are considered unpublished. Oklahoma Supreme Court Rule 1.200(b) (5) provides that unpublished opinions are not citable in briefs, or other supporting documents submitted to a court, except in very limited circumstances such as claims of res judicata, or other claims that would prevent re-litigation of the same issues of the final decision of a case.

Regarding criminal matters, the Oklahoma State Constitution provides that "the Court of Criminal Appeals shall have exclusive appellate jurisdiction in criminal cases until otherwise provided by statute and in the event there is any conflict as to jurisdiction, the Supreme Court shall determine which court has jurisdiction and such determination shall be final."[7] Thus, cases issuing from the Court of Criminal Appeals are typically mandatory authority and binding in other Oklahoma courts.

Primary authorities that are not binding on the court hearing the dispute, along with all secondary sources, will be persuasive. Exam-

---

4. Harvey D. Ellis, Jr., & Clyde A. Muchmore, *Oklahoma Appellate Practice* vol. 5, § 14:122, 525–26 (2011–2012 ed. 2011).

5. *Id.*

6. *Id.* at § 14:124, 530–31.

7. Okla. Const. art. VII, § 4.

ples of primary, persuasive authorities include cases or statutes on point from another state or cases from a court at the same level in the hierarchy of the court structure as the court with jurisdiction in your matter. The savvy researcher must decide how persuasive the authority can be given the issues at hand. The relative persuasiveness of a given authority is sometimes called the "weight" or "value" of the authority, and there are a number of significant factors that help determine an authority's weight.[8] More attention will be given to the weight or value of various authorities in subsequent chapters of this book.

IV. Overview of the Research Process

It is actually somewhat misleading to talk about the research process as though it were a single, well-defined, and immutable set of steps undertaken by anyone exploring a particular legal issue. While there are certainly essential steps in the process, experienced researchers and well-respected authors have varying ways of describing and working through this process. One author suggests that there are five essential steps in the research process.[9] These five steps include formulating a plan and generating search terms, consulting primary authorities, consulting secondary sources, expanding and updating research, and finally analyzing and organizing the results. Another author speaks instead of a task-oriented process, listing eight essential tasks occurring in a clearly identified order.[10] These tasks include some discrete steps such as listing and ranking potential authorities before consulting any sources and knowing when to stop researching. Yet another author adds a critical step: carefully formulating the legal issues

---

8. See Sloan, *supra* note 2, at 5–9 for an excellent discussion of the weight of various authorities. You may also wish to consult David S. Romantz & Kathleen Elliott Vinson, *Legal Analysis: The Fundamental Skill* 15–17 (2d ed. 2009).

9. Mark K. Osbeck, *Impeccable Research: A Concise Guide to Mastering Legal Research Skills* (2010).

10. Kunz et al., *supra* note 1, at 27.

to be researched.[11] Each of these models provides a similar, yet uniquely nuanced, approach to the research process and each can prove both useful and instructive in the course of conducting research.

The essential elements of any research process are summarized in Table 1-1 and explained below.

Table 1-1. Essential Elements of the Research Process

1. Frame the question(s) and develop search terms.
2. Identify, prioritize, and consult relevant sources.
3. Expand and update your research.
4. Make sure your research is responsive to the question(s) presented.
5. Know when to stop.

In an effort to provide an overview of the research process that both appreciates and includes the essential elements present in each of the referenced models, this book will describe the fundamental elements of the legal research process when the researcher has no prior knowledge of the area of law or the research resources best suited to answering the problem. This type of search is called a "fresh search."[12] Those who have worked in a particular area of the law for many years may have developed the knowledge and skills necessary to skip directly to a review of sources with which they are already familiar in seeking answers to their questions. However, it is important to remember that the knowledge and skills they possess were developed

11. Steven M. Barkan, Roy M. Mersky & Donald J. Dunn, *Fundamentals of Legal Research* 15 (9th ed. 2009).

12. Robert C. Berring & Elizabeth A. Edinger, *Finding the Law* 328 (12th ed. 2005).

by engaging in sound research processes and strategies over time. Every great researcher once began with a fresh search.

A. Frame the Questions and Develop Search Terms

Framing the questions that arise from a set of facts is a critically important skill, and one that can only be honed over time and with practice. Because the way in which each question is framed guides the way in which that question is researched, it is vital to give the appropriate amount of attention and energy to framing the questions to be answered. While there is no single correct way to frame a question, there are broader and more narrowly tailored ways of phrasing the issues you wish to address, along with costs and benefits of choosing different ways of identifying the issues.[13] It is often useful to have some background knowledge of the area of law you will be researching before finalizing the way in which you state your issues. Thus, it may make sense when beginning a fresh search to frame each question broadly, engage in some preliminary secondary source exploration, then narrow the language used to identify the question presented. A final element in framing your issue is determining the appropriate jurisdiction for your problem. Again, when conducting a fresh search it is possible that you may need to do some preliminary reading before clearly determining the proper jurisdiction.

Once the issue or issues to be researched are satisfactorily framed, begin the process of creating a search term list. As with descriptions of the research process, there are a variety of effective methods for developing a list of search terms to use during research. A well-written issue statement or question presented might naturally produce an initial list of search terms, which you may supplement by including synonyms, variations on words, and conceptual phrases

13. An excellent discussion of developing questions presented is found in Richard K. Neumann, Jr., *Legal Reasoning and Legal Writing: Structure, Strategy, and Style* 371–79 (5th ed. 2009).

related to the doctrines or remedies that may be involved.[14] Instead, you might consider categories of relevant information in a legal dispute. For example, you could consider the Things, Actions, Relief, and Persons (TARP) involved in your problem.[15] As an alternative, you might take a more journalistic approach to search term development, asking who, what, when, where, and why.[16] Both of these methods are set out in Table 1-2. Whether you adhere to one of these methods, incorporate both of these methods, or develop your own method, you must ensure that you have a working list of search terms prior to beginning in-depth research. Whether consulting a print index or searching a full-text database, the key to every search performed lies in the choice of search terms appropriate to the problem to be resolved.

Consider the following example. Your client is a recently widowed woman in Tulsa, Oklahoma. Prior to his death, her husband consulted with a local attorney who re-drafted his will. The new will provides that a considerable portion of his estate be left to a non-profit organization on whose governing board the drafting attorney currently sits. Your client does not want this new will to be honored and asks if there are grounds for invalidating the will. Table 1-2 provides a list of appropriate search terms using both the TARP method and the journalistic approach.

While neither of these lists is exhaustive, each offers a substantial starting point for conducting secondary source research. Additional appropriate terms will often be revealed as you progress. Here, the phrase "confidential relationship" is likely to emerge as you explore the attorney/client relationship and the fact that the attorney who drafted the will is closely affiliated with one of the will's beneficiaries (the non-profit organization). This new concept should be added to the search term list and may be used to conduct additional research on the issue presented.

---

14. Osbeck, *supra* note 9, at 11.
15. Barkan, Mersky & Dunn, *supra* note 11, at 15–16.
16. Kunz et al., *supra* note 1, at 31.

Table 1-2. Developing Search Terms

TARP Method

Things:	will, probate, estate, assets, inheritance, gift, bequest
Actions:	undue influence, coercion, duress, fraud
Relief:	deny probate, invalidate, void
Persons:	husband, wife, decedent, widow(er), beneficiary, attorney, client, testator, drafter

Journalistic Approach

Who:	husband, wife, decedent, widow(er), beneficiary, attorney, client, testator, drafter
What:	will, probate, inheritance, estate, assets, gift, bequest
When:	before the testator's death, prior to probate
Where:	Tulsa, Oklahoma, attorney's office
Why:	undue influence, coercion, duress, fraud, procurement of a will

B. Identify, Prioritize, and Consult Relevant Sources

1. Secondary Sources

Once you have developed a search term list, the next logical step is to take those search terms either to print or online sources and begin gathering information.[17] In performing a fresh search, you should start with secondary sources. As noted above, secondary sources serve to help a researcher understand and interpret principles of law, find citations to primary authorities, and gather practical ad-

17. We will explore a number of useful online legal research resources throughout this book. We have focused on the resources you are most likely to encounter in research and writing classes, including Lexis, Lexis Advance, Westlaw, WestlawNext, and Bloomberg Law. Chapter 2 contains a fuller exploration of these and other online sources.

vice about handling particular types of legal matters. A thorough discussion of secondary sources can be found in Chapter 3 of this book and will offer guidance as to the types of sources that may be most appropriate depending on the research question at hand.

2. Primary Authorities

Researchers disagree as to which of the available primary authorities to consult first once the review of secondary sources is complete. Some researchers typically turn first to statutes, while others prefer to begin with cases. Some assert that a commitment to diligence in consulting all the relevant primary authorities far outweighs the importance of which primary authority is selected for consultation first. "There are more ways than one to go about legal research, and as long as you are diligent, you will probably reach the right result eventually, even if you don't start out in the best place."[18] That said, it is typically wise to begin with the primary authority that is controlling in the area of law. There are some areas of law that are typically controlled by common law, such as contract law, while other areas of law are predominantly controlled by statutory or regulatory authority, such as environmental law. Secondary sources will help to identify this controlling authority, which is yet another important reason to consult secondary sources at the outset of the research process.

C. Expand and Update

After locating primary authorities that are on point for the research question, expanding and updating these authorities using citators is an absolutely essential follow-up. Chapter 11 provides a detailed analysis of the ways in which citators can be used both to expand the scope of the primary authorities in hand as well as to assure that every primary authority on which you intend to rely is still "good law." The phrase "good law" typically indicates establishing that cases have not been reversed or overruled and that statutes have not

18. Osbeck, *supra* note 9, at 31.

been repealed or amended in ways that would impact the question presented.[19]

D. Make Sure Your Research Is Responsive to the Questions Presented

After gathering the most current and authoritative sources and authorities that are descriptive of and responsive to the research questions presented, the next step in the process is to analyze those authorities to confirm that they do in fact address the specific issue or issues at hand. This is the portion of the research process in which highly developed legal analysis skills are most valuable. Consider revisiting the facts of the case, re-read each question presented, and affirm that it is well-crafted and accurately states the issue(s) at the crux of the dispute. Next, elucidate the way in which each of the sources gathered connects to the issue identified. Not only will this process help to assure that you have gathered useful authorities, it will also provide an opportunity to confirm that each element of the issue has been addressed by an appropriate resource.

E. Know When to Stop

Inexperienced researchers often find that knowing when to stop conducting research is one of the most difficult parts of the process. Because few legal issues are completely discrete and isolated from other peripheral or tangential legal inquiries, novice researchers sometimes have a difficult time determining when they have gathered the material they require. One way to identify when you have reached the proper stopping point for your research problem is to pay careful attention to the steps in the process mentioned above. When the authorities in-hand are fully responsive to the question presented and the legal analysis you have developed to answer the question is thor-

19. The citators explored in this book include Shepard's, available on Lexis; KeyCite, available on Westlaw; and Citationizer, available through the Oklahoma State Courts Network.

ough, you have likely reached an appropriate end to your research. It is also common to see the same sources and authorities appearing over and over again when nearing the end of the research process. When continued research fails to yield new authorities that are responsive to the question, you may need to stop researching even if the issue is not perfectly addressed in the authorities.

V. Organization of This Book

The remaining chapters of this book explore the types of research resources you will encounter, the areas of law you may discover, and the strategic and analytical framework you should incorporate into the research you undertake. Chapters 2 and 3 delve both into the format of available legal research resources as well as the relative value and authority of those materials. Chapters 4 thorough 7 focus on primary authorities essential to Oklahoma state legal research, including the state constitution, judicial opinions, and statutes. Chapters 8 through 10 tackle specific types of research you may need to do, including Oklahoma legislative history and administrative law research, as well as tribal law research. Tribal law is of such incredible importance in Oklahoma that an entire chapter is devoted to this area of legal research. Chapter 11 focuses on updating legal authorities with citators, an essential part of every legal research project.

While this introductory chapter has hinted at some of the strategic and analytical elements involved in conducting excellent legal research, more detailed recommendations are provided throughout this book. Because legal analysis is critical to progressing through every legal research project, each chapter will touch on the basic analytical framework required to undertake Oklahoma legal research in particular types of resources or areas. A final chapter focuses exclusively on research strategy and organization. Because each research problem and jurisdiction is unique, a strategic approach to the problem should be chosen that complements the contours of the issues involved.

Chapter 2

Online Legal Research

I. Introduction

Conducting research online has become the norm in the legal profession.[1] To conduct online research effectively, it is important know how to formulate a keyword search and to understand the types of online services that are available. This chapter will address the major commercial providers of legal material, Westlaw and Lexis, and their modern platforms, WestlawNext and Lexis Advance. The chapter will also introduce the online services Bloomberg Law, HeinOnline, and others, as well as public online research services, like OSCN and Google Scholar.

II. Developing an Effective Online Search

Creating an effective online search can be challenging because legal researchers often need to find *all* of the court opinions, statutes, and regulations relating to a particular issue. At the same time, researchers

1. A current survey of more than 500 Oklahoma law clerks showed that over eighty percent of summer clerks conducted research "mostly online" or "only online" in their summer job, and only thirteen percent used an equal mix of online and print resources. *See* Darin K. Fox, *Survey of Summer Research Experience 2005–2010, University of Oklahoma College of Law* (on file with the author).

don't want to be overwhelmed by a large number of documents that are marginally related to their research question.

A. Generating Search Terms

Creating an effective online search requires a careful consideration of the important facts relating to the issue, the legal concepts at work, and the use of terms of art in cases, statutes, scholarly literature, and practice aids. Also, consider which online service has the best combination of content, features, and value to efficiently locate the required information.

Chapter 1 provides some excellent tips on how to organize your research and how to identify key facts and terms of art. For instance, you might consider the "who, what, when, where, and why" of your legal issues. The answers to these questions will almost always include the keywords you need to conduct an online search.

When considering the facts relating to a particular legal problem, keep in mind the variety and ambiguity of language. There are often several ways to describe a particular problem. For example, if a judge uses the word "canine" instead of "dog" when writing an opinion about dog bite liability, a keyword search for "dog bite" might not find that document, or it might rank that document low in the list of search results. In addition, consider whether there are more general or specific ways to describe a particular issue. For example, dogs are part of the more general category of "animals." There may be court opinions discussing other types of animal bite cases that could be relevant to a dog bite case. Generating search terms that are relevant but not too general or too specific is often the most difficult part of conducting research online. For this reason, many of the major online services provide a thesaurus to help identify the synonyms that might be used in court opinions and other laws. If available, the thesaurus is typically linked near the search box. Westlaw and Lexis both provide a thesaurus feature, which includes an option for automatically inserting synonyms into the search.

The legal profession, just like other professions, has its own specialized terminology. To gain an understanding of the terms of art and legal concepts used in a particular area of law, it is best to begin by looking at a legal encyclopedia or treatise. Legal encyclopedias are written with the novice researcher in mind. They succinctly explain legal rules and are an excellent source for identifying key legal concepts and terms of art relating to a particular issue. For a deeper understanding of the key concepts, a legal treatise can be an excellent source. Legal treatises are written by experts, and they describe a broad area of law, such as contracts or property or tax law, in great detail. Legal encyclopedia and treatises are explained in Chapter 3.

B. Types of Online Searches

There are three ways to conduct keyword searching online: natural language searching, terms and connectors searching, and online indexes and tables of contents searching. Knowing which type of search to conduct is essential to conducting research online. Natural language searching is best used when you are just beginning your research and when you are unfamiliar with the area of law you are researching. Since it ranks search results by relevance, natural language searching is often used to identify a few key cases, statutes, or secondary sources with which to launch a more detailed inquiry. Terms and connectors is a very literal form of searching and is the most difficult to use. However, it is especially helpful when you need to develop a comprehensive list of relevant search results or when you are searching for names and phrases. Finally, tables of contents and indexes should be used to put your issue in context, and they are especially helpful when searching statutes and treatises.

1. Natural Language Searching

Natural language searching is the most common form of searching in use today. Most Internet search engines, such as Google, Yahoo, and Bing, are natural language search engines. To create a natural language search, simply enter a string of keywords. The search engine retrieves documents in the database containing the keywords, evaluates the relevancy of those documents, and presents the results in order of relevancy. Understanding how search engines work and how to evaluate the results they present is essential to conducting an effective natural language search.

a. How Natural Language Search Engines Work

Natural language search engines are designed to calculate the relevancy of documents based on the search terms that are entered. Each natural language search engine uses its own proprietary system for evaluating the relevancy of documents. In fact, if the exact same search is run in both Westlaw and Lexis, the search results are often ranked differently in the two systems. In other words, the top ten search results might not be the same in both services. For this reason, natural language searching should be used as a starting point for research only; do not expect this type of search to produce comprehensive results.

In general, natural language search engines consider the following types of criteria when evaluating documents for relevancy: (1) the number of times the search terms appear in a document, (2) the density of the search terms in a document, (3) the number of times the search terms appear in the title of a document, and (4) the number of documents that cite or link to a particular document that contains the search terms. There can be hundreds of criteria used by search engines to assign a relevancy score to a particular document.

b. Relevancy versus Thoroughness

Natural language search engines are generally very good at presenting the user with a few relevant documents. For this reason, it is often helpful to begin with a natural language search. However, natural language searching should never be used when it is important to identify *every* document that contains a certain word or discusses a certain issue because these search engines are not designed to tell you *exactly* how many documents in the database contain all of the search terms. For example, in Westlaw Classic and Lexis, a natural language search for court opinions relating to dog bite will always retreive 100 search results,[2] even though there are only about two dozen opinions in Oklahoma that discuss dog bites. This happens because the natural language search engine in Westlaw Classic is programmed to return the 100 most relevant cases, even if 80 of those are minimally relevant to the issue. As a result, even though experienced researchers may begin with a natural language search, they will always use secondary sources (discussed in Chapter 3) and additional tools, such as digests (discussed in Chapter 6), citators (discussed in Chapter 11), annotated codes (discussed in Chapter 7), and terms and connectors searches (discussed in this chapter) to complete their research.

c. Mandatory Search Terms

Since natural language searching presents documents based on their relevancy, some of your search results might not contain one or more of the keywords you entered. For instance, even though a search for dog bite cases in Oklahoma will return dozens of search results on WestlawNext, many of those opinions do not contain the phrase "dog bite." This happens because the search engine will retrieve all of the documents that it considers relevant even if it needs to drop or omit certain search terms to generate those results. In most research services that provide natural language searching, this problem can be minimized by indicating that specific search terms are mandatory or required. This prevents the retrieval of documents which don't contain that keyword. This option can typically be found in the advanced search page of these services.

2. Terms and Connectors Searching

Terms and connectors searching, also called Boolean searching, is a very precise and literal form of keyword searching. It gives the re-

2. The number of search results retrieved by a natural language search can be changed, but the same principle applies. If number of natural language search results is changed to 25, the search engine will always return 25 results, even if there are, in fact, many more or many fewer relevant documents.

searcher complete control over how the search engine will evaluate and return search results. A terms and connectors search will only return those documents that contain *exactly* the search terms provided by the researcher and in *exactly* the relationship described by the connectors. For this reason, terms and connectors searching can be used to determine the exact number of documents that contain a certain word or phrase.

a. Key Uses of Terms and Connectors Searching

Terms and connectors searching is very helpful in the following circumstances:

- searching for documents containing a particular phrase
- searching for documents containing a specific name
- searching for documents containing unique facts
- searching for every document that contains certain keywords.

Table 2-1 shows the most commonly used connectors that are provided by three of the major online services, Westlaw, Lexis, and Bloomberg Law.

Here is an example of how a terms and connectors search is developed. Assume that a client was bitten on the leg by his neighbor's dog after the dog jumped the fence and came onto your client's property. Begin by thinking about the key facts and the terms that describe those facts. In this case, they are "dog," "bite," and perhaps "injury." Some courts may use the word "canine" instead of "dog," and the word "harm" could be used in place of "injury." Next, consider the legal concepts at issue. A legal encyclopedia can be very helpful for learning that a dog owner has a "duty" to control his animal, and the owner may be "liable" for "damages" if he doesn't control the animal. In addition, specific rules apply to "vicious" dogs with a known history of biting people. With these ideas in mind, an initial terms and connectors search might look like this:

> (dog or canine) /2 bit! and liab! and (injury or harm) and damages

In plain English, this search will find every court opinion that contains the word dog or canine within two words of bite, bit, bitten, and

Table 2-1. Common Connectors Used in Boolean Searching

Goal	Westlaw	Lexis	Bloomberg Law
To find both terms in a document	&, AND	AND	AND
To find either term in a document	Space, OR	OR	OR
To find a phrase	Place phrase in quotation marks	No quotation marks required	Place phrase in quotation marks
To find terms within 10 words of each other	w/10	w/10	N/10
To find terms within the same sentence	/s	w/s	S/
To find terms within the same paragraph	/p	w/p	P/
To find documents that do not include a term	%	AND NOT	NOT
To find terms with a variety of endings	!	!	!
To hold the place of a character in a term	*	*	*

all other words that begin with the root "bit." Additionally, the following words must be contained anywhere within the document: (1) words that begin with the root "liab," such as liable or liability and (2) injury or harm and (3) damages.

b. Field Searching

Field searching is a specialized type of terms and connectors search. Every document in a legal database is composed of specific fields. For instance, a court opinion has fields for the name of the judge who wrote the opinion, the names of the attorneys, the headnotes,[3] and the text of the opinion. Field searching facilitates looking for keywords within a specific part of a document. For instance, to find all Oklahoma court opinions on WestlawNext that were written by Justice Taylor, use the judge field in the following way: JU(taylor). The field names vary from one online service to another, but a complete list of fields can generally be found in a drop-down menu near the terms and connectors search box in each service. For instance, in WestlawNext, fields can be searched in the advanced search page for each database. In Westlaw Classic, fields are shown in a drop-down menu just below the terms and connectors search box. More detail on field searching can also be found within the online guides for each service.

3. Online Tables of Contents and Indexes

All of the major research services in Oklahoma provide expandable tables of contents as an alternative method for locating information. This is especially helpful when searching for information in statutes and treatises. For example, each title of the statutes can be expanded to show the chapters and sections within that title. Since statutory codes are arranged by subject and since each title, chapter, and section of the statutes is identified by a descriptive heading, ex-

---

3. Headnotes are the key points of law stated in a court opinion. They are discussed in more detail in Chapter 6.

amining the statutes in this way can help to provide context that keyword searching alone might not provide.

In addition, an online index can be an effective way to gain access to online content. For instance, the Oklahoma statutes on Westlaw Classic and WestlawNext include an index, similar to what you find at the back of most print books. An index can often be an efficient way to locate relevant statutes when a researcher is not familiar with the terms of art used to describe a particular issue or when a keyword search is returning large numbers of results. For example, you can easily find the Oklahoma statutes relating to dog bite by browsing the online index to the Oklahoma statutes. If you begin by looking for the term "Dogs," and then "Bites," you are immediately directed to "OK ST T. 4 §42.1 et seq." which is the key Oklahoma statute on dog bite.

III. Types of Online Legal Research Services

Technology has greatly facilitated the distribution of legal information online. Today, researchers have access to dozens of online legal research services that provide a wide range of materials from primary law (cases, statutes, and regulations) to secondary sources (law reviews, legal journals, and treatises) to practice-oriented materials (form books and practice guides). These materials are published by commercial publishers (Westlaw, Lexis, Bloomberg Law), federal and state governments, and other law-related organizations (law schools and bar associations).

Online legal research services can be divided into two categories—commercial services and public services. Commercial services like WestlawNext, Lexis Advance, Bloomberg Law, Fastcase, and HeinOnline are owned by major legal publishers. These publishers typically require an annual subscription fee to access their content. Public research services are owned by a variety of organizations, including federal and state governments, non-profit organizations, law schools, and law libraries. Public services, like the Oklahoma State Court Network (OSCN), are typically free to access, though registration is required to gain access to some public services.

Selecting the appropriate online service requires a careful balance of cost, features, availability, and coverage. For instance, OSCN would be a good database to use when looking for a few recent Oklahoma court opinions discussing a particular issue. However, to conduct a more comprehensive national survey of all state court opinions on a long-standing issue in the law, a commercial service would be a better choice. Services such as Westlaw and Lexis provide coverage of court opinions across all jurisdictions, more editorial enhancements, and more sophisticated search options.

A. Commercial Research Services

Since the development of the first online resources, two commercial services have dominated the online legal research landscape, Westlaw and Lexis. Today, they remain the most widely used research services in the legal profession.[4] However, there are now a host of competitors in the marketplace. When deciding which online service to use, think about the features, cost, and scope of content provided by each service.

1. Westlaw (WestlawNext and Westlaw Classic) and Lexis (Lexis Advance and Lexis)

Westlaw[5] and Lexis[6] stand apart from the growing crowd of online legal research services. They are the premier research services in the legal profession today for two reasons. First, they offer access to a vast amount of legal information—much more than any of their competitors. Second, they offer unique features designed to make research more efficient. Some of the content and features that distinguish Westlaw and Lexis from other online legal research services are listed below:

- *Access to Primary Law*: While many online services claim to provide access to the primary law of all 50 states and the fed-

4. ABA Legal Tech. Resource Ctr. *2010 American Bar Association Legal Technology Survey Report*, V-50 (2010).

5. Westlaw, http://www.westlawnext.com.

6. Lexis, http://www.advance.lexis.com.

eral government, many services do not provide access to older court opinions available on Westlaw and Lexis. They also often do not provide access to session laws, bills, and administrative decisions.

- *Headnotes and Digests*: Headnotes encapsulate the key points of law stated in a court's opinion. Both Westlaw and Lexis create headnotes and list them at the beginning of court opinions. Headnotes make it much easier for researchers to determine whether a case is relevant to their client's issue. In addition, headnotes are arranged in subject order within a tool, called a digest, which makes it easier to find related cases. Most other research services do not have this feature.
- *Annotated Statutes*: Case annotations are brief summaries of court opinions that interpret a statute. Westlaw and Lexis provide case annotations for the statutes of all 50 states and the federal government. In addition, Westlaw also provides references to related law review articles, treatises, and other practice aids. Annotations are conveniently located at the bottom of each statute section.
- *Legal Treatises*: Legal treatises are major works of scholarship and analysis prepared by professors, lawyers, and judges that explain the law and identify key cases, statutes, and regulations governing a particular issue. Westlaw and Lexis have, by far, the largest treatise libraries with approximately 2,000 and 1,000 titles respectively.
- *Comprehensive Citators*: Westlaw and Lexis include the two most comprehensive citators available, KeyCite on Westlaw and Shepard's on Lexis. Citators are essential tools for determining whether a case or statute is still "good law." They are also helpful research tools because they list authorities that cite the case or statute that the researcher is currently reading; those authorities are likely to be relevant to the issue. Citators are discussed in detail in Chapter 11.
- *Sophisticated Search Interfaces*: Both Westlaw and Lexis provide powerful search interfaces with a wide variety of features

designed to support both simple natural language searches and advanced terms and connectors searches.

- *Database Directories and Scope Notes*: Westlaw and Lexis each contain thousands of databases.[7] Both services provide searchable directories designed to help researchers locate relevant databases. Also, both services provide "scope notes" next to the name of each database, which describe the content, coverage dates, and other details specific to each database.

2. WestlawNext and Lexis Advance

The publishers of Westlaw and Lexis, Thomson Reuters and Reed Elsevier, released the current versions of their popular research services in the fall of 2010 and the spring of 2011. Both of these services are designed to make it easier to begin the research process. In the original or "classic" versions of Westlaw and Lexis, a database or set of databases must first be selected to begin searching. This initial step is often difficult for students, new associates, and members of the public who are not familiar with the types of publications available in the legal field. WestlawNext and Lexis Advance automatically select databases to search based upon the keywords entered into the search box. This makes it easier to begin researching since only the jurisdiction needs to be selected.

WestlawNext and Lexis Advance have also added several new productivity features, including (1) a highlighter to mark important passages of documents, (2) a way to add notes to online documents, and (3) a folder system which can be used to organize research materials and collaborate with others online.

The cost of providing access to all of these features and services can be considerable. Both companies offer multiple ways to pay for access, including flat-fee annual contracts, transactional billing (where customers pay per search), and hourly billing (where customers pay by the minute).[8] In Oklahoma, access to Westlaw is pro-

---

7. *Westlaw Database Directory* (Pam Larson, compiler, 2007).

8. More information on the cost of these services can be found in Chapter 25 of Kendall F. Svengalis, *The Legal Information Buyer's Guide and Reference Manual* (2010).

vided free of charge by the county law library system throughout the state. However, researchers must use dedicated computers located at the county law libraries to access this service. Remote access is not provided.

3. *Bloomberg Law*

Bloomberg Law is a relatively new product for legal research, but it is fast-growing and already offers an impressive array of features and content.[9] Bloomberg L.P., the publisher of Bloomberg Law, is a well-known publisher of financial and business information. In 2010, Bloomberg launched its first legal research platform, and in 2011, Bloomberg purchased Bureau of National Affairs (BNA), perhaps the most highly valued legal news service in the country. Bloomberg offers access to primary source materials nationwide, and through the BNA products, it now offers commentary, analysis, and legal news with more than one hundred titles. However, Bloomberg's strength is in providing access to very current information. Bloomberg provides perhaps the best interface for tracking court dockets. If you need to follow the developments of court cases, Bloomberg provides a very robust interface for accomplishing this. Bloomberg also boasts an impressive array of news and business databases.

4. *HeinOnline*

HeinOnline is the online service of the well-established legal publisher W.S. Hein & Co. Launched in 2000, it has quickly become an important source for law journals.[10] It is the only legal database that has digitized nearly all English-language law journals and made them available in image-based PDF format beginning with the first volume of each journal. In contrast, other commercial publishers only provide coverage of most law journals beginning in the late 1980s and

9. Bloomberg BNA, http://www.bloomberglaw.com.

10. HeinOnline, http://heinonline.org/HOL/Welcome.

early 1990s. In recent years, HeinOnline has added full-text databases for the *U.S. Code*, the *Code of Federal Regulations*, the *Federal Register*, the *Statutes at Large*, and state session laws. HeinOnline also contains a "*Legal Classics Library*," which contains the full text of more than 2,500 historic legal treatises. Finally, HeinOnline contains a wealth of foreign and international law resources, such as treaties, international agreements, and world constitutions. HeinOnline is a commercial service and requires a personal or institutional subscription, but it can be accessed free of charge by patrons at most academic and county law libraries.

5. *Fastcase, Casemaker, and VersusLaw*

Fastcase, Casemaker, and VersusLaw are low-cost research services that provide access to primary law from all 50 states and the federal government. Significantly, these services do not provide access to older state court opinions. Coverage for most state court opinions and federal district courts begins in 1950. All three services support natural language searching and terms and connectors searching, and all three include a basic citator for checking the validity of court opinions. The citator in Fastcase provides a unique feature, called an Interactive Timeline, which presents a visual map of court opinions that cite to an earlier case. The visual map is made up of small and large circles arranged chronologically. The large circles make it easy to identify a case that has a significant amount of discussion about the earlier case. Many state bar associations provide attorneys access to these services as a part of their bar membership.[11] Due to their low cost, they are a good choice for cost-conscious researchers who mainly need access to primary law.[12]

---

11. The Oklahoma Bar Association provides Fastcase to its members at no extra charge. Casemaker has partnerships with twenty-seven state bars. Casemaker, http://www.casemakerlegal.com.

12. VersusLaw subscriptions start at $167.50 per year. *VersusLaw Research Database, Products and Services*, http://www.versuslaw.com/products/all.aspx.

6. Loislaw

Loislaw[13] is the online research service from another large legal publisher, Wolters Kluwer. Launched in 1998, Loislaw has become a low-cost alternative to Westlaw and Lexis. Like the two major online services, Loislaw contains primary law for all 50 states and the federal government. Loislaw is superior to other low-cost providers in two ways. First, it provides access to older court opinions. Second, it includes a treatise library of approximately 150 expert-authored works on a variety of topics from agriculture to zoning. Loislaw also provides access to bar publications and public records that are not available from other low-cost providers. However, Loislaw's search interface is more limited than either Westlaw or Lexis, and it does not support natural language searching. It supports only terms and connectors searching, which makes Loislaw more difficult for novice researchers to use. Finally, Loislaw does not provide editorial features, like headnotes and case annotations within statutes.

7. Google Scholar

In 2009, Google added court opinions and some law journals to its Google Scholar database.[14] This service is free, and it provides an easy way to search for cases using the familiar Google search interface. Using Google Scholar's advanced search interface, searches can be limited to a specific jurisdiction.[15] Google has also added freely accessible law journals to the database, along with a basic citator, called "How Cited."

13. Loislaw, http://www.loislaw.com.

14. *See* Google Scholar, http://scholar.google.com.

15. After selecting the "Legal Documents" option on the Google Scholar page, you can narrow your search to a specific jurisdiction.

Coverage in Google Scholar is limited. Older state court opinions are not present in the database. Statutes and regulations are also not available, and only those law journals that publicly post their issues online are included in the Google database. Finally, Google does not provide the range of advanced search features provided by the services mentioned above (e.g., terms and connectors searching and field searching), other than date and title searches.

B. Public Research Services

The Internet has been a boon for publication of legal information. Today, the primary law of all 50 states and the federal government can be obtained freely online. For example, the State of Oklahoma maintains a comprehensive legal research service, called the Oklahoma State Court Network (OSCN), which provides access to all published Oklahoma court opinions, statutes, legal forms, and more. In addition to government sites, law schools, law firms,[16] and other non-profit organizations have created free, public websites designed to facilitate locating legal information online.

1. Oklahoma State Court Network (OSCN)

The most important public online service in Oklahoma is the Oklahoma State Court Network (OSCN), which is managed by the Supreme Court of Oklahoma. It offers access to a wealth of Oklahoma legal information. OSCN includes the full text of all major primary law sources, including Oklahoma court opinions, state statutes, and state regulations. It also provides access to a variety of secondary sources, including forms, jury instructions, fee schedules, and law journals. It even includes a free citator, called Citationizer, which can be used to locate Oklahoma court opinions that have interpreted a statute or discussed an earlier court opinion. Figure 2-1 shows the "Legal Research" section of the OSCN services and the wide variety of resources available to the public free of charge.

---

16. Some law firms provide freely accessible online guides relating to their particular area of practice.

Figure 2-1. Legal Resources Available on the Oklahoma State Courts Network

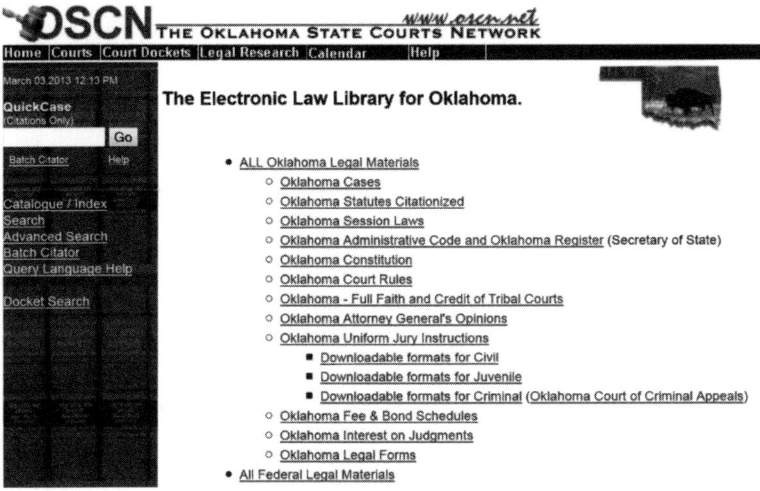

Source: Oklahoma State Court Network, www.oscn.net.

OSCN provides access to legal information in a variety of ways. Basic and advanced search interfaces are available. The advanced search page supports both natural language searching and terms and connectors searching. Note, however, that the basic or "Quick Search" interface supports only terms and connectors searching. Further, the advanced search page supports "field searching" for locating documents by case number, date, party names, etc. OSCN also offers an easy and straightforward method for browsing through the table of contents of sources. For statutes, OSCN includes an expandable table of contents, which can be used to browse through each chapter and subchapter to locate individual sections.

In addition to providing primary authority, OSCN provides one of the most advanced court docketing systems in the country, the Oklahoma Court Information System (OCIS). OCIS is used in the counties encompassing the state's major metropolitan areas. In this system, court documents are scanned shortly after they are filed with the court and made available online. Each scanned document is an exact replica of the original print document filed with the court and is linked to an online docket for each case. For other counties in Oklahoma, a docket for each case is available online, but court documents are not freely available. Researchers must purchase an account for access to scanned court documents in the "non-OCIS" counties. Court documents can also be obtained in print by contacting the court clerk for that county.

In 2010, the Oklahoma Supreme Court approved the creation of a new "unified case management system" for the Oklahoma courts.[17] When completed, the new system will support modern features, such as electronic filing, trial and appellate court case management, electronic payments, jury management, electronic warrants and citations, and more.[18]

2. Oklahoma State Legislature Website

The Oklahoma State Legislature website provides access to current bills, statutes, and the Oklahoma Constitution.[19] The site includes a sophisticated search engine for locating bills. The full text of bills can be searched by keyword, by subject, and by author. Coverage of bills begins in 1993. The site also includes legislative calendars and information about state representatives and state senators. The legislature recently added live video from the House and Senate floors. There is no charge to access the site, and no registration is required. Figure 2-2 shows the Advanced Bill Search interface, which easily allows you to find current bills by subject.

---

17. Chief Justice James Edmonson, *On the Horizon: Oklahoma's Unified Case Management System: Connecting Oklahoma Courts*, 81 Okla. B.J. 2810–14 (Dec. 2010).

18. *Id.* at 2813.

19. Oklahoma State Legislature, http://www.oklegislature.gov/index.aspx.

Figure 2-2. Searching for Bills by Subject on the Oklahoma Legislature Site

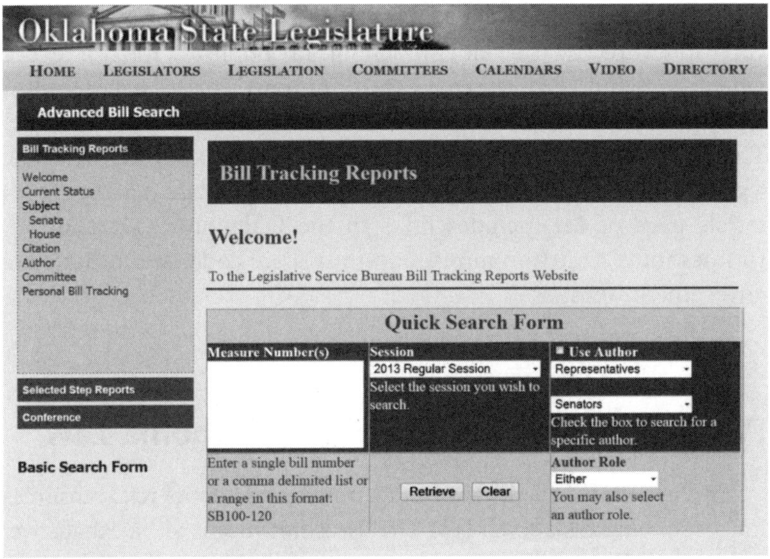

Source: Oklahoma State Legislature, www.oklegislature.gov/advancedsearchform.aspx.

3. Oklahoma Secretary of State Website

The Oklahoma Secretary of State makes administrative rules and regulations available through its website.[20] The *Oklahoma Administrative Code* and the *Oklahoma Register* can be searched here. However, the online versions of the Code and the Register are unofficial. The print and CD-ROM versions of the Code and the Register are the official versions. Coverage of the *Oklahoma Register* online begins in 2001. Using the site is free, and registration is not required. The search engine supports only terms and connectors searching.

---

20. Oklahoma Secretary of State, Office of Administrative Rules, https://www.sos.ok.gov/oar/default.aspx.

4. *Legal Information Institute*

Perhaps the most widely-known and freely accessible public website for conducting online research is the Legal Information Institute (LII) sponsored by Cornell Law School. LII publishes the full text of federal laws and U.S. Supreme Court opinions. It also includes tools to help researchers locate and understand legal information online. The "Wex" legal encyclopedia is a "community-built, freely-available legal dictionary and legal encyclopedia."[21] The Oklahoma Legal Materials page of LII includes links to the Oklahoma Constitution, statutes, bills, court opinions, administrative code, and other state government websites.

IV. Appendix: Where to Find Oklahoma Law

This appendix lists the key online public and commercial resources for researching Oklahoma law. The list is not meant to be exhaustive. It is meant as a starting point for research. A link to the publicly available sources is provided along with the database identifiers for Westlaw and Lexis. Database identifiers are short codes that allow researchers on Lexis to Westlaw to quickly locate a database and begin searching.

- **Oklahoma Constitution**
  Oklahoma State Court Network: http://www.oscn.net/
  Oklahoma Legislature: http://www.oklegislature.gov/index.aspx
  Lexis: OKCODE
  Westlaw: OK-ST, OK-ST-ANN
- **Oklahoma Statutes**
  Oklahoma State Court Network: http://www.oscn.net/
  Oklahoma Legislature: http://www.oklegislature.gov/index.aspx
  Lexis: OKCODE
  Westlaw: OK-ST, OK-ST-ANN

---

21. Legal Information Institute, *Wex*, http://www.law.cornell.edu/wex.

- **Oklahoma Regulations**
  Oklahoma Secretary of State: https://www.sos.ok.gov/oar/default.aspx
  Lexis: OKADMN
  Westlaw: OK-ADC
- **Oklahoma Court Opinions**
  Oklahoma State Court Network: http://www.oscn.net/
  Lexis: OKCTS
  Westlaw: OK-CS
- **Oklahoma Court Rules**
  Oklahoma State Court Network: http://www.oscn.net/
  Lexis: OKRULE
  Westlaw: OK-RULES
- **Oklahoma Bills and Legislative Information**
  Oklahoma Legislature: http://www.oklegislature.gov/BasicSearchForm.aspx
  Lexis: OKTEXT, OKLH
  Westlaw: OK-BILLS, OK-LH

Chapter 3

Secondary Sources

Primary law ... is like a farm. And on this farm are cattle (bulls and cows), chickens, pigs, crops of all sorts, barns with hay bales stacked to the ceiling, tractors, combines, trucks, silos filled with grain, a woodshop, a metal shop, dogs, cats, mice, a farmer (of course) and his wife. Secondary sources are like cheeseburgers.—Jason Wilson[1]

I. Introduction

Everyone who conducts legal research, at one time or another, feels overwhelmed by the amount of legal information available on their topic. A simple search in the Oklahoma federal and state case law database for "medical malpractice" returns 462 court opinions in the last three years alone! So, how do lawyers and legal researchers find the answers to legal questions without having to read dozens or hundreds of court opinions, statutes, and regulations to find the relevant information? They begin with secondary sources.

Secondary sources serve two important functions in legal research. First, if you are unfamiliar with the subject area that you are re-

1. Jason Wilson, *Dear Law Students, Secondary Sources are Like Cheeseburgers. You like those, right?*, http://www.jasnwilsn.com/2010/08/25/dear-law-students-secondary-sources-are-like-cheeseburgers-you-like-those-right/.

searching, secondary sources are an excellent place to start because they explain the law and provide important references to key cases, statutes, etc. Second, even if you are familiar with the subject area you are researching, secondary sources allow you to avoid manually sifting through search results; another expert has already done that and summarized the results in a secondary source. As law librarians are fond of the saying, "Don't reinvent the wheel." The role of secondary sources in legal research is to keep you from having to recreate the work that has been done by another researcher.

As explained in Chapter 1, there are two categories of legal information. Primary sources are publications that contain the rules of law produced by the government, such as statutes, regulations, and court opinions. Case reporters and annotated codes are examples of primary sources of law. Secondary sources are those publications that discuss or explain the law. This chapter covers many types of secondary sources: legal encyclopedias, treatises, law review articles, *American Law Reports*, form books, continuing legal education (CLE) materials, and Restatements. These secondary sources—the "cheeseburgers" of legal research—are sure to be among your favorite resources.

II. Legal Encyclopedias

Legal encyclopedias are an excellent place to begin a research project, especially when you have little knowledge of the subject area being researched. Legal encyclopedias summarize the law. As a result, they are concise and to the point. They typically provide a brief discussion of a particular issue with references to a few key cases, statutes, and regulations.

A. National Legal Encyclopedias

There are two legal encyclopedias with a national scope, *American Jurisprudence 2d* (AmJur) and *Corpus Juris Secundum* (CJS). Both are commercial publications. So they are not freely available on the Internet. Both are published by Thomson Reuters and are available in print and on Westlaw and WestlawNext. AmJur is also available on Lexis and Lexis Advance.

AmJur and CJS cover a broad range of legal topics, which are arranged alphabetically. Volume 1 begins with Abandoned Property, and the final volume ends with Zoning. In AmJur, each of the more than 400 topics is broken down into specific sub-issues. As a result, it is very important to examine the Table of Contents after finding one relevant section because related topics are discussed in nearby sections. AmJur and CJS cover both federal and state law issues.[2]

Both AmJur and CJS can be searched by keyword on Westlaw and Lexis. Natural language searching and terms and connectors searching can be used. Both databases are prominently linked from the home screens of Westlaw and Lexis. In WestlawNext, simply begin typing the title of the encyclopedia into the search box, and a link to the database will appear. To go directly to these databases in Westlaw Classic, use the database identifier AMJUR for *American Jurisprudence 2d* and CJS for *Corpus Juris Secundum.*

When using an encyclopedia in print, refer to the index at the very end of the set to begin your research. The index can be used to find legal topics by keyword, much like you would use an index at the back of any book. References in the index will be to a particular topic and section number. In the print version of the encyclopedia, the topics covered by each volume are printed on the spine. Once you have found the correct volume, you can find the specific section you need by referring to the section number printed in the top corner of each page.

B. State Legal Encyclopedias

Many states with large populations have a legal encyclopedia dedicated to the laws of that specific state. Unfortunately, there is no legal encyclopedia dedicated to discussing Oklahoma law alone. However,

---

2. Both encyclopedias include extensive references to topics and key numbers on Westlaw. See Chapter 6 on Researching Judicial Opinions for more discussion of topics and key numbers.

Vernon's Oklahoma Forms (discussed in detail later in this chapter) fills this role to some degree. *Vernon's* is a multi-volume form book set that is published by Thomson Reuters. It is available on Westlaw Classic and WestlawNext. In addition to providing forms, it is annotated and includes practice tips and commentaries, drafting advice, and citations to relevant cases and statutes. Subjects covered include commercial and consumer law, criminal law, civil procedure, business organizations, and real estate.

III. Legal Treatises

Treatises (not to be confused with *treaties*—which are agreements between countries) are legal publications that provide in-depth coverage of a broad area of law, such as property, contracts, criminal law, or taxation. The term "treatise" encompasses a wide range of publications from single-volume works primarily directed at law students and new attorneys to massive multi-volume sets intended to serve as "one-stop" resources for experienced practitioners and law firms. Treatises are often the first place an experienced attorney will look for information because they provide detailed analysis, practice tips, references to critical court opinions, and a broad context of an entire area of law. You will often hear attorneys speak affectionately about a particular treatise as "the bible" in that particular area of law. These treatises, often named after the scholar who originally wrote the work, are among the most persuasive secondary sources available in that subject area. Although no secondary sources are binding authority, court opinions and other legal documents will sometimes cite to legal treatises for their analysis of specific issues.

A. How to Locate and Evaluate Treatises

There are literally thousands of treatises. Both Westlaw and Lexis each have at least one treatise on any given subject area, and they very frequently have multiple treatises per topic. For example, Westlaw has more than ten treatises on civil rights litigation alone.

One of the most difficult tasks for a new legal researcher is locating treatises in a particular subject area. Both Westlaw and Lexis have multiple methods for locating treatises. On WestlawNext, all treatises can be found by clicking the "Secondary Sources" link on the home page. From there, click on the link for "Texts and Treatises." You will then be presented with a list of topic areas and state jurisdictions. Select a topic area or state to see a list of relevant treatises. Treatises can also be located on WestlawNext by subject. Click the Topics tab on the home page and then select a topic area, such as Family Law. All of the primary and secondary source databases related to family law will be listed there. Finally, if you already know the title of a treatise, you can simply begin typing it into the main search box on the home page. A drop-down list of titles that match what you have typed will appear. Click the link for the database you want, and a new tab will appear over the search box allowing you to search only that title.

Figure 3-1 shows how treatises are arranged and accessed on WestlawNext by topic or by jurisdiction.

On Westlaw Classic, there is a directory of all databases linked at the top of the page. The link is called simply "Directory," and it is always present at the top of each page. After clicking the Directory link, you can search for a treatise by next clicking "Treatises, CLEs, and Other Practice Materials." A search box within the Directory will then allow you to search for treatises by keyword, such as "copyright law" or "criminal procedure."

On Lexis Advance, treatises can be found by clicking the "Browse Sources" link at the top-right corner of the search box. Next, click "Secondary Materials" under Content Type on the left-hand margin, then click "Treatises." You will then be presented with an A–Z list of treatises available, which you can narrow down by keyword or jurisdiction. Similar to WestlawNext, if you already know the title of a treatise, you can simply type the title into the main search box on the home page and select the database from a drop-down list of titles containing those keywords.

Figure 3-2 shows how treatises can be found on Lexis Advance using the "Browse Sources" feature.

Figure 3-1. Accessing Treatises on WestlawNext

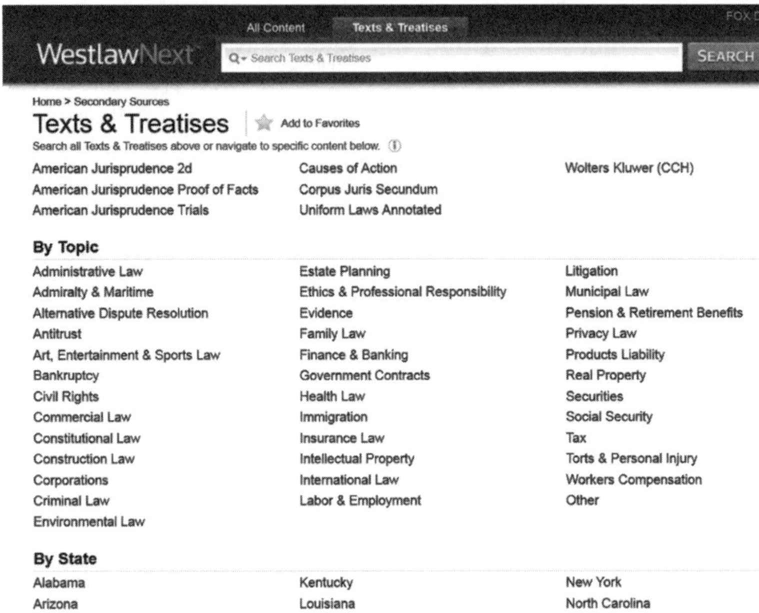

Reprinted with permission of Thomson Reuters.

On Lexis, the best way to locate treatises is to begin by clicking the "Area of Law—By Topic" link on the "Legal" tab. You will be presented with a long list of topics. After you have selected a topic, one section of the screen will be labeled "Search Analysis & CLE Materials." The top treatises are typically listed here. You can use the "View more" link to see a more detailed listing of treatises in this subject area. Treatises can also be located through the "Find a Source" link located on the menu bar under the "Search" tab. You can search for treatises by keyword here.

Another way to locate treatises on Westlaw and Lexis is by using the subject-oriented "tabs" of those services. Each tab brings together important sources for that subject area on one screen. Look for a link called "add/edit tabs" on both services to add a subject-oriented tab to the main search screen.

On both WestlawNext and Lexis Advance, treatises are automatically selected and included in your search based on the search terms

Figure 3-2. Accessing Treatises on Lexis Advance

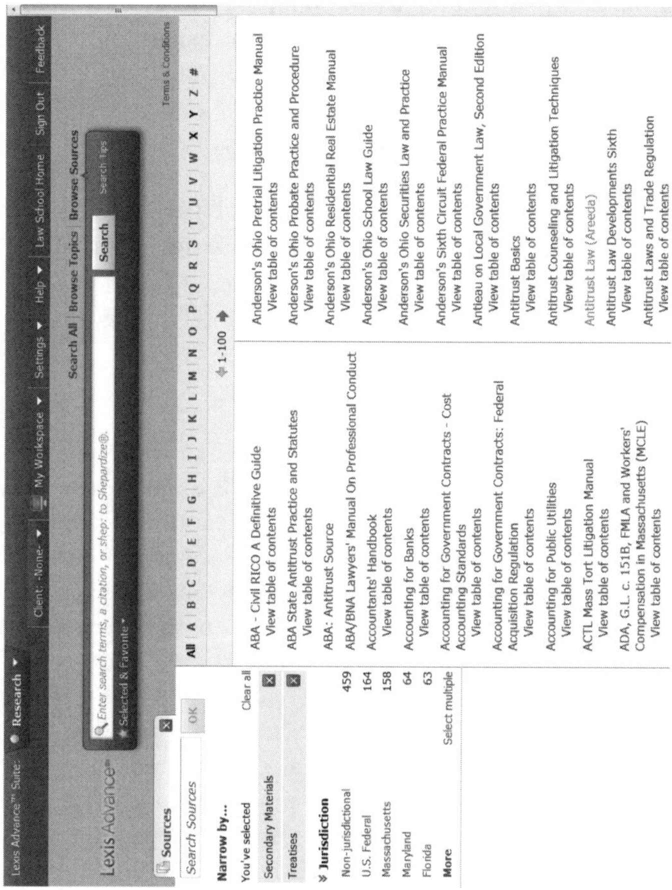

provided. After running a keyword search, treatises can be selected from the "Content Type" box on the left side of the screen. This will narrow the search results to treatises and other secondary sources only.

Since there are so many legal treatises, it is often helpful to have an expert tell you which treatise is most authoritative and best suited to your needs. Law librarians and experienced practitioners can be good sources for identifying treatises. However, there are two publications that specialize in evaluating legal treatises. *The Legal Infor-*

mation Buyer's Guide and Reference Manual by Kendall F. Svengalis provides detailed reviews and descriptions of major treatises. Most law libraries have a copy of this reference work, and it can also be accessed in full text on Lexis. Another source for locating treatises is IndexMaster,[3] an online database that includes descriptions of secondary sources along with the table of contents and index of each source. Note that IndexMaster is a commercial database. So, it is not freely accessible on the Internet. Many law libraries subscribe to this service.

B. State versus National Treatises

In terms of content, treatises can be broken down into two categories: those that focus on a particular state's law and those that have a national scope. State law treatises tend to be one-volume or two-volume works, and are typically written by practitioners, judges, or law professors from that state. State treatises tend to be focused on subject areas involving state law, including family law, probate, criminal law, business organizations, practice and procedure, and evidence. However, they may also address federal court opinions and laws that are relevant to practitioners in that particular state. State law treatises typically provide a narrative summary that explains how key statutes, regulations, and common law rules are applied by courts and in practice. In contrast, national treatises tend to be much larger multi-volume sets, and they often focus on both federal and state law issues. National treatises often summarize the law in every jurisdiction and identify trends.

3. IndexMaster, http://www.indexmaster.com/.

Table 3-1. Titles Included within the Oklahoma Practice Series

- *Courtroom Guide to the Oklahoma Evidence Code* by Whinery
- *Commentary on the Law of Evidence* by Whinery
- *Oklahoma Family Law* by DeLacerda
- *Oklahoma Appellate Practice* by Ellis and Muchmore
- *Oklahoma Trial Practice* by Rolls, Giles, and Jones
- *Oklahoma Probate Law and Practice* by Huff and Taylor
- *Oklahoma Product Liability Law* by MacDougall
- *Oklahoma Construction Law* by Donaldson

Oklahoma attorneys can take advantage of titles included within the Oklahoma Practice Series, listed in Table 3-1, and a number of Oklahoma-specific treatises, some of which are noted in Table 3-2.

C. Checking the Currency of a Treatise

Treatises are updated on a wide variety of schedules. For this reason, it is very important to check the currency of any treatise that you are using for research. There are three ways that treatises are kept up-to-date. First, smaller treatises, like the Nutshells and Hornbooks discussed below, are updated every few years through the publication of new editions. These treatises tend to be one volume, and they are sometimes published as paperback books. Second, some treatises are kept current through the use of "pocket parts" or supplemental paperback volumes. Pocket parts are supplemental inserts that fit into a slot in the back of a hardbound book. This form of supplementation is used for treatises that are kept current on a more regular basis, typically with annual updates. Third, larger treatises with editorial boards are often published in looseleaf format

Table 3-2. Other Oklahoma-Specific Treatises

- *Oklahoma Business Organization Forms and Practice* by Arnold and Cooper
- *Oklahoma Civil Procedure* by Adams and Boudreau
- *Oklahoma Commercial and Consumer Forms* by Miller and Harrell
- *Oklahoma Criminal Law: Statutes and Rules Annotated* by Cantrell
- *Oklahoma Criminal Practice and Procedure* by Jones
- *Oklahoma DUI Defense: The Law and Practice* by Hunsucker, Edge, and Nesci
- *Oklahoma Estate Planning* by Taylor
- *Oklahoma Family Law: Statutes and Rules Annotated* by Spector
- *Oklahoma Family Law: Direct and Cross Examination, Suggested Questions, Ideas and Outlines* by Harrington
- *Oklahoma Family Law: The Handbook* by Spector
- *Oklahoma Jury Instruction Handbook* by Adams
- *Oklahoma Real Estate Forms and Practice* by Epperson
- *Oklahoma Secured Transactions Under Revised Article 9 of the Uniform Commercial Code: Forms and Practice Manual* by Adkins

and updates are filed into the three-ring binders on a frequent basis. Some looseleaf treatises, like the enormous tax treatises, are very current, and new updates are filed every two weeks. Online versions of treatises tend to follow the same update schedule as their print counterparts.

D. Nutshells and Hornbooks

Nutshells and hornbooks are smaller, one-volume treatises used by law students, beginning practitioners, and anyone who is just beginning research in a particular subject area. Like treatises in general, Nutshells provide an overview of a broad subject area, such as constitutional law, contracts, or torts. Nutshells are available for virtually every legal topic. They provide more detail than legal encyclopedias but less detail than larger single or multi-volume treatises. Nutshells are published in paperback and are available on Westlaw and WestlawNext. New editions are issued every few years. This makes them a relatively inexpensive source for the beginning researcher. Nutshells are written in a narrative fashion and generally provide a short two-to-three page summary of each important court opinion that discusses a particular issue.

Hornbooks are slightly larger works than Nutshells, and they are intended primarily as teaching aids for law students. They are often written by law professors and other scholars who also write "casebooks" (textbooks) for law schools. Like Nutshells, they provide more detail than encyclopedias, but less than other treatises. Since they are teaching aids, they are written in a narrative and descriptive manner and provide summaries of landmark cases.

Because they are teaching tools and study aids, Nutshells and hornbooks are generally not cited in formal legal documents.

E. Looseleaf Treatises

Looseleaf treatises are a special form of treatise used in subject areas that require frequent updating. The term "looseleaf" means that the treatise is (or historically was) published in three-ring binders so that pages can be easily added and removed as new content becomes available. Looseleaf treatises are directed at practitioners who specialize in a particular area of law. They sometimes serve as a complete research library by including the full text of primary sources of law (such as the entire Internal Revenue Code) and secondary analytical material, such as case summaries, practice pointers, forms, tables, and news.

Looseleafs in print usually have many different types of finding aids, including very detailed and thorough indexes and tables of cases. Since they contain so much information, it can take time and effort to learn their arrangement. Many looseleafs are also available electronically so that they can be searched by keyword. Looseleafs are available on Westlaw, WestlawNext, Lexis, and Lexis Advance, and from the Bureau of National Affairs (BNA),[4] Commerce Clearinghouse (CCH),[5] Loislaw,[6] and Law Journal Press.[7]

IV. Law Journals and Law Reviews

Law journals, often called law reviews, publish scholarly articles written by law professors, law students, practicing attorneys, judges, and other legal experts. Most articles in law reviews provide an in-depth analysis of a specific legal issue and are heavily footnoted with references to key cases, statutes, regulations, and related scholarly articles written by other experts. Law review articles often present a summary of the current state of the law on a particular issue and then discuss the public policy implications. They are often written with legislators, judges, and other legal officials in mind, and they frequently recommend a particular course of action, such as the amendment of a law, the need for a new law, or the reversal of an important court decision.

There are more than 1,500 law journals and law reviews published in English alone. In the United States, most law reviews are published by law schools and are edited by top law students at those institutions. Table 3-3 lists law reviews and journals published by law schools in Oklahoma. Some law journals are published by commercial publish-

---

4. Bloomberg BNA, http://www.bna.com.
5. Commerce Clearinghouse, Inc., http://intelliconnect.cch.com.
6. Loislaw, http://www.loislaw.com.
7. Law Journal Press, http://www.lawjournalpress.com.

Table 3-3. Law Reviews and Journals Published by Oklahoma Law Schools

- *American Indian Law Review*—University of Oklahoma College of Law
- *Consumer Finance Law Quarterly Report*—Oklahoma City University School of Law
- *Energy Law Journal*—University of Tulsa School of Law
- *Oklahoma City University Law Review*—Oklahoma City University School of Law
- *Oklahoma Journal of Law and Technology*—University of Oklahoma College of Law
- *Oklahoma Law Review*—University of Oklahoma College of Law
- *Tulsa Law Review*—University of Tulsa School of Law

ers or by professional associations. These journals tend to be edited by law professors and other legal experts.

A. Types of Law Journals

In terms of content, there are essentially two types of law journals: general law reviews and subject-specific journals. General law reviews tend to carry the name of the publishing institution, such as the *Oklahoma Law Review*, produced by the University of Oklahoma College of Law. Although general law reviews may focus on issues specific to that school or state, they can include articles on any topic.

Subject-specific law reviews, such as the *American Indian Law Review*, focus on topics in a particular area. There are several ways to find law journals that focus on a specific topic. An excellent resource for finding law reviews is the Washington and Lee Law Journal database.[8] On the home page of this site, there is a drop-down menu la-

8. Wash. & Lee U. Sch. of Law, *Law Journals: Submissions and Rankings 2005–2012*, http://lawlib.wlu.edu/LJ/index.aspx.

beled "All Subjects." When choosing a subject from that menu, such as Energy Law, the researcher is provided with a list of energy-related journals in the database. The database includes a link to each journal's home page, contact information for the journal, and a description of whether the full text of the journal is available online. Law journals can also be located through a general Google search. Including the term "law review" or "law journal" along with keywords describing the subject area, such as energy law, will locate law reviews in that area.

B. Finding Law Review Articles by Citation

Often a researcher will have a citation to a particular law review article in hand. Most law reviews use the following citation format: 61 Okla. L. Rev. 257 (2010). In this example, "61" refers to the volume of the law review. "257" is the starting page, and "Okla. L. Rev." is the abbreviation for the journal's title, *Oklahoma Law Review*. With that citation in hand, a researcher can easily find the article on the journal's web site or in subscription databases such as Westlaw, Lexis, or, as discussed below, HeinOnline.

C. Finding Law Review Articles by Keyword

Since law reviews are generally published in chronological order, it's not efficient to find articles on a particular subject simply by browsing the bookshelves or looking at tables of contents online. To find articles by subject, a researcher needs to conduct a keyword search online or consult a print index. Although Westlaw and Lexis contain substantial law journal databases, there are a few other sources that are very important and helpful to researchers looking for legal scholarship in law journals.

1. HeinOnline

The most important source for locating law review articles today is a commercial database called HeinOnline, produced by William S. Hein & Co., Inc.[9] HeinOnline is unique in at least two ways. First, HeinOnline contains page images of the print versions of law reviews in PDF format. This has the benefit of keeping footnotes in law review articles on the same page as the text that discusses them. Second, HeinOnline has scanned over 1,500 law journals into its database beginning with the very first volume of each journal. Although Westlaw and Lexis also contain substantial full-text law journal databases, they include very few issues published before 1990. HeinOnline does have one limitation, however. Many law journals "embargo" their most current issues for a year or more. In other words, they require HeinOnline to wait one to three years before including the full text of recent issues in the database. This means that very current issues will need to be obtained through another source, such as the journal's own website, Westlaw, or Lexis. There has been a trend to reduce embargo periods among journals, but this is still an important consideration when searching for very new scholarship online.

2. LegalTrac and Index to Legal Periodicals

LegalTrac is an online index for law journals that is published by the major educational publisher, Gale. LegalTrac is not intended to be a comprehensive, full-text database of law journals, though it does contain the full text of articles for about 250 law journals.[10] LegalTrac's strength is its indexing of law journals. LegalTrac indexes more than 1,500 law journals from 1980 to the present. For most journals, it provides only bibliographic information, including article title, author, journal title, citation, and a link to other full-text databases that contain the article. The unique feature of LegalTrac is its subject indexing. The record for each law review article in LegalTrac includes a topic outline on the left side of the screen that shows the specific

9. HeinOnline, http://home.heinonline.org.
10. LegalTrac, http://www.gale.cengage.com/pdf/facts/legal.pdf.

topic where this article has been classified. With a simple click, you are then presented with other relevant documents that have been categorized in the same subject as the original article. The concept is similar to browsing books on a library shelf. All books on a particular subject are brought together for easy browsing. LegalTrac's subject indexing makes it extremely easy and efficient to locate related articles without having to worry if your keyword search has captured all relevant articles.

Index to Legal Periodicals (ILP) is a competing product to LegalTrac and is published by EBSCO. It indexes 1,025 legal journals, law reviews, yearbooks, institutes, bar association publications, and other materials. Coverage varies by journal, but coverage of most journals begins on January 1, 1981. EBSCO also offers a historical index to law journals, called Index to Legal Periodicals Retrospective: 1908–1981. This database indexes approximately 750 journals.

3. Law Journals on Westlaw and Lexis

As mentioned above, Westlaw and Lexis include substantial full-text law journal databases. WestlawNext and Lexis Advance have the same journal content as the "classic" version of these systems. The primary law journal database on Westlaw is called "TP-ALL," which stands for "Texts and Periodicals—All." On Lexis, the primary law journal database is simply called "Law Reviews & Journals," and a link is available on the "Legal" tab when you first log into the system. As mentioned above, the primary limitation of these services is their scope of coverage. The full text of few journals is available prior to 1990. However, assuming you primarily need to search for articles from the past twenty years, there are many advantages to using Westlaw, WestlawNext, Lexis or Lexis Advance. All of these services have very powerful search interfaces that make it possible to quickly find a few relevant articles or alternatively conduct a very specific survey of the entire landscape of legal scholarship on a given issue. In addition, they also have powerful citator features, KeyCite and Shepard's.

These features make it easy to locate later articles that have cited to an earlier article. Using a citator, researchers can follow the scholarly debate on a particular issue as more recent scholarship cites back to earlier scholarship.

4. *Google Scholar*

In 2009, Google added legal content, including court opinions and legal journals, to its Google Scholar service. Google Scholar can be used to search the full text of those law journals that make their content available for free on the Internet. To locate articles from *legal* periodicals, as opposed to other disciplines, available on the Internet, click the "Legal Documents" button just below the main Google Scholar search box.[11] Once your results are retrieved, you can use the filtering options on the left-hand side of the screen to limit your search results to articles only. You can also filter your search results by date and change the sorting method from relevance to date. Note also that Google scholar is able to "discover" the full text of some journals that are actually contained in commercial databases. For instance, articles can be found through Google Scholar that are included in the commercial databases HeinOnline and JSTOR.[12] Access to those articles through Google Scholar will depend upon the subscription provided by the institution where the researcher is located.

5. *Bar Journals*

Bar journals are periodicals published by county, state, and federal bar associations. They are typically published monthly or bi-weekly and distributed to each member of the bar association. Bar journals are very practitioner-oriented. Although, they do contain articles on current legal issues, the articles tend to be much shorter than those in law reviews and often are written by practicing attorneys or judges.

---

11. Google Scholar, http://scholar.google.com/.

12. JSTOR, http://www.jstor.org. This is a multi-disciplinary journal database that also includes several law-related titles in full-text PDF format.

Bar journals also contain lots of practical information for attorneys, such as events calendars, important notices for bar members, summaries of recent court opinions, notices of unpublished court opinions, advertising from legal service providers, continuing legal education information, classified advertising, and more.

In Oklahoma, the *Oklahoma Bar Journal* is the official publication of the Oklahoma Bar Association. PDF versions of the journal from 1994 to the present are freely available online at the Oklahoma Bar Associate website.[13] Two issues are published each month, which contain appellate court opinions and bar association information. Ten special issues are published each year addressing a specific theme; these issues contain articles on current legal topics, information on trends in the legal profession, and ethics and practice management tips. The counties with the two largest metropolitan areas in Oklahoma, Oklahoma County and Tulsa County, also have bar associations that produce monthly bar journals. The Oklahoma County Bar Association produces a journal called *Briefcase*,[14] which is available online free-of-charge from 2006 to the present. The Tulsa County Bar Association also produces a monthly bar journal called *Tulsa Lawyer*.

The national bar journal of the American Bar Association is called the *ABA Journal*. The *ABA Journal* can be accessed for free online at the ABA's website. Issues from 2004 to the present are available in PDF format online. Similar to state bar journals, the *ABA Journal* contains a lot of practical information. However, it contains much more scholarship on legal issues and trends nationwide.

The most comprehensive full-text collection of bar journals online can be found in HeinOnline. As with its law journal database, HeinOnline has scanned the full text of most bar journals beginning with the first issue of each journal. Both the *ABA Journal* and the *Ok-*

---

13. Okla. Bar Ass'n, Oklahoma Bar Journal, http://www.okbar.org/members/barjournal.aspx.

14. Okla. County Bar Ass'n, Casebriefs, http://www.okcbar.org/.displaynewsletter.cfm.

lahoma Bar Journal are available in full text on HeinOnline. HeinOnline should be used for searching the full text of the *Oklahoma Bar Journal* because the Oklahoma Bar Association website does not provide an interface for searching the full text. Furthermore, HeinOnline contains the *Oklahoma Bar Journal* from 1930 to the present. Bar journal articles for some jurisdictions can also be searched online using Westlaw, WestlawNext, Lexis, and Lexis Advance, and many state bar journals are now freely available on the internet in PDF format, usually as a publication within the state bar association website.

V. *American Law Reports*

American Law Reports (ALR) is published by Thomson Reuters and is composed of individual articles written by lawyers, judges, and law professors on very specific legal issues. These articles summarize or "annotate" court opinions on a specific matter and provide a wealth of helpful research references.[15] Each ALR article can be thought of as mini-treatise addressing a particular legal question.

ALR articles have a national scope, and they seek to identify and summarize relevant cases, statutes, and regulations on point for a particular topic from every jurisdiction in the country. This approach makes it easy to locate key Oklahoma cases, statutes, and regulations, and it allows researchers to determine how Oklahoma's laws compare to national trends. ALR articles are different from law review articles in that they attempt to objectively summarize cases and identify trends among the various jurisdictions. They also provide a wealth of library references. ALR authors add helpful features like cross-references to related annotations, references to Westlaw databases, practice pointers, and even sample keyword searches used by the author on Westlaw to gather the relevant authority.

15. "Annotation" is used in legal research to refer to a case summary. The word is used in two contexts. Most commonly, it is used to refer to case summaries that appear at the end of statutory code sections. However, ALR articles, which are compilations of case annotations, are also referred to as annotations.

ALR articles address each aspect of a particular issue in outline fashion, and where different jurisdictions have adopted different approaches, the cases from each jurisdiction are sorted based on their outcome and analysis. This organization allows you to identify easily how the courts in your home jurisdiction have ruled, and it makes it easy to find other court opinions that have ruled in a way that supports your client's case. A keyword index of the article is also provided.

ALR is available on Westlaw, WestlawNext, Lexis, and Lexis Advance, and it is also published in print. There are three ways to locate ALR articles. First, all ALR volumes are contained within a database on Westlaw and Lexis, which can be searched by keyword. Second, ALR articles can be found through the KeyCite and Shepard's services on Westlaw and Lexis. If you have already found a relevant case or statute through prior searching, the KeyCite or Shepard's report for that case will provide references to each ALR article that mentions the case. This is one of the most powerful ways that researcher can find additional cases addressing a legal question. Third, when using the print version of ALR, index volumes located at the end of the set allow you to find the citation to relevant ALR articles by keyword.

ALR has been published in six successive "series" of volumes, called ALR, ALR 2d, ALR 3d, etc. The series numbers simply indicate how recently an ALR article was published. Articles in the sixth series are the most recent. Articles in the first series are the oldest. Note, however, that many of the older articles are kept current by pocket parts in print and by updates to the online database. Just because an ALR article is old does not mean that it is irrelevant or discontinued. Whenever an older article is superseded, ALR will provide an indication of the newer article in the supplement to the superseded article. Finally, there are also two ALR sets devoted specifically to federal issues. They are called *American Law Reports, Federal* and *American Law Reports, Federal 2d*.

In 2010, ALR *International* was created by West. The international set provides analysis of legal issues and case law from countries around the world. ALR *International* covers both English and non-

English-speaking countries and focuses on international legal issues that have been litigated in the U.S. and global courts.

VI. Form Books

The saying "don't reinvent the wheel" is especially true for the production of legal documents, such as pleadings, contracts, wills, and leases. Imagine for a moment the number of people over the years who have filed litigation documents, who have started a business, who have needed a will, or who have signed a lease for an apartment. Since many people and companies have similar needs, lawyers have drafted legal documents with similar provisions countless times. For this reason, anyone who is preparing a legal document should consult a legal form book.

Legal form books, as the name suggests, contain the full text of legal forms, which allow individuals to "fill in the blanks" relating to their own factual situation. However, some form books also contain important practice tips, and some even contain substantive discussions of the law relevant to the legal issue for which the form was created.

Legal form books are available in a variety of formats. Traditional print form books are frequently used by members of the public to photocopy forms from local law libraries. Like most legal publications, most form books are now also available online, which facilitates the document creation process even more. Westlaw and Lexis both allow researchers to download forms in Microsoft Word format, which allows them to be easily manipulated and edited. Finally, large law firms manipulate forms in highly sophisticated software packages, like HotDocs.[16] These systems allow forms to be automatically populated with information from client questionnaires, court documents, and legal memos.

16. HotDocs, http://www.hotdocs.com/.

A. Oklahoma Form Books

The most comprehensive form book set in Oklahoma is *Vernon's Oklahoma Forms 2d*, which is published by Thomson Reuters. *Vernon's* is available in print, online via Westlaw and WestlawNext, and on CD-ROM. In addition to containing the forms themselves, *Vernon's* is annotated to include practice tips and commentaries, drafting advice, and citations to relevant cases and statutes. Subjects covered include commercial and consumer law, criminal law, civil procedure, business organizations, and real estate. The publisher states that the set is created by locally prominent attorneys.

The Oklahoma Bar Association produces a form book specifically designed for Oklahoma practitioners. The book is simply called the *OBA/CLE Form Book.*[17] The book is described by the Oklahoma Bar Association as a "must have" for the Oklahoma general practitioner, and some of the forms contained in it are heavily requested at local law libraries. At only $195, it is a bargain compared to many legal publications. The book comes in the form of a large three-ring binder with an accompanying CD-ROM that includes all of the forms in both Microsoft Word and WordPerfect formats. The forms contained in the book cover a wide range of legal topics, including general civil litigation, business organizations, divorce and adoption, criminal law, and probate. A complete listing of the table of contents for the OBA Form Book can be found on the OBA website.

Another excellent source for Oklahoma forms is the Oklahoma State Courts Network (OSCN).[18] Here you can obtain forms produced by the various departments of state government and adopted by the Oklahoma Supreme Court. Many heavily used forms can be

---

17. *OBA/CLE 2013 Form Book*, http://www.okbar.org/members/cle.aspx. Note that this form book was most recently published in 2013. Before using the forms in this book, you would need to make sure that the law underlying a particular form has not been changed by the courts or the legislature since the date of publication.

18. Oklahoma State Court Network (OSCN), *Forms*, http://www.oscn.net/static/forms/start.asp.

Table 3-4. Oklahoma Form Books

- *OBA/CLE Form Book* by the Oklahoma Bar Association
- *Oklahoma Civil Procedure Forms and Practice* by Muchmore and Ellis
- *Oklahoma Corporate Forms* by Mock and Holloman
- *Oklahoma Employment Law Forms and Practice Manual* by Whatley
- *Oklahoma Estate Planning: Will Drafting and Estate Administration Forms* by Coffman and Jones
- *Oklahoma Probate Law and Practice with Forms* by Huff
- *Oklahoma Real Estate Forms* by Durbin and Bixler
- *Oklahoma Secured Transactions Under Revised Article 9 of the Uniform Commercial Code: Forms and Practice Manual* by Adkins
- *Vernon's Oklahoma Forms 2d* compiled by many local authors

found here. Forms are provided on a wide variety of subjects, including general civil litigation, family law, property, workers' compensation, corporations and business organization, and much more.

In addition to the sources mentioned above, there are a multitude of subject-specific form books. These form books can be found by searching your local law library's catalog, the Directory on Westlaw, or the "Find a Source" feature of Lexis. Table 3-4 lists several subject-specific Oklahoma form books. Some of the treatises in the *Oklahoma Practice Series* (mentioned earlier) also contain forms.

B. National Form Book Sets

Some form book sets are multi-jurisdictional and provide generic forms that can be modified for use in different courts. The largest and most comprehensive form book set is *American Jurisprudence Pleading and Practice Forms Annotated.* This set contains over 44,000 forms. In addition to the form itself, this resource also includes practitioner advice, commentary, "how-to" guidance, and references to statutes and procedural rules that support the form. Other major multi-jurisdictional form sets include the *West's Legal Forms*, *Nichols Cyclopedia of Legal Forms Annotated*, and *American Jurisprudence Legal Forms 2d.* Some form sets focus specifically on federal litigation. Those include *West's Federal Forms*, *Federal Procedural Forms*, and *Nichols Cyclopedia of Federal Procedure Forms.*

These large form book sets are available in print and on both Westlaw and Lexis. On Westlaw Classic, click the "Directory" link at the top of the page, then click on "Forms." Westlaw Classic has a special "FormFinder" feature that attempts to guide you to the appropriate form by subject matter, jurisdiction, and keyword. On WestlawNext, simply click on the "Forms" link on the home page. On Lexis Advance, you can search for forms by clicking the "All Content Types" drop-down menu directly beneath the main search box on the home page. From there, you can check a box to search forms only. On Lexis, view the "Legal" tab, then look in the "Secondary Sources" heading and click on "Forms and Agreements."

VII. Continuing Legal Education Materials

Most attorneys are required by state laws and bar association rules to attend continuing legal education (CLE) programs every year. In Oklahoma, attorneys must attend twelve hours of continuing legal education programs every year to retain their license to practice law.[19]

---

19. Okla. Bar Ass'n, *Mandatory Continuing Legal Education*, http://www.okbar.org/members/mcle.aspx.

Experienced attorneys who are experts in a particular subject area often teach continuing education programs. These programs are usually recorded and/or transcribed for later publication by the bar association or by an independent commercial publisher of CLE programs. CLE programs on popular themes are often taught every year or every few years. For instance, in Oklahoma, a program titled *The Criminal Trial from Start to Finish* is offered and published every few years and, as indicated by the title, covers opening statements, examination of witnesses, ethics, presenting evidence, closing statements, and more. These publications can be very helpful resources because they present practical advice from experienced attorneys.

In Oklahoma, the two major publishers of CLE programming are the Department of Continuing Legal Education at the Oklahoma Bar Association and the National Business Institute (NBI). CLE publications can generally be purchased directly from the state bar association that accredits the programming or from a commercial publisher like NBI. For bar members, CLE offerings are increasingly available online. Oklahoma has a wide array of CLE programming available on its website.

Most academic law libraries purchase CLE publications relevant to the state where they are located. To find CLE materials in a local law library, consult the library catalog. In Oklahoma, CLE materials in the library catalog can be found by conducting an advanced search. Use the publisher's name as one search term ("National Business Institute" or "Oklahoma Bar Association") and then add search terms for the CLE subjects you want to find, such as "criminal," or "divorce," or "business." A quick search of the University of Oklahoma Law Library catalog for the terms "Oklahoma Bar Association" and "criminal" returns 34 CLE titles on criminal law.

VIII. Restatements

Restatements are a unique type of secondary source. The American Law Institute, a prestigious group of approximately 4000 law professors, judges, and lawyers, publishes the Restatements. The ALI describes itself as "the leading independent organization in the United States producing scholarly work to clarify, modernize, and otherwise improve the law."[20] While no secondary sources are ever binding upon a court, Restatements are perhaps the most persuasive secondary sources to judges because of the role they serve. They seek to make the law more accessible by distilling common law rules, developed in the courts, into succinct "black letter" rules. This is extremely helpful to practitioners, lawyers, and judges because of the amount of work involved in surveying common law rules nationwide. The process of developing a new Restatement takes many years. For instance, the original *Restatement of Contracts* was published in 1932. The *Restatement (Second) of Contracts* was published in 1981.

After each black letter rule, Restatements include extensive commentary and illustrations. The comments provide discussion and explanation about each black letter rule. The illustrations apply the black letter rule to different fact scenarios and explain how the rule will operate and what the outcome would likely be. Figure 3-3 shows the rule, commentary, and illustration for a Restatement section as it appears on WestlawNext.

Restatements are available for the following subject areas: agency, conflict of laws, contracts, foreign relations law, judgments, law governing lawyers, property, restitution, suretyship and guaranty, torts, trusts, and unfair competition. Restatements are available on both Westlaw and Lexis. On Westlaw Classic, the database identifier is "REST." On WestlawNext, they can be found within the "Secondary Sources" link on the home page. Likewise, on Lexis, the Restatements can be found within the "Secondary Sources" link. On Lexis Advance, Restatements can be found through the "Browse Sources" link in the top-right corner of the home page.

---

20. American Law Institute, http://www.ali.org.

Figure 3-3. Excerpt from *Restatement (Second) of Contracts*, § 278 Substituted Performance

Chapter 12. Discharge By Assent Or Alteration
Topic 2. Substituted Performance, Substituted Contract, Accord And Account Stated

§ 278. Substituted Performance

Link to Case Citations

(1) If an obligee accepts in satisfaction of the obligor's duty a performance offered by the obligor that differs from what is due, the duty is discharged.

(2) If an obligee accepts in satisfaction of the obligor's duty a performance offered by a third person, the duty is discharged, but an obligor who has not previously assented to the performance for his benefit may in a reasonable time after learning of it render the discharge inoperative from the beginning by disclaimer.

Comment:

a. Substituted performance by the obligor. If the obligor offers a performance that differs from what is due in full or partial satisfaction of his duty, the obligee need not accept it. If he chooses to accept it, however, the obligor is discharged in accordance with the terms of the offer. The obligee generally cannot avoid the consequences of such an exercise of dominion by a declaration that he does not assent to the condition attached by the debtor. Uniform Commercial Code § 1-207, providing for acceptance of performance under reservation of rights, need not be read as changing this well-established rule. See Comment *d* to § 281.

Illustration:

1. A owes B $1,000. A offers B a machine in full satisfaction of his debt, and B accepts it. A's debt is discharged. The result is the same if, before accepting the machine, B writes A that he does not accept it in full satisfaction of the debt.

Chapter 4

The Constitution

I. Introduction

Under the authority of the Oklahoma Enabling Act of 1906,[1] an Oklahoma Constitutional Convention was convened on November 20, 1906.[2] The resulting document was the original constitution of Oklahoma, ratified on September 17, 1907. The Constitution of the State of Oklahoma became effective on November 16, 1907, following President Theodore Roosevelt's signature of the proclamation announcing Oklahoma statehood.[3]

The Oklahoma Constitution was not, in fact, the first constitution drafted and ratified in the territory that was to become the state of Oklahoma. The first such document was the Choctaw Constitution, drafted in 1834, followed by similar constitutions drafted by the majority of the other tribes in Indian Territory.[4] In the first few years of the 20th century, it was uncertain whether Oklahoma was to become one single state or two separate states. The majority of the tribes in Indian Territory gathered and ratified the Sequoyah Constitution in 1905 in an effort to form the state of Sequoyah, which

---

1. Pub. L. No. 59-234, 34 Stat. 267 (1906).

2. For a detailed history of the Oklahoma Constitutional Convention, consult Albert H. Ellis, *A History of the Constitutional Convention of the State of Oklahoma* (1923).

3. Exec. Procl. of Nov. 16, 1907, 35 Stat. 2160 (Nov. 16, 1907).

4. Danny M. Adkison & Lisa McNair Palmer, *The Oklahoma State Constitution: A Reference Guide* 2 (2001).

would exist separate and apart from the state of Oklahoma. Though Congress did not ultimately approve the state of Sequoyah, several members of the Sequoyah Convention involved in the drafting of its constitution were later involved in the drafting of the Constitution for the state of Oklahoma, and they took significant inspiration from this earlier document.[5]

Though Oklahoma's constitution was not necessarily atypical of state constitutions ratified in the early 1900s, its content and length indicated trends in state constitutional drafting favoring an almost statutory code-like detail and progressive policies.[6] The Oklahoma Constitution was among the first to include an initiative and referendum process (discussed in greater detail later in this chapter), a prohibition on debtor's prison, and strict regulation of corporations.[7] The detailed nature of the provisions in the Constitution, coupled with the inclusion of the initiative and referendum process, are most often attributed to a fundamental mistrust of the legislative branch of government held by those involved in the drafting of the document.[8]

Table 4-1 lists the articles of the Oklahoma Constitution. Though the Oklahoma Constitution is not amended often, amendments are frequent enough that it is best to consult one of the resources listed in this chapter to confirm the precise language and content of constitutional articles and sections prior to citing them. Additionally, the highly detailed nature of the provisions of the Oklahoma Constitution makes it necessary to consult the Constitution for relevant provisions when beginning research in the event that the particular subject matter is covered by a constitutional provision.

---

5. William H. Murray, *Chronicles of Oklahoma* vol. 9, 126 (1931), http://digital.library.okstate.edu/chronicles/v009/v009p126.html.

6. Adkison & McNair Palmer, *supra* note 4, at 15.

7. *Id.*

8. *Id.*; Frederick F. Blachly & Miriam E. Oatman, *Government of Oklahoma* 15, 26 (2d ed. 1929).

Table 4-1. Articles of the Constitution of Oklahoma

Article I	Federal Relations
Article II	Bill of Rights
Article III	Suffrage
Article IV	Distribution of Powers
Article V	Legislative Department
Article VI	Executive Department
Article VII	Judicial Department
Article VII A	Court on the Judiciary
Article VII B	Selection of Justices and Judges
Article VIII	Impeachment and Removal from Office
Article IX	Corporations
Article X	Revenue and Taxation
Article XI	State and School Lands
Article XII	Homestead and Exemptions
Article XII A	Homestead Exemptions from Taxation
Article XIII	Education
Article XIII A	Oklahoma State System of Higher Education
Article XIII B	Board of Regents of Oklahoma Colleges
Article XIV	Banks and Banking
Article XV	Oath of Office
Article XVI	Public Roads
Article XVII	Counties
Article XVIII	Municipal Corporations
Article XIX	Insurance
Article XX	Manufacture and Commerce
Article XXI	Public Institutions
Article XXII	Alien and Corporate Ownership of Lands
Article XXIII	Miscellaneous
Article XXIV	Constitutional Amendments
Article XXV	Social Security
Article XXVI	Department of Wildlife Conservation
Article XXVIII	Alcoholic Beverage Laws and Enforcement
Article XXIX	Ethics Commission
Article XXX	Official Actions of the State of Oklahoma

II. Sources for Accessing the Oklahoma Constitution

A. The Constitution in the *Oklahoma Statutes*

The *Oklahoma Statutes* is the official compilation of the constitution and statutes of the State of Oklahoma. It is currently published by West and is fully reprinted every decade, during years ending in one (e.g., 2001, 2011). Supplemental volumes are published annually and include updates to the Constitution and statutes since the prior full publication of the set or most recent supplemental volume. Additionally, the supplement volumes contain proposed amendments to the Constitution that are pending at the time of publication of the volume. Supplemental volumes are cumulative. Thus, each supplemental volume includes the contents of prior supplemental volumes since the most recent publication of the full set. Remember, however, that this set is updated only once per year. Thorough research practices dictate consulting at least one online resource discussed in this chapter to confirm the text of the most current version of the provision.

Research regarding how the language of a constitutional provision was written on a particular date may require reference to multiple volumes. This type of research should begin in the volume containing the Constitution for the year in question. If the volume consulted is from a year in which the entire statutory code and Constitution are reprinted, every constitutional provision in force will be included in the volume. Look closely at the history information that follows the text of the provision, as shown in Figure 4-1. That history information will indicate whether or not the constitutional provision has been amended, and if so, the effective date of the amendment.

If the volume consulted is a supplement, any new language of the constitutional provision of interest will appear in the volume only if the constitutional provision has undergone a change within the year. History information about the amendment and its effective date will be placed just below the text of the section. If the article and section do not appear in the supplement volume, this indicates that there has

Figure 4-1. Oklahoma Constitutional Provision

IN GENERAL

§ 1. Executive officers enumerated—Offices and records—Duties

A. The Executive authority of the state shall be vested in a Governor, Lieutenant Governor, Secretary of State, State Auditor and Inspector, Attorney General, State Treasurer, Superintendent of Public Instruction, Commissioner of Labor, Commissioner of Insurance and other officers provided by law and this Constitution, each of whom shall keep his office and public records, books and papers at the seat of government, and shall perform such duties as may be designated in this Constitution or prescribed by law.

B. The Secretary of State shall be appointed by the Governor by and with the consent of the Senate for a term of four (4) years to run concurrently with the term of the Governor.

Amended by State Question Nos. 509 to 513, Legislation Referendum Nos. 209 to 213, adopted at election held on July 22, 1975, eff. Jan. 8, 1979; State Question No. 594, Legislative Referendum No. 258, adopted at election held on Aug. 26, 1986; State Question No. 613, Legislative Referendum No. 270, adopted at election held on Nov. 8, 1988.

Amendment proposed by Laws 1988, p. 1851, H.J.R. No. 1044.

Amendment proposed by Laws 1985, p. 1676, H.J.R. No. 1018.

Amendment proposed by Laws 1975, p. 731, S.J.R. No. 37, § 1. Section 3 provides that this resolution shall become effective on January 8, 1979.

St.1931, § 13518.

States ⚿41.

Construction and application

Love v. Boyle, 72 Okl. 300, 180 P. 705 (1919); State v. Huston, 27 Okl. 606, 113 P. 190 (1910), 34 L.R.A.,N.S., 380.

This section makes insurance commissioner part of executive branch of government and expresses intent that legislature may vest in him executive power to adjust all matters growing out of disputes between companies and policyholders. Oklahoma Benefit Life Ass'n v. Bird, 192 Okl. 288, 135 P.2d 994 (1943).

Corporation Commissioners

Corporation Commissioners are included in the language "* * * and other elective State officers, * * *" contained in constitutional article relating to impeachment and are liable and subject to impeachment. State ex rel. Blankenship v. Freeman, Okl., 440 P.2d 744 (1968).

been no amendment to the section within the last year. Choose the volume from the prior year and search again. Continue looking at each prior year's publication until the language of the constitutional provision appears and examine the history information following that article and section.

Though the title of this statutory compilation does not indicate that it is annotated, the *Oklahoma Statutes* do contain limited annotations. Following each constitutional section, there are references to significant case law that applies, interprets, or construes the section. There is also at least one West Digest System topic and key number assigned to each constitutional provision to assist with additional case law research.

B. The Constitution in *West's Oklahoma Statutes Annotated*

The Oklahoma Constitution is included in the first five volumes of *West's Oklahoma Statutes Annotated* (WOSA) set. The initial volume contains a number of significant documents, including the original Constitution of the State of Oklahoma, the Constitution of the United States, the Organic Act, the Enabling Act, and an Initiative and Referendum table. The volumes in this annotated set are updated with pocket parts.

The complete Oklahoma Constitution with accompanying annotations is found in the remaining four volumes. Annotations include cases from both federal and Oklahoma state appellate courts, cross-references from other state and federal constitutional provisions and Oklahoma statutes, relevant law journal references, and additional selected secondary source references. Pay careful attention to the Preface of the main volume (or pocket part if there is one) to determine the precise currency of the information in the volume. Amendments to the Oklahoma Constitution approved following the publication of the volume and pocket part will not be included. Thus, it is critical to consult an online source to determine the most current version of the provisions at hand.

The final volume in the WOSA set related to the Constitution contains an index for the provisions of the Constitution. Additionally, constitutional provisions are indexed in the annual General Index pamphlet found at the end of the set. Also included in this final constitutional volume is the Schedule, drafted to assure the orderly transition from Indian Territory and the Territory of Oklahoma to the State of Oklahoma in 1907.

C. Free Online Access to the Oklahoma Constitution

The full text of the Oklahoma Constitution is available via the Oklahoma State Courts Network (OSCN) at www.oscn.net, under the "Legal Research" tab. OSCN allows the researcher to browse the Constitution by Article and section or search by keyword. Historical data which indicates whether a section has been repealed, amended, or added as a result of an initiative or referendum is provided.

The full text of the Constitution is also available at the Oklahoma Legislature's website at www.oklegislature.gov, under the "Legislation" link. This site provides access to the Constitution in Microsoft Word format and includes the same historical data provided by OSCN. However, the legislature's site does not give information about other documents that cite to each constitutional section.

D. The Constitution on Lexis and Westlaw

Both Westlaw and Lexis include the Oklahoma Constitution in their respective state statutory databases for Oklahoma. In Westlaw Classic, you need only search for a database with the phrase "Oklahoma Statutes." Using WestlawNext, you may either select the link for Statutes & Court Rules and then choose Oklahoma, or you may click on the tab for State Materials and choose Oklahoma. Either selection will allow you to view the Oklahoma Statutes & Court Rules database, in which you will find the Constitution. When using Lexis, simply select States Legal and then click the link for Oklahoma. Access via Lexis Advance requires only that you select "browse sources" and search for Oklahoma Statues. Again, the Oklahoma Constitution is found in the same database as the Oklahoma Statutes. Both systems allow for browsing and searching within the text and annotations of the Constitution.

Westlaw has compiled annotations for the Constitution including relevant secondary authorities; cross-references to other statutory or constitutional sections; and cases that interpret, apply, or construe constitutional provisions. Additionally, the KeyCite feature of Westlaw provides access to documents that cite a specific article and section of the Constitution. KeyCite, an electronic citator service available through Westlaw Classic and WestlawNext, is discussed in Chapter 11.

Lexis has a somewhat less robust system of annotations for the Oklahoma Constitution, which include only case citations to individual articles and sections. Additionally, it is difficult to Shepardize the Oklahoma Constitution using Lexis. You must go directly to the Shepard's feature of Lexis and enter a citation for a Constitutional provision in order to Shepardize it. If you retrieve a constitutional provision and then attempt to Shepardize it using the *Shepardize* link at the top of the page, you will not receive any results, even if the provision has been cited.

III. Amendments to the Oklahoma Constitution

Attention to constitutional amendments is particularly important in light of the way in which the Oklahoma Constitution has served as both an object of and vehicle for reform since its ratification.[9] One of the more progressive elements of the Oklahoma Constitution is the inclusion of the initiative and referendum process as a means for enacting laws and amending the Constitution.[10] "Initiative means the power of the people to propose bills (or constitutional amendments),

---

9. Ann-Marie Szymanski, *Oklahoma Constitutional Revision, Revisited*, 2 Okla. Policy Stud. Rev. 13 (2001).

10. Okla. Const. art. XXIV.

and to enact or reject them at the polls. Referendum is the right of the people to have bills passed by the legislature submitted to the voters for their approval."[11] Under Article XXIV of the Oklahoma Constitution, amendments proposed by either house of the state legislature and agreed to by a majority of both houses must be referred to the people for their approval or rejection. No legislative proposal for a constitutional amendment may encompass more than a single subject to be amended. Section 3 of this Article explicitly recognizes the right of the people to amend the Constitution through the initiative petition process. Interestingly, the Oklahoma Constitution also provides for amendment via constitutional convention, yet there has not been a constitutional convention in Oklahoma since the first in 1907.[12]

An excellent source for details about the initiative and referendum process and exploration of both successful and unsuccessful attempts to amend the Oklahoma Constitution can be found on the Oklahoma Secretary of State's website at www.sos.ok.gov. Those matters submitted for consideration and vote of the people by the initiative and referendum process are called state questions. Examine the "Executive/Legislative" area of the site to review the petition process and proposed state questions. A complete and searchable state question table is also provided which details the summary, disposition, type, and date of all initiatives and referenda since statehood. Patricia Monk has also authored a useful article entitled "Researching Initiatives and Referenda: A Guide for Oklahoma."[13]

IV. Research Questions Related to the Oklahoma Constitution

Oklahoma courts generally interpret constitutional provisions by focusing on the language of the provision itself and applying the stan-

---

11. Adkison & McNair Palmer, *supra* note 4, at 299.
12. *Id.* at 9.
13. 26 Leg. Ref. Servs. Q. 265 (2008).

dard rules of statutory construction.[14] Additionally, some case law advances the proposition that the best method for interpretation is an attempt to give effect to the intent of the drafters.[15] As a general matter, such inquiries focus on the plain language of the statute, following the "plain meaning rule."[16] Yet, there are instances in which constitutional provisions may either be ambiguous on their face or in their application. In these rare instances, it is possible that the intent of the drafters may be drawn from the debate reflected in the minutes of the constitutional convention, available in the collection of the Oklahoma Historical Society.[17] It should be noted, however, that complex searches for the drafters' intent are unlikely to yield substantial or useful results in all but a few unique cases. Thus, a more straightforward approach is often the best course for any researcher asked to inquire into the interpretation or application of a provision of the Oklahoma Constitution.

When faced with a research problem that requires interpretation of an Oklahoma constitutional provision, you should first review existing case law that interprets, construes, or applies the provision. An initial list of cases can be located in print by consulting the constitutional article and section in either the official *Oklahoma Statutes* or *West's Oklahoma Statutes Annotated* and reviewing the "Notes of Decision" following the section text and other research references. When conducting research in print, remember that the cases included are only as current as the publication date of the volume and/or pocket part consulted. You should next consult an online resource for the Constitution. Westlaw and Lexis both provide relevant case law for articles and sections of the Oklahoma Constitution. After reviewing these initial cases, remember to consult the *Oklahoma Digest* or an

---

14. *Draper v. State*, 621 P.2d 1142 (Okla. 1980).

15. *Wimberly v. Deacon*, 144 P.2d 447 (Okla. 1944).

16. An excellent discussion of the "plain meaning rule" can be found in Norman J. Singer & J.D. Shambie Singer, *Statutes and Statutory Construction* vol. 2A, § 46.1, 137–58 (3d ed. 2007).

17. Visit http://okhistory.cuadra.com/star/public.html and search the archives for the Oklahoma Constitutional Convention minutes.

online database to expand the search for cases interpreting the constitutional article and section.[18]

Should review of the case law related to the constitutional provision in question fail to clarify the way in which it should be interpreted, additional methods for interpretation should be considered. Another element of Oklahoma constitutional interpretation involves the nature of the section in question. Because Oklahoma's Constitution provides for its amendment through the initiative and referendum process,[19] take care to determine if the provision in question is the product of a public initiative or legislative referendum. If so, it may be useful to engage in legislative history research on the particular initiative or referendum to get a greater sense of the context for the amendment.[20]

V. State versus Federal Constitutions

Recent challenges to Oklahoma constitutional amendments based on the United States Constitution illustrate an additional way in which state constitutional research may be undertaken. Any claim questioning the federal constitutionality of a state constitutional provision must necessarily be researched using federal research resources. While a complete discussion of federal constitutional research is outside the scope of this chapter, note that an examination of the United States Constitution article and section in question and the law interpreting that provision will play a central role in determining whether or not the state constitutional provision comports with federal constitutional principles. The United States Constitution with annotations can be found in the *United States Code Annotated* (published by West), in the *United States Code Service* (published by Lexis), on Westlaw, and on Lexis.

---

18. Case law research methods are covered in Chapter 6.

19. Okla. Const. art. V.

20. A more detailed discussion of Oklahoma legislative history research can be found in Chapter 8.

Chapter 5

Judicial Opinions

> *I am pleased that you have noticed my efforts to produce opinions which are clear, succinct and without footnotes, where possible. Opinion writing is something which leaves room for different styles, and I have no illusions that my approach will be widely copied. Nevertheless, in my view we write for a rather wide "audience" here at the Supreme Court, and clarity and simplicity can be virtues.—Sandra Day O'Connor*[1]

A judicial opinion, also called a case, is written by a court to explain its decision in a particular dispute. Unlike statutes, which are published both chronologically, by date of enactment, and topically in codified formats, judicial opinions are published in rough chronological order in books called reporters.

This chapter begins with an overview of the Oklahoma court system. Next, because the federal court system also operates within Oklahoma and affects Oklahoma law, this chapter provides an overview of the federal court system. The chapter then explains the precedential value of cases within Oklahoma and the availability of print reporters and online sources for Oklahoma and federal judicial opinions.

---

1. Ray Forrester, *Supreme Court Opinions-Style and Substance: An Appeal for Reform*, 47 Hastings L.J. 167 (1995–1996), citing Letter from Justice Sandra Day O'Connor, United States Supreme Court, to Ray Forrester, Professor, Hastings College of the Law (May 11, 1988).

I. Court Systems

The basic court structure involves a trial court, an intermediate appellate court, and an ultimate appellate court (often referenced as the Supreme Court in many state court systems).

A. Oklahoma Courts

The organization of Oklahoma courts is depicted in Figure 5-1. In Oklahoma, trial courts are called district courts.[2] These courts are located in each of Oklahoma's seventy-seven counties. Oklahoma's intermediate court for civil issues is the Oklahoma Court of Civil Appeals. The Oklahoma Court of Civil Appeals is composed of twelve judges, who sit in four permanent divisions. Two divisions sit in Oklahoma County and two divisions sit in Tulsa County.[3]

Unique to Oklahoma,[4] the Oklahoma Court of Criminal Appeals has "exclusive appellate jurisdiction in criminal cases."[5] As such, the Oklahoma Court of Criminal Appeals serves as the court of last resort for criminal matters. The Oklahoma Supreme Court is thus the ultimate appellate court in matters of a civil nature, while the Court of Criminal Appeals decides criminal matters. The Oklahoma Court of Criminal Appeals consists of five judges, "any three of whom shall

2. Okla. State Court Network, *The Oklahoma Court System*, http://www.oscn.net/applications/oscn/start.asp?viewType=COURTS.

3. 20 O.S.2011, § 30.2.

4. The Oklahoma court system "is different from all other states, with the exception of Texas" because Oklahoma employs a system employing two courts of last resort. Jerry E. Stephens, Judiciary, http://digital.library.okstate.edu/encyclopedia/entries/J/JU001.html.

5. Okla. Const. art. VII, § 4 provides:

> The appellate jurisdiction of the Supreme Court shall be coextensive with the State and shall extend to all cases at law and in equity; except that the Court of Criminal Appeals shall have exclusive appellate jurisdiction in criminal cases until otherwise provided by statute and in the event there is any conflict as to jurisdiction, the Supreme Court shall determine which court has jurisdiction and such determination shall be final.

Figure 5-1. Organizational Chart of the Oklahoma Judicial System

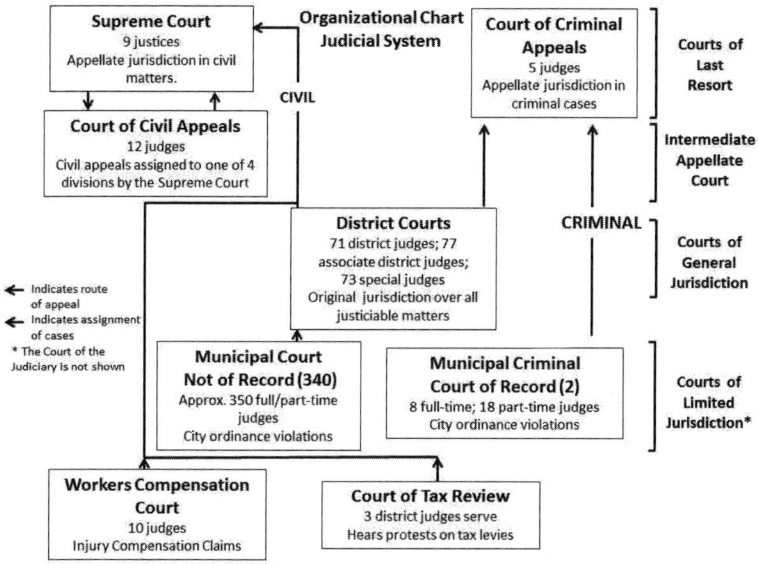

Source: The Oklahoma Supreme Court Brochure, http://www.oscn.net/oscn/schome/appelate.htm.

constitute a quorum, and the concurrence of three judges shall be necessary to a decision."[6] As established by the Oklahoma Constitution and state statute, the Oklahoma Supreme Court consists of nine justices.[7] The nine justices sit *en banc* to hear cases.[8] The Oklahoma State Court's website provides a significant amount of information about Oklahoma courts. The information provided includes:

- a map of Oklahoma counties, which links to information about the district court for the county;
- images of the district judges; and

6. 20 O.S. 2011, § 31.

7. Okla. Const. art. VII, § 2; 20 O.S. 2011, § 1.

8. The term "*en banc*" is derived from the French meaning "on the bench." An *en banc* sitting is a "court session in which all the judges (or a quorum) participate." *Black's Law Dictionary* 606, 1513 (9th ed. 2009).

Figure 5-2. Map Reflecting U.S. District Court Jurisdiction in Oklahoma

Source: United States District Court for the Western District of Oklahoma, *General Information,* http://www.okwd.uscourts.gov/courtinfo.htm.

- for district court clerk offices with an existing website, links to the websites.

B. Federal Courts

In the federal judicial system, the trial courts are also designated as district courts. There are ninety-four federal district courts, including at least one district in each state, the District of Columbia and Puerto Rico, as well as the three territories of the United States—the Virgin Islands, Guam, and the Northern Mariana Islands.[9]

As indicated in Figure 5-2, three federal district courts are located within the State of Oklahoma. The three district courts are the U.S. District Court for the Western District of Oklahoma, which includes forty Oklahoma counties and is seated in Oklahoma City; the U.S District Court for the Northern District, which contains eleven coun-

9. United States Courts, *District Courts*, http://www.uscourts.gov/FederalCourts/UnderstandingtheFederalCourts/DistrictCourts.aspx.

ties and is located in Tulsa;[10] and the U.S. District Court for the Eastern District of Oklahoma, which includes twenty-six counties and is located in Muskogee.[11]

Intermediate appellate courts in the federal system are called United States Courts of Appeals. Twelve of the thirteen circuit courts are established on a geographical basis. Eleven of the regional circuit courts cover all of the states and the twelfth geographically based circuit is responsible for the District of Columbia. See Figure 5-3. The thirteenth federal circuit, the Court of Appeals for the Federal Circuit "has nationwide jurisdiction to hear appeals in specialized cases, such as those involving patent laws and cases decided by the Court of International Trade and the Court of Federal Claims."[12]

Oklahoma is in the Tenth Circuit. This means that cases from the three United States District Courts in Oklahoma are appealed to the United States Court of Appeals for the Tenth Circuit. Along with Oklahoma, the Tenth Circuit includes Colorado, Kansas, New Mexico, Utah, and Wyoming.

The highest court in the federal system is the United States Supreme Court. The United States Constitution provides that "[t]he judicial Power of the United States, shall be vested in one supreme Court, and in such inferior Courts as the Congress may from time to time ordain and establish."[13] Although the jurisdiction of the court encompasses final settlement of controversies involving a variety of issues,[14] including cases concerning the United States Constitution

---

10. *Id.*

11. United States District Court for the Eastern District of Oklahoma, *General Information—Oklahoma Counties and Jurisdictions*, http://www.oked.uscourts.gov/juris_right.htm.

12. United States Courts, *Understanding the Federal Courts—Court of Appeals*, http://www.uscourts.gov/FederalCourts/UnderstandingtheFederalCourts/CourtofAppeals.aspx.

13. U.S. Const. art. III, § 1.

14. "The judicial Power shall extend to all Cases, in Law and Equity, arising under this Constitution, the Laws of the United States, and Treaties made, or which shall be made, under their Authority—to all Cases affecting Ambassadors, other public Ministers and Consuls—to all Cases of admiralty and maritime Jurisdiction—to Controversies to which the United States shall

Figure 5-3. Map Reflecting Geographical Boundaries of U.S. Courts of Appeals & U.S.

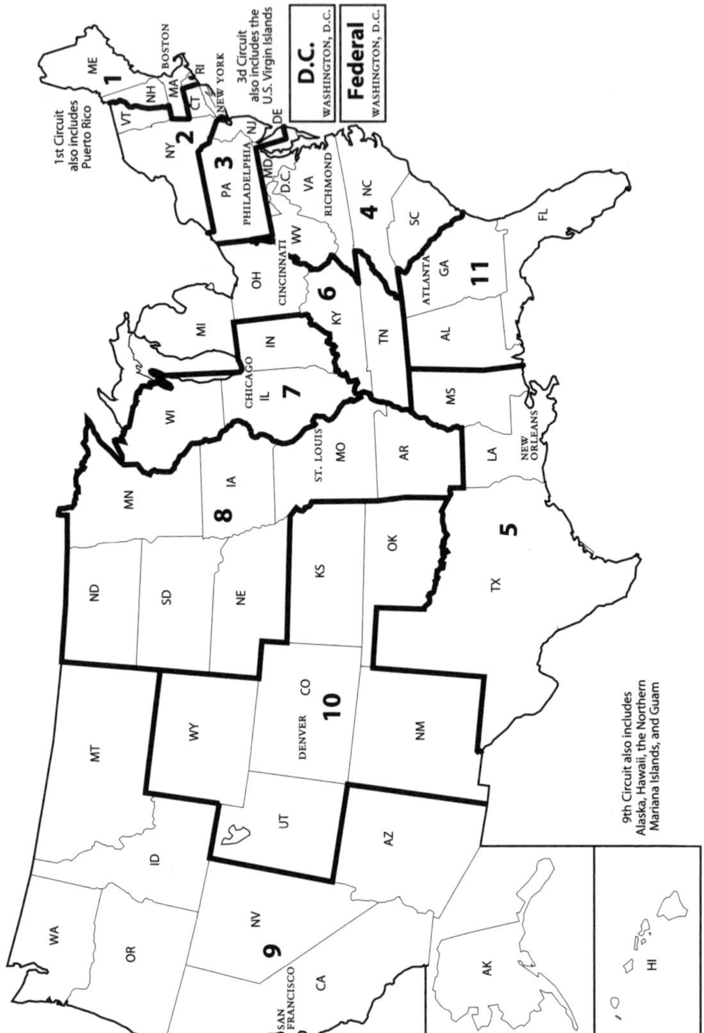

Source: Federal Judicial Center, *Federal Courts & What They Do*, http://www.fjc.gov/public/pdf.nsf/lookup/FCtsWh06.pdf/$file/FCtsWhat.pdf/$file/FCtsWhat.pdf. Map on page 3.

---

be a Party; to Controversies between two or more States; between a State and Citizens of another State; between Citizens of different States; between Citizens of the same State claiming Lands under Grants of different States, and between a State, or the Citizens thereof, and foreign States, Citizens or Subjects." U.S. Const. art. III, § 2.

and federal statutory law, matters involving solely state law issues are not within the jurisdiction of the United States Supreme Court. Further, the court does not hear all matters that may be within its jurisdiction. Rather, parties desiring for the United States Supreme Court to hear their case or to appeal decisions of the intermediate federal appellate courts must petition the court to do so.[15]

II. Citation to and the Precedential Value of Published and Unpublished Judicial Opinions in Oklahoma Courts

Similar to other states,[16] Oklahoma has court rules governing the publication of opinions and in turn the citation of unpublished opinions as precedent in Oklahoma state courts. Before discussing these rules, note that generally the term "unpublished opinion" does not mean that the decision is not available.[17] Rather, unpublished opinions are those "that [a] court has specifically designated as not for publication."[18]

A. Oklahoma Supreme Court and Oklahoma Court of Civil Appeals Decisions

The basis for the Oklahoma Supreme Court's rule is the Oklahoma Constitution, which directs the Oklahoma Supreme Court to establish rules for the form of its opinions and the opinions of the inter-

---

15. A petition seeking discretionary review from an appellate court is known as a certiorari petition. *Black's Law Dictionary* 1261 (9th ed. 2009).

16. Karen S. Breda, *Citation of Unpublished Opinions As Precedent in the State Courts*, http://www.aallnet.org/sections/rips/pdfs/17th-legal-research-teach-in/BredaStateCourtOpinions.pdf.

17. For example, the *Federal Appendix*, one of the West reporter series, includes federal decisions that have been designated as not published.

18. *Black's Law Dictionary* 1202 (9th ed. 2009).

mediate Oklahoma Court of Civil Appeals.[19] As provided by Oklahoma Supreme Court Rule, opinions are to be prepared and issued in memorandum form "without a formal published opinion," (meaning each opinion is to be unpublished) unless the opinion:

(1) Establishes a new rule of law or alters or modifies an existing rule;
(2) Involves a legal issue of continuing public interest;
(3) Criticizes or explains existing law;
(4) Applies an established rule of law to a factual situation significantly different from that in published opinions of the courts of this state;
(5) Resolves an apparent conflict of authority; or
(6) Constitutes a significant and non-duplicative contribution to legal literature:

(a) by an historical review of the law; or (b) by describing legislative history.[20]

The publication of opinions occurs only when one of the established criteria is met. Further, Supreme Court Rule 1.200 sets forth the "[e]ffect of publication" as follows:

(1) Opinions of the Supreme Court designated For Official Publication when adopted will be published in the unofficial reporter, (Oklahoma Bar Journal), on the Oklahoma Supreme Court World Wide Web site, and published after mandate in the official reporter (Pacific Reporter 2d). **Such opinions may not be cited as authority in a subsequent appellate opinion nor may they be used as authority by a trial court until the mandate in the matter has been issued.**

(2) Opinions of the Court of Civil Appeals which resolve novel or unusual issues may be designated for publication, at the

---

19. "The Supreme Court and intermediate appellate court decisions shall be in such form as the Supreme Court shall specify by rule and the Court of Criminal Appeals decisions shall be in such form as it shall specify by rule, until otherwise provided by statute." Okla. Const. art. VII, § 5.

20. Okla.Sup.Ct.R. 1.200, http://www.oscn.net/applications/oscn/DeliverDocument.asp?CiteID=73621.

> time the opinion is adopted, by affirmative vote of at least two members of the division responsible for the opinion. Such opinions shall remain unpublished until after mandate issues, after which time they shall be published in the unofficial reporter, (Oklahoma Bar Journal), the Oklahoma Supreme Court World Wide Web site, and in the official reporter (Pacific Reporter 2nd). Such opinions shall bear the notation "Released for publication by order of the Court of Civil Appeals", **and shall be considered to have persuasive effect.** Any such opinion, however, bearing the notation "Approved for publication by the Supreme Court" has been so designated by the Supreme Court pursuant to 20 O.S.1991 § 30.5, and **shall be accorded precedential value.** The Supreme Court retains the power to order opinions of the Court of Civil Appeals withdrawn from publication.[21]

Thus, researchers must be aware of whether an opinion has been designated for publication, whether mandate has issued—in order to effectively determine if a case may be cited, and whether the court opinion will have only persuasive effect or be followed as precedent. The Oklahoma Supreme Court requires notice to be posted with a decision when the decision has not been "released for publication in the permanent law reports."[22]

---

21. *Id.* (emphasis added).

22. Section (d) of Rule 1.200 provides further information:

Opinions of the Supreme Court designated for official publication shall be published on the Court's World Wide Web site. They shall be published on the web site when filed with the Clerk of the Supreme Court.

Supreme Court opinions shall contain the following notice: "NOTICE: THIS OPINION HAS NOT BEEN RELEASED FOR PUBLICATION IN THE PERMANENT LAW REPORTS. UNTIL RELEASED, IT IS SUBJECT TO REVISION OR WITHDRAWAL." Okla. Sup. Ct. R. 1.200(d), *supra* n. 20. The rule further provides "[s]uch opinions may not be cited as authority in a subsequent appellate opinion nor may they be used as authority by a trial court until the mandate in the matter has been issued. The date of the effectiveness of opinions in original proceedings is governed by Okla. Sup. Ct. R. 1.193. When opinions published on the web site are modified or withdrawn the text of the opinion shall be deleted and any subsequent opinion

B. Oklahoma Court of Criminal Appeals Decisions

The Constitution similarly provides for the establishment of such a rule by the Oklahoma Court of Criminal Appeals.[23] The Oklahoma Legislature has, however, mandated that "[a]ll opinions of the Criminal Court of Appeals must be given in writing and recorded in the journal." [24] Notwithstanding the requirement that all opinions be given in writing, the Court of Criminal Appeals may nonetheless designate an opinion as an unpublished opinion and thus not binding on the Court.[25] Yet, an unpublished opinion may be cited and brought to the Court of Criminal Appeals "attention" if "counsel states that no published case would serve as well the purpose for which counsel cites it, and provided further that counsel shall provide opposing counsel and the Court with a copy of the unpublished decision."[26]

---

in the matter shall be published on the web site if it meets the requirements of Rule 1.200." *Id.*

23. Okla. Const. art. VII, § 5.

24. 22 O.S.2011, § 1071 (2011), http://www.oscn.net/applications/oscn/DeliverDocument.asp?CiteID=70858.

25. "In all instances, an unpublished decision is not binding on this Court." Okla. Ct. Crim. App. Rule 3.5(c)(3), http://www.oscn.net/applications/oscn/DeliverDocument.asp?CiteID=451229 and http://www.okcca.net/online/rules/rulesrvr.jsp?r=26.

26. *Id.* This conditional citation rule would likely withstand challenges, such as that mounted against the California no-citation rule, that claim a Constitutional rationale for negating rules that restrict the citation of unpublished cases. *E.g., Schmier v. Justices of Cal. Super. Ct.*, 408 Fed. Appx. 17 (9th Cir. 2010), http://law.justia.com/cases/federal/appellate-courts/ca9/09-17195/09-17195-2011-04-18.html.

III. Citation to and the Precedential Value of Unpublished Judicial Opinions in Federal Courts

In 2007, Rule 32.1 of the Federal Rules of Appellate Procedure was modified to allow parties to cite to unpublished opinions. As modified, the rule states that a court "may not prohibit or restrict the citation of federal judicial opinions, orders, judgments, or other written dispositions that have been: (i) designated as 'unpublished,' 'not for publication,' 'non-precedential,' 'not precedent,' or the like; and (ii) issued on or after January 1, 2007."[27] While the rule allows for citation of unpublished opinions, it does not address the authoritative value to be afforded these opinions. Rather, the determination of the value of an unpublished decision is left to the individual circuit courts. The Tenth Circuit, which includes Oklahoma, affords no precedential value to unpublished decisions, but allows citation of unpublished decisions for their "persuasive value."[28]

IV. Trial Court Opinions

When conducting case research, you will primarily be attempting to locate appellate court opinions. However, occasionally, you may find it desirable to review a trial court decision or order. For example, you may have a citation to the decision provided by a secondary

27. Fed. R. App. P. 32.1, http://www.law.cornell.edu/rules/frap/rule_32-1.

28. Tenth Cir. R. 32.1, http://www.ca10.uscourts.gov/downloads/2012-rules.pdf. "The citation of unpublished decisions is permitted to the full extent of the authority found in Fed. R. App. P. 32.1. Unpublished decisions are not precedential, but may be cited for their persuasive value. They may also be cited under the doctrines of law of the case, claim preclusion, and issue preclusion." *Id.*

Figure 5-4 Map Reflecting Use of KellPro and OCIS by County

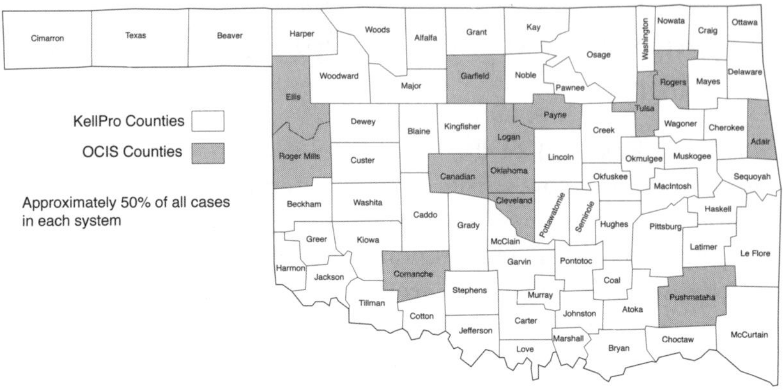

Source: Oklahoma Supreme Court, Administrative Office of the Courts, Unified Case Management System (UCMS) Pre Bid Conference, http://www.docstoc.com/docs/113127889/UCMS-Pre-Bid-Conference.

source. The fact that a citation is available does not ensure ready access to a state trial court decision.

A. Oklahoma Trial Court Decisions

Case management in Oklahoma is provided by two different systems, Oklahoma Court Information System (OCIS) and KellPro. As illustrated in Figure 5-4, the counties with the most populous areas of the state, including Oklahoma City and Tulsa, utilize the OCIS system while the more rural counties utilize the KellPro system.[29]

For cases in counties utilizing OCIS, locating a case docket, which is a formal record of the proceedings and filings in an action, is not a complex task. At www.oscn.net, you may search the docket by party names, view daily cases filed, and view the judges' dockets. In 2001, OCIS added functionality by making it possible to view images of

29. Unified Case Management System, *Supreme Court of Oklahoma Administrative Office of the Court Pre-Bid Conference, Jan. 13, 2010*, at 4, http://www.docstoc.com/docs/42065408/Unified-Case-Management-System.

documents filed in cases at the trial court level, including trial court orders, judgments, and decisions. The documents may be downloaded and printed by clicking on the hyperlink associated with the entry on the case docket.[30] Appellate court dockets are also available via OCIS; however, documents and filings of appellate courts are not available.

Access to case documents through the KellPro system is also more limited. KellPro dockets are available via On Demand Court Records at www.odcr.com. While the searching function is similar to that available via OCIS, advanced searching tools are only available via a five-dollar monthly subscription and actual viewing of documents requires a fifty-dollar monthly subscription.[31] Additionally, not all Oklahoma counties and district courts support image viewing of documents. Further, ODCR notes that it is "currently mandated to only provide image access to members of the Oklahoma Bar Association in good standing."[32]

In November 2010, it was announced that a vendor had been selected to establish a unified case management system,[33] with improved access to case documents for all Oklahoma counties. However, conversion to the improved system will take several years. Case information is available in pilot counties and final "rollout" to all Oklahoma counties is anticipated by Fall 2015.[34]

Westlaw and Bloomberg services also may provide limited access to select Oklahoma trial court orders and judgments or to the dockets that reference these documents. In Westlaw Classic, the Oklahoma State Civil Trial Court Orders (OK-TRIALORDERS) database pro-

---

30. Lisa S. Lambert, *Technology Enhances Services Provided by Court Clerks*, 79 Okla. B.J. 2543 (2008), http://www.okbar.org/members/BarJournal/archive2008/Novarchive08/obj7929tec.aspx.

31. On Demand Court Records, http://www.odcr.com/pricing.

32. *Id.*

33. James Edmondson, *On the Horizon: Oklahoma's Unified Case Management System Connecting Oklahoma Courts*, 81 Okla. B.J. 2810 (2010), http://www.okbar.org/members/barJournal/Archive2010/DeCArchive10/obj8133Edmondson.aspx.

34. Frank Holdsclaw, *Oklahoma Administrative Office of the Court OBA–UCMS Meeting, Aug. 31, 2011*, at 10 (on file with the author).

Figure 5-5. Trial Court Orders on WestlawNext

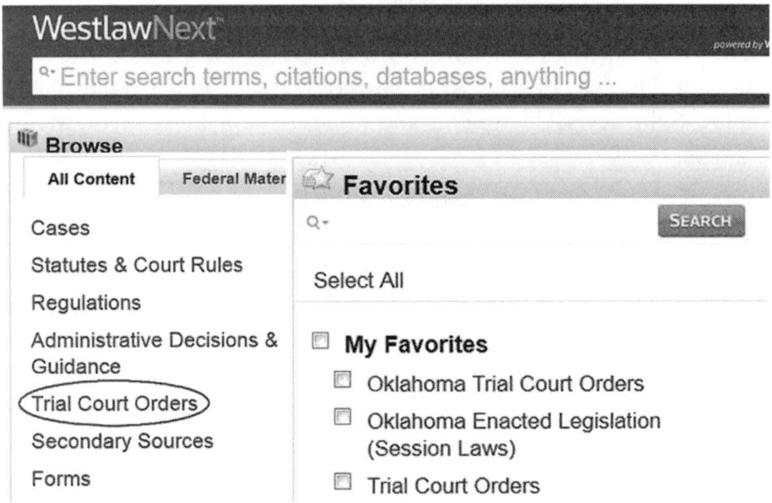

Source: Reprinted with permission of Thomson Reuters.

vides access to available orders in Oklahoma civil cases. As shown in Figure 5-5, Oklahoma Trial Court Orders may be accessed on WestlawNext by selecting the "Trial Court Orders" link on the All Content Tab and then selecting the Oklahoma link when the Trial Court Orders tab displays. Alternatively, access may be made simpler by saving the database as a favorite. Select coverage on Westlaw and WestlawNext begins in 2001 with more limited coverage for the years preceding 2001. Westlaw services also provide not only access to the text but also to the PDF image of the order.

Bloomberg, similar to ODCR, allows searching dockets at no cost, but additional cost must be incurred to access an actual document, such as a judgment or order.[35]

35. The notice actually states, "Documents from this court require onsite retrieval by a courier. Additional fees for sending a courier to the court will be added to your Bloomberg account."

Figure 5-6. Opinions & Dockets on Health Practice Center Tab on Bloomberg Law

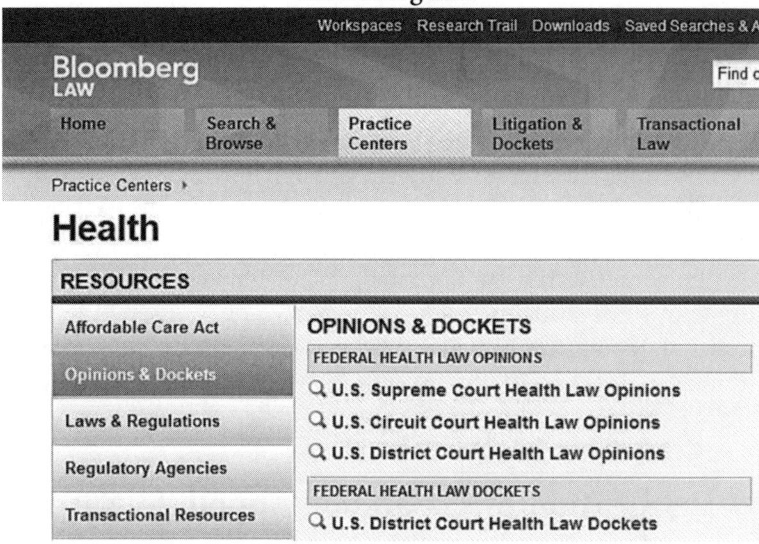

Source: Bloomberg Law BNA. Reprinted with permission.

B. Federal Trial Court Opinions

Although the task of locating trial court opinions in the federal system can be accomplished with more ease than locating trial court opinions at the state level, the task is not uncomplicated. Select federal district court decisions are included in West's *Federal Supplement* reporter. These decisions can be accessed in the print reporter or easily searched or retrieved by citation using online research services provided by West and Lexis. Additionally, Bloomberg Law allows retrieval of select federal trial court opinions based on the practice area addressed in the case. As illustrated in Figure 5-6, select U.S. District Court opinions related to Health Law can be searched in via the Bloomberg Practice Centers Tab.

Additionally, for some time, case opinions were available for free through a court's website. While some courts may continue the practice of posting their decisions, federal trial court opinions[36] must now be accessible through the Public Access to Court Electronic Records (PACER) system. To use PACER, you must register an account. Registration and access to opinions is free, but requires the provision of credit card information.[37]

An alternative to using PACER is to access dockets using Bloomberg Law. See Figure 5-7. Unlike PACER, Bloomberg Law is not a free/low cost resource; however, Bloomberg Law's docket search adds value through its more robust search functionality. For example, the docket search on Bloomberg includes a keyword search feature that is not available in PACER. Once you have located the case docket on Bloomberg Law, you may be able to click on the document number associated with the court opinion to display the opinion.

V. Publication of Oklahoma Appellate Cases

A. Slip Opinions

As indicated previously, the goal of case law research is primarily to locate appellate court opinions. After an appellate court reaches its

---

36. Opinions, consistent with the E-Government Act of 2002, must be made available without cost. However, as noted on the U.S. District Court for the Northern District of Oklahoma's website,

> An opinion is defined by the Judicial Conference of the United States as any document issued by the court "that sets forth a reasoned explanation for a court's decision." The definition excludes routine, non-substantive orders, such as scheduling orders or rulings on motions for extension of time. For the purposes of posting opinions online, judges decide, on a document-by-document basis, whether what they have written qualifies as an opinion.

U.S. Dist. Ct. Case Info. N. Dist. of Okla., *Viewing Case Opinions Online*, http://www.oknd.uscourts.gov/okndpublic/caseinfo.nsf/e1df95432b8fe773862567ca00573ae3/1da6ba39ce0c760d8625718e0053469c?OpenDocument (emphasis added).

37. "To access the court's opinions, you must register for PACER. You will be asked for a credit card number. Viewing the opinions is free, but viewing case docket sheets and other records through PACER costs 10 cents per page." *Id.*

Figure 5-7. Dockets Search on Bloomberg Law

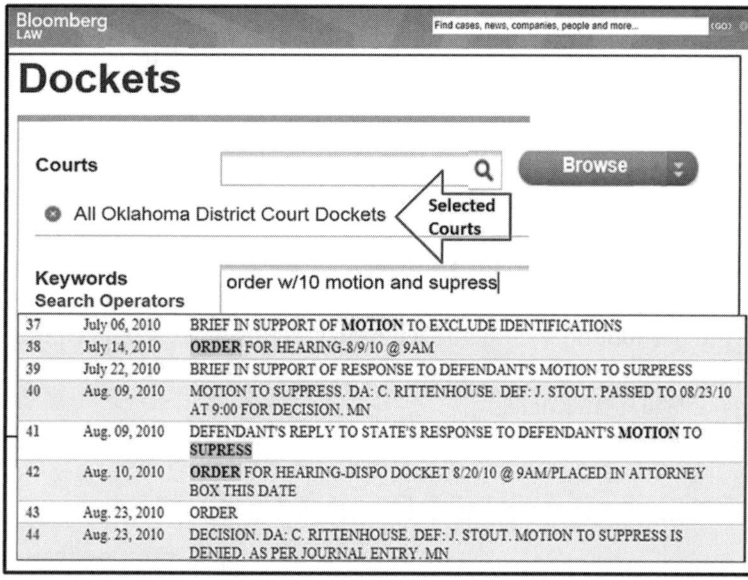

Source: Bloomberg Law BNA. Reprinted with permission.

decision, the case is published as a *slip opinion*. As will be discussed in the next chapter, the opinion can be located on the Internet via the Oklahoma State Court Network (OSCN). In states with a less robust state legal network, the slip opinions may be accessed on the issuing court's website. These slip opinions are also made available via commercial online legal information service providers, such as Lexis, Westlaw, Bloomberg Law, and Fastcase. The opinions are usually available within a day of being issued. Further, the Oklahoma Court of Criminal Appeals has established a mailing list which allows researchers to sign up to receive newly published decisions of this court on the day they are handed down.[38]

38. Researchers may sign up by emailing maillistmgr@oscn.net. Okla. Court of Criminal Appeals, *OCCAOnline*, http://www.okcca.net/online/.

B. Advance Sheets

Because it may take a significant amount of time to publish the bound volumes of the print reporters, legal publishers provide subscribers with the softbound advance sheet booklets to make opinions available in print as soon as possible. These booklets can be printed and distributed more quickly than the bound reporters. The advanced sheets for the *Pacific Reporter*, the regional reporter in which Oklahoma decisions are included, are received on a weekly basis. The pagination reflected in the advance sheets is identical to the pagination in the hardbound volume of the reporter allowing a single citation for both the advance sheet and the hardbound volume that will be available at a later date.

C. Print Reporters for Oklahoma Cases

Oklahoma Supreme Court Rule 1.200 designates the *Pacific Reporter* as the official reporter for decisions of the Oklahoma Supreme Court and the Oklahoma Court of Civil Appeals. While the Oklahoma Court of Criminal Appeals does not specifically state that the *Pacific Reporter* is the official reporter for its decisions, Oklahoma Court of Criminal Appeals Rules do provide that "[c]itation to opinions of the Oklahoma Court of Criminal Appeals shall include citations to Pacific, Pacific 2nd, and Pacific 3rd Reporters."[39]

The *Pacific Reporter* is a regional reporter, meaning that it publishes the opinions of courts in a number of states. Designation of the regional reporter, the *Pacific Reporter*, as the official reporter, indicates that there is no state reporter series. Publication of *Oklahoma Reports*, which began in 1890 prior to Oklahoma statehood, was discontinued in 1953.[40] However, West continues the publication of *Oklahoma Decisions*, an offprint reporter, that contains the decisions of a single state, in this case Oklahoma, but with regional reporter pagination.

---

39. Okla. Ct. Crim. App. Rule 3.5(c)(2), *supra* note 25.

40. Association of Legal Writing Directors & Darby Dickerson, *ALWD Citation Manual: A Professional System of Citation* 438 (4th ed. 2010).

The official reporter of the Oklahoma Court of Criminal Appeals from 1908 to 1953 was the *Oklahoma Criminal Reports*; until 1959 this court was known as the Oklahoma Criminal Court of Appeals. Similar to the process of publication for Oklahoma Supreme Court decisions, in 1953, the *Pacific Reporter* began serving as the official reporter.[41]

Other reporters have historically contained opinions of courts located in the geographic area of Oklahoma. For example, from 1896 to 1907, *Indian Territory Reports* served as the official reporter for the Oklahoma Court of Appeals of the Indian Territory, and the *South Western Reporter* was the unofficial reporter containing select opinions.[42]

As a regional reporter, the *Pacific Reporter* contains the decisions of not only Oklahoma courts but also courts in Alaska, Arizona, California, Colorado, Hawaii, Idaho, Kansas, Montana, Nevada, New Mexico, Oregon, Utah, Washington, and Wyoming. With the inclusion of opinions from these multiple jurisdictions, the number of volumes in a regional reporter quickly expands. When the number of volumes for a reporter begins to become large, West may begin another series. For example, after the *Pacific Reporter* reached 300 volumes in 1931, West began publishing the Second Series of the *Pacific Reporter* with volume 1. Similarly, in 2000, the volumes in the Second Series had become sufficiently numerous that West began publishing a Third Series of the *Pacific Reporter*.[43] As of May 2012, the Third Series of the *Pacific Reporter* had reached 275 volumes. While each volume of the reporter contains a table of cases reported in that volume, without a volume and series citation, it is difficult to locate a case in a reporter published in multiple series. The volume and series number is printed on the spine of each hardbound volume to assist researchers in locating the correct volume within a series.

The availability of Oklahoma cases through online resources will be covered in the next chapter.

41. *Id.*
42. *Id.*
43. *Id.*

VI. Publication of Federal Cases

Opinions and decisions of the United States Supreme Court are reported in the *United States Reports*, which is the official reporter of the Supreme Court. Opinions of the United State Supreme Court are also published by commercial publishers. The *Supreme Court Reporter*, a West publication, and the *United States Supreme Court Reports Lawyers' Edition,* published by LexisNexis, both contain United States Supreme Court decisions. A number of famous cases that initiated in state and federal district courts in Oklahoma have been reviewed by the United States Supreme Court, and the opinions of the Court in these cases are reported in the above mentioned reporters.[44] While use and citation to the official reporter is preferred, lawyers often use the commercially published reporters because there is a several year delay in publication of cases in the official reporter. The commercial reporters have the added advantage of providing editorial enhancements to facilitate research.

Cases decided by the United States Courts of Appeals, which serve as the intermediate appellate courts, are included in the *Federal Reporter*, a West publication. As discussed previously, reporters are often published in series and newly issued judicial opinions are now being included in the Third Series of the *Federal Reporter.* Select unpublished decisions from the intermediate appellate courts are also included in the *Federal Appendix.* Opinions of the United States Tenth Circuit Court of Appeals concerning cases appealed from the state court system and federal district courts in Oklahoma are included in the *Federal Reporter and Federal Appendix.*

Select cases from the United States District Courts are reported in the various series of the *Federal Supplement.* These cases may also be available through the services of online providers such as Lexis, Westlaw, Bloomberg Law, PACER, and Fastcase.

---

44. *E.g., Nat'l Collegiate Athletic Ass'n v. Bd. of Regents of the U. of Okla.*, 468 U.S. 85, 107 (1984).

VII. Composition of a Case

Opinions published in a reporter or available electronically reflect the exact language of the judicial opinion as issued by the court. Additionally, supplemental information intended to assist the researcher in understanding the procedural and substantive issues addressed in the case may also be available. This supplemental information may reflect the court record, or it may be authored by the editorial staff of the publisher of the reporter. This section of the chapter explains the various items included in a case. To assist in visualizing some of the items included in the print reporters and online sources, Figures 5-8 through 5-11 provide labeled excerpts of an Oklahoma case included in the *Pacific Reporter.*

Case Citation. Cases are often published in multiple reporters and online databases. As explained in more depth in the next chapter and the book's appendix, the traditional case citation contains a volume number, the reporter name, and the page number of the beginning page of the case. For example, in the *Pacific Reporter*, the citation to *Berman v. Laboratory Corporation of America* is 268 P.3d 68. Oklahoma Supreme Court Rules require *parallel citation*, which is an additional citation to a case that is reported in more than one publication or form, not only to the *Pacific Reporter* but also to the Oklahoma Supreme Court's official paragraph citation.[45] The paragraph citation for the *Berman* case is 2011 OK 1106. The paragraph citation format is illustrated in Figures 5-8 and 5-11.

Page Numbers. When citing to information appearing on a specific page in a print reporter, include that page number in the case citation. Researchers using online resources should be aware that page numbers from print reporters are embedded in the text. To assist researchers in recognizing the embedded page numbers, the online providers will place an asterisk before the page number. However, as illustrated in Figure 5-8, Lexis Advance allows the researcher to select the reporter in which she would like to view the opinion and places

45. Okla.Sup.Ct.R.1.200(e), *supra* note 20.

the page number for the selected reporter in brackets. Moreover, West's online services allow researchers to download PDF versions of West reporters, making it easy to identify the print page for citation purposes.

Case Number/Docket Number. The case number, also referred to as the docket number, is the number assigned to a case by a court. Each court assigns a different number to a case. In the appellate process, each court will assign a number to the case as the case proceeds from one court to the next higher court. As discussed in the section on trial court opinions, docket numbers are useful in locating documents filed in the case and reflected on the docket. Because some case filings are not published, they may be obtained only through electronic systems, such as OCIS, or only from the court that decided the case. In either case, the researcher must have the appropriate docket number and/or party names to retrieve or request the documents.

Synopsis. The synopsis of the case provides a summary of the facts, procedure, legal issues, and disposition of the case. This summary can help a researcher efficiently determine if further review of the case is warranted. Although the synopsis can be helpful to the research process, neither the synopsis nor the headnotes, both of which are prepared by the publisher's editorial staff, are authoritative. As a result, neither synopsis nor headnotes should be cited.

Headnotes. A headnote is a brief statement about a single point of law in a case. Because almost all cases address more than one issue, cases often have more than one headnote. Headnotes are organized in a sequential manner. The number at the beginning of the headnote represents its order in the sequence. As shown in Figure 5-8, in the print format of the *Pacific Reporter*, within the text of the opinion the number of each headnote is enclosed in brackets at the point of the discussion of the issue covered by the headnote. West headnotes also include topic and key number references that can be used to assist in locating other sources and cases using West publications, including the West digests. The use of digests to locate cases will be addressed in the next chapter. Figure 5-10 illustrates that, in Lexis Advance headnotes, the opinion's discussion of the issue covered by the headnote is indicated by the number of the headnote in a square. Researchers should be aware that headnotes, which are prepared by the commercial publishers' editorial staff, are not included in the case opinions accessed via the OSCN website.

Disposition. There are a variety of actions a court may take to decide a case. The action taken is often referred to as the disposition of the case. For example, a trial court may decide to grant or deny a motion. An appellate court may decide to affirm, reverse, or affirm in part and reverse in part the judgment of a lower court. If the higher court affirms a judgment of the lower court, the appeal is dismissed, regardless of whether the decision of the court below is expressly affirmed. Similarly, a higher court may reverse the judgment of a lower court, irrespective of whether the higher court sends the matter back for further adjudication. The term for the action of sending the matter back to the lower court for additional proceeding is remand. The higher court may also *vacate*, which includes making the null and void by expressly overruling the judgment of a lower court. As indicated by the explanation of the actions, the court may include several actions in the final disposition of the case. For example, as illustrated in the case included in Figure 5-10 and Figure 5-11, the disposition included vacating, reversing, and remanding the lower court's decision.

Opinion. The first opinion appearing in the case is the majority opinion. As the name implies, the majority opinion is that opinion supported by a majority of the judges hearing the case. In the example provided in Figure 5-11, the names of the concurring justices, who agreed with the opinion, appear at the bottom of the opinion. In the case provided as an illustration, neither the concurring justices nor the dissenting justices, who did not agree with the majority opinion, wrote separate opinions. In some cases, justices agreeing with the outcome announced in the majority opinion will nonetheless select to set forth in a separate opinion their reasons for agreeing with the outcome. Such opinions are referred to as concurring opinions. Similarly, dissenting justices may select to suggest alternative outcomes and to elaborate on the reasoning they have followed. Opinions of this type are known as dissenting opinions.

Figure 5-8. *Pacific Reporter* Case with Labels

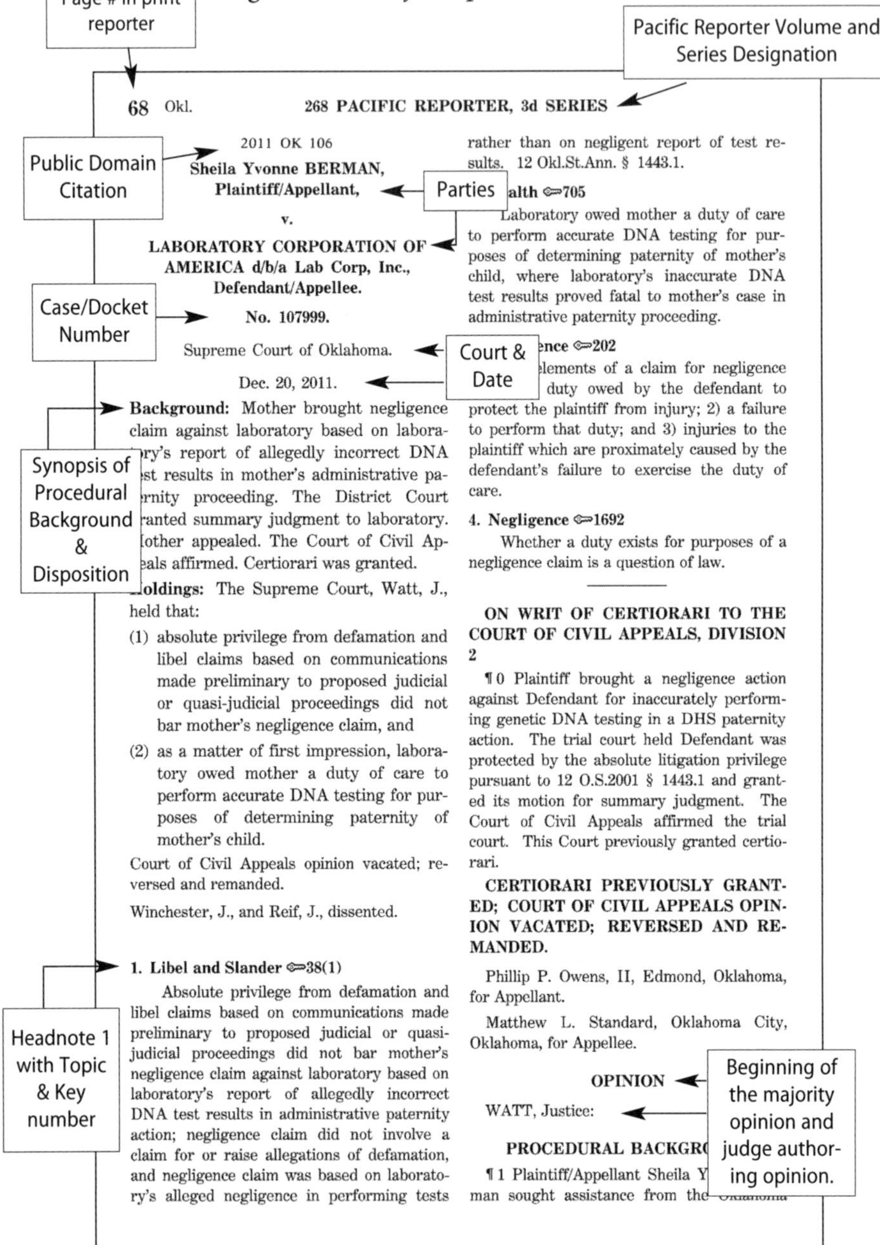

68 Okl. 268 PACIFIC REPORTER, 3d SERIES

2011 OK 106

Sheila Yvonne BERMAN, Plaintiff/Appellant,

v.

LABORATORY CORPORATION OF AMERICA d/b/a Lab Corp, Inc., Defendant/Appellee.

No. 107999.

Supreme Court of Oklahoma.

Dec. 20, 2011.

Background: Mother brought negligence claim against laboratory based on labora-ry's report of allegedly incorrect DNA st results in mother's administrative pa-rnity proceeding. The District Court anted summary judgment to laboratory. other appealed. The Court of Civil Ap-als affirmed. Certiorari was granted.

oldings: The Supreme Court, Watt, J., held that:

(1) absolute privilege from defamation and libel claims based on communications made preliminary to proposed judicial or quasi-judicial proceedings did not bar mother's negligence claim, and

(2) as a matter of first impression, laboratory owed mother a duty of care to perform accurate DNA testing for purposes of determining paternity of mother's child.

Court of Civil Appeals opinion vacated; reversed and remanded.

Winchester, J., and Reif, J., dissented.

1. Libel and Slander ⚿38(1)

Absolute privilege from defamation and libel claims based on communications made preliminary to proposed judicial or quasi-judicial proceedings did not bar mother's negligence claim against laboratory based on laboratory's report of allegedly incorrect DNA test results in administrative paternity action; negligence claim did not involve a claim for or raise allegations of defamation, and negligence claim was based on laboratory's alleged negligence in performing tests rather than on negligent report of test results. 12 Okl.St.Ann. § 1443.1.

alth ⚿705

Laboratory owed mother a duty of care to perform accurate DNA testing for purposes of determining paternity of mother's child, where laboratory's inaccurate DNA test results proved fatal to mother's case in administrative paternity proceeding.

nce ⚿202

lements of a claim for negligence duty owed by the defendant to protect the plaintiff from injury; 2) a failure to perform that duty; and 3) injuries to the plaintiff which are proximately caused by the defendant's failure to exercise the duty of care.

4. Negligence ⚿1692

Whether a duty exists for purposes of a negligence claim is a question of law.

ON WRIT OF CERTIORARI TO THE COURT OF CIVIL APPEALS, DIVISION 2

¶ 0 Plaintiff brought a negligence action against Defendant for inaccurately performing genetic DNA testing in a DHS paternity action. The trial court held Defendant was protected by the absolute litigation privilege pursuant to 12 O.S.2001 § 1443.1 and granted its motion for summary judgment. The Court of Civil Appeals affirmed the trial court. This Court previously granted certiorari.

CERTIORARI PREVIOUSLY GRANTED; COURT OF CIVIL APPEALS OPINION VACATED; REVERSED AND REMANDED.

Phillip P. Owens, II, Edmond, Oklahoma, for Appellant.

Matthew L. Standard, Oklahoma City, Oklahoma, for Appellee.

OPINION

WATT, Justice:

PROCEDURAL BACKGR

¶ 1 Plaintiff/Appellant Sheila Y man sought assistance from the

Reprinted with permission of Thomson Reuters.

Figure 5-8. *Pacific Reporter* Case with Labels (*continued*)

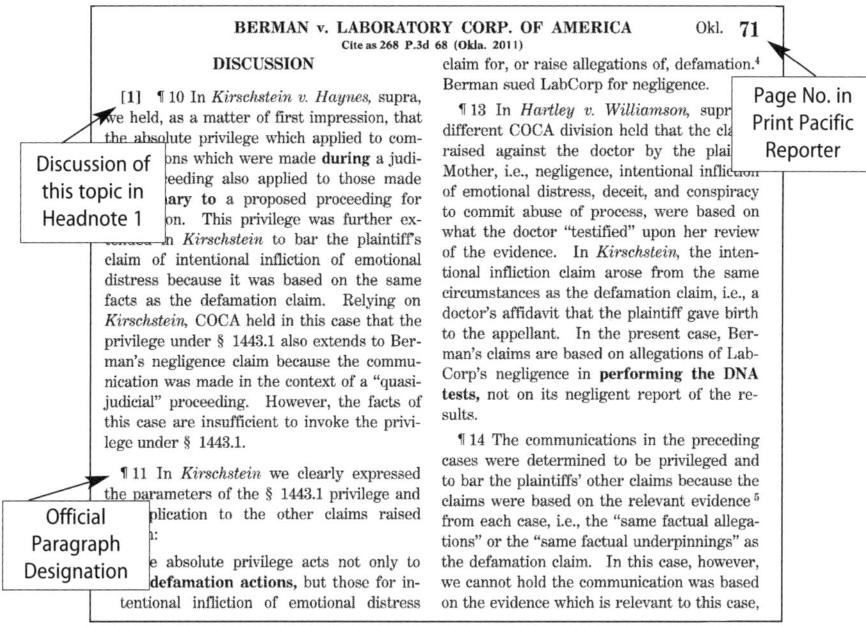
BERMAN v. LABORATORY CORP. OF AMERICA Okl. 71
Cite as 268 P.3d 68 (Okla. 2011)

DISCUSSION

[1] ¶ 10 In *Kirschstein v. Haynes*, supra, we held, as a matter of first impression, that the absolute privilege which applied to com-ons which were made **during** a judi-eeding also applied to those made ary **to** a proposed proceeding for on. This privilege was further ex-n *Kirschstein* to bar the plaintiff's claim of intentional infliction of emotional distress because it was based on the same facts as the defamation claim. Relying on *Kirschstein*, COCA held in this case that the privilege under § 1443.1 also extends to Berman's negligence claim because the communication was made in the context of a "quasi-judicial" proceeding. However, the facts of this case are insufficient to invoke the privilege under § 1443.1.

¶ 11 In *Kirschstein* we clearly expressed the parameters of the § 1443.1 privilege and plication to the other claims raised :

e absolute privilege acts not only to **defamation actions,** but those for intentional infliction of emotional distress

claim for, or raise allegations of, defamation.[4] Berman sued LabCorp for negligence.

¶ 13 In *Hartley v. Williamson*, supr different COCA division held that the cl raised against the doctor by the plai Mother, i.e., negligence, intentional inflic of emotional distress, deceit, and conspiracy to commit abuse of process, were based on what the doctor "testified" upon her review of the evidence. In *Kirschstein*, the intentional infliction claim arose from the same circumstances as the defamation claim, i.e., a doctor's affidavit that the plaintiff gave birth to the appellant. In the present case, Berman's claims are based on allegations of LabCorp's negligence in **performing the DNA tests,** not on its negligent report of the results.

¶ 14 The communications in the preceding cases were determined to be privileged and to bar the plaintiffs' other claims because the claims were based on the relevant evidence[5] from each case, i.e., the "same factual allegations" or the "same factual underpinnings" as the defamation claim. In this case, however, we cannot hold the communication was based on the evidence which is relevant to this case,

Figure 5-9. Case Excerpt from Lexis with Related Content

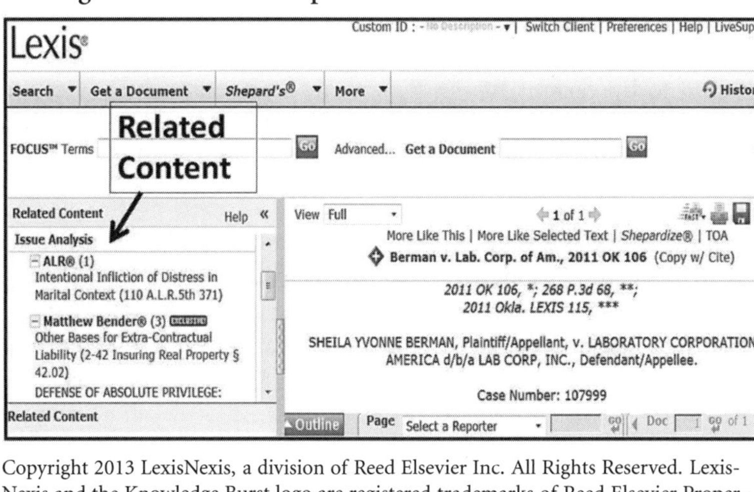

Figure 5-10. *Pacific Reporter* Case Excerpt in Lexis Advance

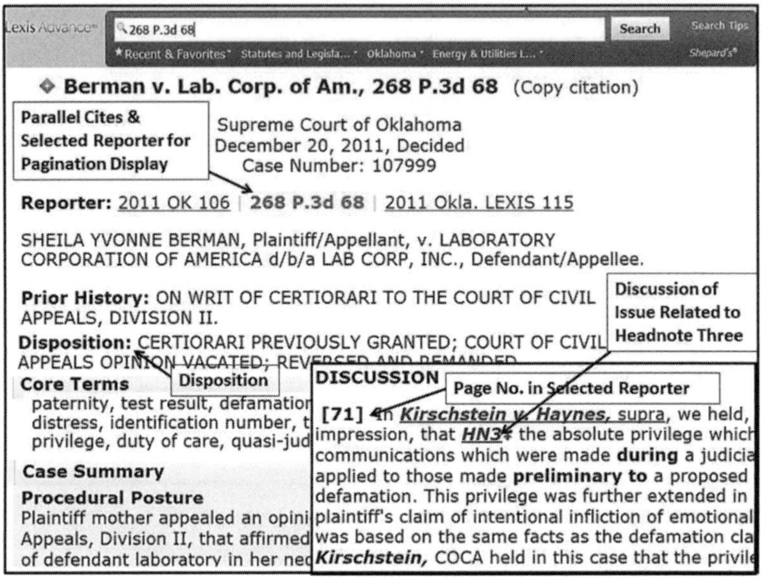

Related Content. Various online sources, including Lexis and West services, provide related content to assist researchers. This content is referred to by various names by specific services, such as "Results Plus." The related content links to a variety of secondary sources that may help the researcher understand the issues addressed in a particular case.

These related resources, such as a legal encyclopedia or *American Law Reports* annotation, may include discussions of the law in multiple jurisdictions. Other resources, such as resources included the Oklahoma Practice Series, may be jurisdiction specific. Much of the related content is discussed in Chapter 3 on Secondary Sources.

Figure 5-11. Oklahoma Case Excerpts with Labels from the Oklahoma State Court Network

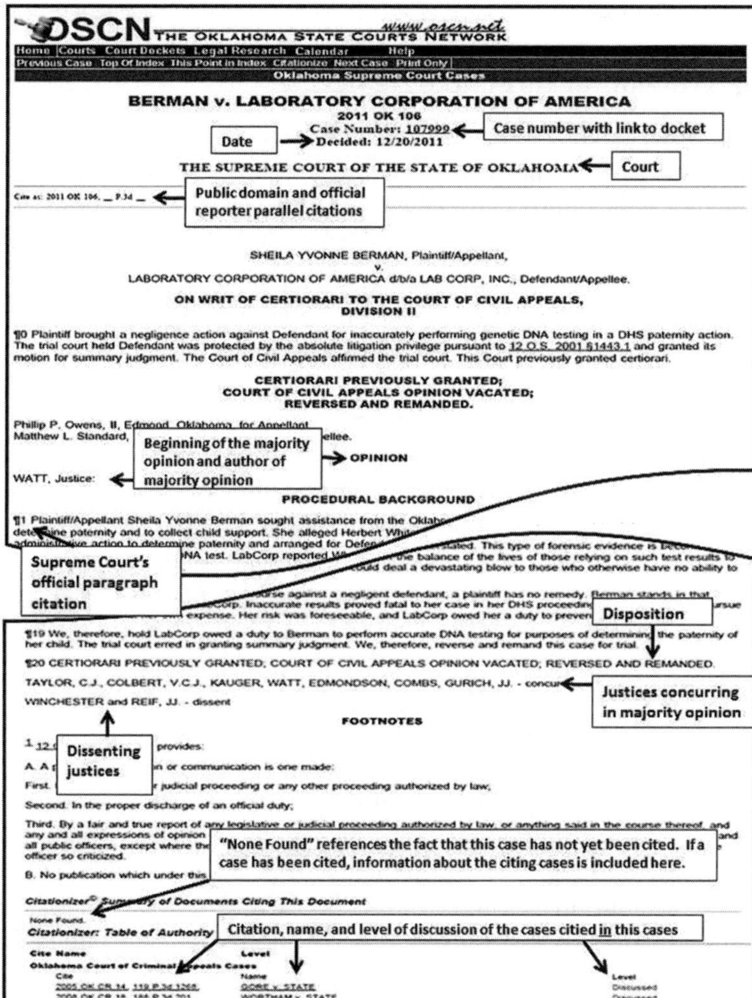

Source: Oklahoma State Court Network, www.oscn.net.

VIII. Strategies for Reading and Analyzing Cases

A. Procedural Terminology

In order to effectively read and understand case law, a researcher must have a basic understanding of the procedural aspects of the case. While civil and criminal procedure are topics beyond the scope of this text, a few basic terms involving civil procedure are briefly discussed in this section.

- *Petition* (complaint)—The document filed by the plaintiff alleging harm by the defendant and asking for relief. Because Oklahoma is a notice pleading jurisdiction,[46] the requirements for the information that must be included in the petition are less stringent than in some other jurisdictions. However, the information in the petition must be sufficient to "give fair notice of the nature of the claim asserted."[47]
- *Answer*—The response of the defendant to the petition. The answer should include admissions and denials to the allegations contained in the petition; specific defenses set forth by statute; and affirmative defenses to the plaintiff's claims for relief.[48]
- *Judgment*—A court's determination of the parties' rights and obligations in a case.[49] There are a number of types of judgments. If the defendant fails to file a response to a petition within the period prescribed by statute, the court may enter a default judgment, which grants the plaintiff the relief sought without further proceedings. Similarly, "if the pleadings, the discovery and disclosure materials on file, and any affidavits

46. David C. Clark & Charles Adams, *Oklahoma Civil Pretrial Procedure: Jurisdiction Service of Process*, Venue § 1.2 (1995).

47. 12 O.S.2011, § 2008 (committee comment).

48. Charles W. Adams & Daniel J. Boudreau, 1A *Vernon's Okla. Forms 2d*, Civ. Proc. Ch. 3 B Introduction (2000).

49. *Black's Law Dictionary* 918 (9th ed. 2009).

show that there is no genuine issue as to any material fact" and the party making a motion for the judgment "is entitled to judgment as a matter of law," a summary judgment may be entered without further proceedings.[50]

- *Appellant / Respondent*—The procedural designations of parties on appeal. The unsuccessful party at the trial level may appeal a case. The appealing party is the appellant and the other parties are the respondents.
- *Disposition*—The final settlement or determination of a case by a court.[51] As previously discussed in this chapter, an appellate court may dispose of a trial court's action by affirming, reversing, vacating, overruling, or remanding the case.

B. Reading Cases

The figures and explanations contained in the previous section of the chapter should assist researchers in identifying those elements of the decision that should be reviewed initially to determine if more in-depth reading and review of the case will be helpful. Below is some additional guidance on reading and reviewing cases.

- If possible, organize search results and cases according to jurisdiction and decision date. Locating the current rule of law will be facilitated by reading the most recent case first. However, to understand how the law developed in a particular jurisdiction, you may desire to read the cases in a chronological or a reverse chronological order.
- Review the synopsis or case summary provided in the opinion to determine if a case has similar facts or addresses the issues being researched. If so, skim the headnotes to find those portions of the case that discuss the issues relevant to the research.
- If you determine, after reviewing those portions of the case identified by the relevant headnote, that the case is important to the research, skim the entire case to develop an under-

50. 12 O.S.2011, §2056.

51. *Black's Law Dictionary* 539 (9th ed. 2009).

standing of the essential facts in the case. Also skim the disposition of the case and the rationale for the court's handling of the case. Again, pay particular attention to the relevant portions of the case as identified by the headnotes.

- Carefully and deliberately read the case. Portions of the case that are obviously not pertinent to the issue being researched may be skipped. During this reading, take notes regarding the decision. The notes should summarize the portions of the discussion of the case that you have previously identified as important. If you have difficulty summarizing the material, another review of that section of material is warranted. The notes may also include language from the case that is stated in such a way that a quote of the material would add to the persuasive nature of legal documents, such as briefs, addressing the topic. Remember that one of the features provided by some online providers is the ability to highlight portions of a decision electronically and to attach notes to the opinion.[52] These highlights and notes are retained by the provider and can also be shared. Further, some online providers provide a functionality that allows the notes to be searched at a later time.
- As you read more cases, pay particular attention to how the cases fit together to form trends. You may find that certain factual situations virtually guaranteed a specific outcome. Additionally, you may find that you need to synthesize a rule from the decisions in several cases. Alternatively, there may be one case that summarizes the current rule and/or provides an historical overview of the development of the current rule.

C. Case Analysis

While research may reveal a number of cases with facts that are similar to the facts involved in your situation, rarely will you identify a case that has exactly the same facts. As a result, you must engage in

52. Both WestlawNext and Lexis Advance will provide this capability. OSCN does not have this added functionality.

analysis to determine if the facts are similar enough that the court is likely to apply the law in the same way and to reach an outcome that is consistent with the disposition in a previous case. If the disposition in a previous case is the same as the desired outcome in your situation, you should emphasize the similar facts when preparing legal documents based on the research. However, if the outcome in a previous case is not favorable, your legal arguments should emphasize the differences between the case and your situation. Efforts to emphasize the differences between cases are often referred to as "distinguishing" the facts and outcome from the case at hand. It is important to remember that attorneys have an ethical duty to disclose the existence of a case that is directly on point regardless of whether the case supports the desired outcome.

Most causes of action have several elements or factors that the court will review to determine if the proper outcome has been reached. Elements are required parts of the legal action. For instance, the elements of a conversion action in Oklahoma include (1) the plaintiff was the owner or possessor of the property, (2) the defendant intentionally took possession of, prevented the plaintiff's access to, or destroyed the property, (3) the plaintiff did not consent to the defendant's conduct, and (4) the plaintiff was harmed because of the defendant's conduct.[53]

In contrast, factors are important but not required parts of an action. For example, in determining if a use of copyrighted material is an infringement or a fair use the following factors are to be considered:

> (1) the purpose and character of the use, including whether such use is of a commercial nature or is for nonprofit educational purposes; (2) the nature of the copyrighted work; (3) the amount and substantiality of the portion used in relation to the copyrighted work as a whole; and (4) the effect of the use upon the potential market for or value of the copyrighted work.[54]

53. Okla. Unif. Civ. Jury Instruction 27.1 (3d ed. rev., 2009), http://www.oscn.net/forms/lawlibrary/Civil/adobe/Chapter27.pdf.

54. 17 U.S.C. § 107 (2006), http://www.law.cornell.edu/uscode/text/17/107.

Applying these factors, the court may determine that a use is a fair use regardless of the amount of the work used if there is no effect on the value of the work.

Although the distinction between elements and factors is central in the analysis of the researcher, such a distinction will not likely affect the necessity for continued research. If a court decides that one element of an action is not established, the court may elect not to address other elements in its opinion. As a result, the researcher will have to locate other cases to properly analyze the law and its application to the current situation. If, as illustrated in the fair use discussion above, a court decides that application of a single factor is determinative and that other factors have no impact, the court may similarly decide not to discuss the other factors. As a result, the researcher will again need to locate additional cases addressing the other factors.

Finally, the application of the doctrine of stare decisis will affect the researcher's analysis. Stare decisis, which in Latin means "to stand by things decided," is the "doctrine of precedent, under which a court must follow earlier judicial decisions when the same points arise again."[55] As previously discussed in this chapter, court rules will often determine if a case serves as binding precedent or whether a case may be cited as persuasive authority. Beyond the court rules, a researcher must determine if the particular language she desires to rely upon is part of the holding of the case or simply a non-binding statement, often referred to as dictum.[56]

---

55. *Black's Law Dictionary* 1537 (9th ed. 2009).

56. *Dictum* is a "statement of opinion or belief considered authoritative because of the dignity of the person making it." *Black's Law Dictionary* 519 (9th ed. 2009). Judicial *dictum* is defined as an "opinion by a court on a question that is directly involved, briefed, and argued by counsel, and even passed on by the court, but that is not essential to the decision. Several statements of such opinion are referred to as *dicta*." *Id.*

Chapter 6

Researching Judicial Opinions

Locating judicial opinions can be one of the most difficult parts of any research project. In contrast to statutes and regulations, which are updated frequently and organized neatly into subject arrangements, judicial opinions are simply published in chronological order, and literally thousands of new opinions are issued by courts every year.[1] Yet, in order for our legal system, which is based on the concepts of precedent and stare decisis,[2] to function properly, attorneys and other researchers must be able to efficiently and accurately find court opinions that establish legal rules.

The judicial opinions of all Oklahoma state courts, dating back to 1890, are available online through government, commercial, and free databases. All published Oklahoma court opinions are available through the Oklahoma State Courts Network (OSCN),[3] a government service managed by the Oklahoma Supreme Court. Oklahoma court opinions are also available through commercial services like Westlaw, Lexis, Bloomberg Law, and Fastcase. Even Google, through its Google Scholar site,[4] makes Oklahoma state court opinions from the last sixty years available online for free. Court opinions are added to online databases very quickly, often within hours of when the opinions are released by courts. With the development of these easily accessible

1. More than 250 new court opinions were published in 2010 in Oklahoma alone, and there were many more unpublished opinions.

2. "The doctrine of precedent, under which a court must follow earlier judicial decisions when the same points arise again in litigation." *Black's Law Dictionary* 1537 (9th ed. 2009).

3. Oklahoma State Court Network, http://www.oscn.net.

4. Google Scholar, http://scholar.google.com.

and powerful services, attorneys and other researchers have increasingly turned to online resources for retrieval of court opinions.

The twenty-first century has seen an explosion in the number of services providing access to court opinions. Each vendor has created its own unique approach to helping researchers find the cases they need. However, there are essentially three ways to locate court opinions in electronic resources: (1) by citation, (2) by keyword, and (3) by subject area. Each of these approaches is discussed in detail in this chapter, with the unique features offered by each vendor highlighted.

I. Retrieving Court Opinion by Citation

The legal profession has a unique citation system that enables researchers to quickly and easily locate court opinions.[5] Figure 6-1 explains the various parts of a citation for an Oklahoma Supreme Court

Figure 6-1. Sample Citation to Oklahoma Court Opinion

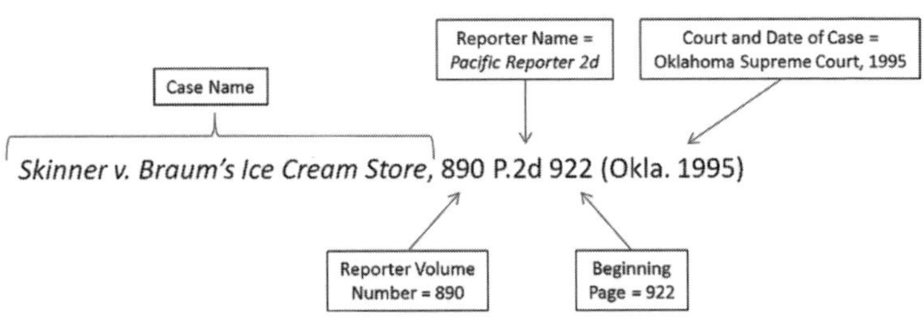

5. For more information, see *The Bluebook: A Uniform System of Citation* (19th ed. 2010), which has been widely adopted as a citation guide by courts nationwide. *See also ALWD Citation Manual: A Professional System of Citation* (4th ed. 2010).

Figure 6-2. QuickCase Feature in OSCN

Source: Oklahoma State Court Network, www.oscn.net.

opinion published in the *Pacific Reporter.* With the information contained in the citation, the court opinion can be easily retrieved online in the OSCN database using the QuickCase feature (see Figure 6-2) or in one of the commercial services. Typically, you only need to know three pieces of information to retrieve a court opinion: (1) the reporter volume number, (2) the name and series of the reporter in which the opinion is published, and (3) the starting page number. Note that most legal databases do not require exact punctuation or spacing when entering legal citations for retrieval. The case used as an example in Figures 6-1 and 6-2 can be found in volume 890 of the *Pacific Reporter, Second Series* beginning on page 922.

In 1997, the Oklahoma Supreme Court began requiring attorneys to cite court opinions using an "official paragraph citation form" as described in the Oklahoma Supreme Court Rule 1.200.[6] As a result, you may encounter citations that use the vendor-neutral paragraph citation form in Oklahoma shown in Figure 6-3. This figure identifies the individual parts of the paragraph citation format.

In plain language, the citation in Figure 6-3 says that the court opinion in *Skinner v. Braum's Ice Cream Store* was the eleventh decision of the Oklahoma Supreme Court during the year 1995. It can be retrieved through the QuickCase feature of the OSCN service using

6. Okla.Sup.Ct.R. 1.200(e), Opinions of the Supreme Court and the Court of Civil Appeals, http://www.oscn.net/applications/oscn/DeliverDocument.asp?CiteID=73621.

Figure 6-3. Sample Oklahoma Citation with Paragraph Citation Format

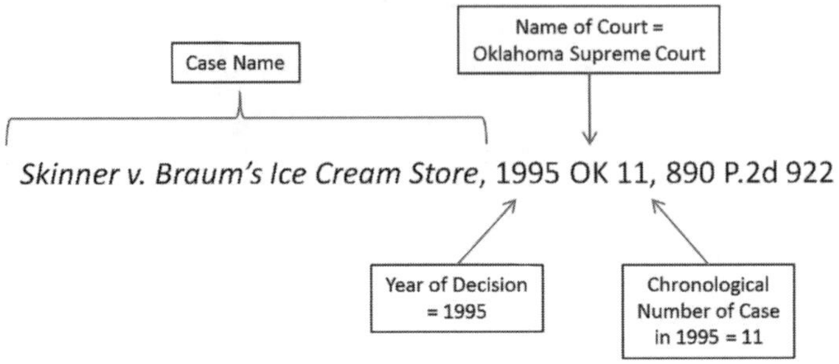

either the *Pacific Reporter* citation (890 P.2d 922) or the Oklahoma paragraph citation format (1995 OK 11).

II. Searching for Court Opinions by Keyword

With easy and free access to all Oklahoma court opinions online via OSCN and with powerful keyword search features available on commercial services like Westlaw, Lexis, Bloomberg Law, and Fastcase, researchers often choose to locate court opinions by keyword search. Searching for cases by keyword can be especially helpful in the following circumstances: (1) when searching for court opinions that contain a specific phrase or term of art, (2) when compiling a comprehensive list of court opinions that mentions specific facts or names, and (3) to locate a few relevant court opinions at the beginning of the research process that can be used as a launching point for further research.

Figure 6-4. Searching for a Phrase in Oklahoma Cases Database in OSCN

Source: Oklahoma State Court Network, www.oscn.net.

A. Searching for a Specific Phrase or Term of Art

Most modern databases contain powerful search interfaces that enable you to search for a specific phrase. When searching in terms and connectors search mode (also called Boolean searching), a phrase can be placed in quotes to instruct the search engine to return *every* court opinion—and *only* those specific court opinions—with a certain phrase. This can be extremely helpful when you want to locate every case that mentions a specific term of art. For example, OSCN can be used to locate every Oklahoma court opinion that mentions the phrase "greater latitude rule," as seen in Figure 6-4.

By placing the phrase in quotes, you can determine that exactly six Oklahoma court opinions mention this rule. Locating every case that discusses a specific rule can be extremely important in situations where one court has established a rule and another court has established an exception to or criticism of the earlier rule.

B. Searching for Specific Names or Facts

Keyword searching can be a very effective way to find court opinions that mention the name of a person or company. The terms and connectors search interface of OSCN, Westlaw, Lexis, and other major databases all contain options for name searching.

When searching for names, keep in mind that people often refer to themselves in different ways. Nicknames, abbreviations, and middle initials must all be considered when searching for court opinions that contain names. For example, if you needed to locate every court opinion that mentioned "Joseph Harroz," you would construct the following keyword search using the terms and connectors search box in a database of court opinions: Jo! w/2 Harroz. This search will locate any document that contains the words "Joseph" or "Joe" within two words of the word "Harroz." The connector "w/2" tells the database that the two parts of the name can occur in any order. For instance, the name may be written "Harroz, Joseph" or "Joseph Harroz" or simply "Joe Harroz." The "w/2" connector will retrieve court opinions that contain any of those variations because "Joseph" simply needs to occur within two words of "Harroz." In addition, the truncation symbol (!) will tell the search engine to retrieve any name that begins with the letters "Jo." So, it will retrieve instances of "Joe" or "Joseph." Note, though, that it will also retrieve Joel and John since those names also contain the two letters "Jo."

In addition to keyword searching using the terms and connectors search box, most legal research systems provide forms or templates for locating cases by party name. These templates generally prompt you to provide one or more party names, the jurisdiction of the court, and sometimes the date (if known). Figure 6-5 shows the Advanced Search options in WestlawNext. Cases can be located by party name, citation, and date. This form can also be used to search the specific "fields" of information contained in every case, including the judge, the attorneys, the docket number, and several others. If you know one piece of information, such as the party names, it is generally more efficient to search just the "name" field of all court opinions than to search the entire text of all court opinions.

Keyword searching can also be useful for locating court opinions that discuss specific facts. For instance, if you need to review every court opinion in Oklahoma that discusses methamphetamine, a terms and connectors search would be very effective because it literally retrieves *every* case which mentions that word and *only* those cases which mention that word.

Figure 6-5. Search by Party Name Field in WestlawNext

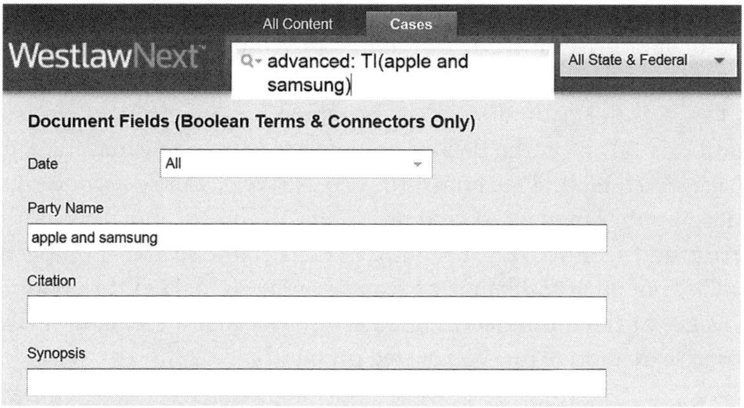

Reprinted with permission of Thomson Reuters.

C. Conducting a Natural Language Search for Court Opinions

When beginning a research project, the best place to start is by looking at a relevant secondary source, such as a treatise or law review article written by an expert on the topic.[7] Consider, for a moment, the reasoning behind this approach. When you begin your research by conducting a keyword search for court opinions, you have committed yourself to the very time-consuming and manual process of evaluating all of the cases retrieved by the search—a process that may have already been completed by an expert in the field. So, in general, if a relevant secondary source is available, you should begin by "standing on the shoulders" of the expert who has previously evaluated and identified the key court opinions that govern a specific issue. The relevant secondary source may point you to one or more key court opinions which can make the research process much more efficient.

Even so, there may be occasions where no current secondary source is available or where the only relevant secondary sources are

7. Research strategy is discussed in more detail in Chapter 1, 2, and 12.

several years old, and you will need to conduct a keyword search to begin the research process. A natural language search can often reveal one or more relevant court opinions that can serve as a launching point for further research. Both versions of Westlaw and Lexis, as well as OSCN, offer natural language searching options. In WestlawNext and Lexis Advance, the default method for searching is natural language searching. In Oklahoma, the OSCN service can be used to conduct natural language searching of all Oklahoma court opinions. Terms and Connectors searching is the default search method in OSCN, but a natural language search can be conducted through the Advanced Search interface. Figure 6-6 shows where the natural language search mode can be selected on OSCN.

After locating one or more relevant court opinions using a keyword search, you can use additional tools, like a digest (described later in this chapter), annotated statutes (described in Chapter 7), and citators (described in Chapter 11) to find other relevant opinions and to make sure each opinion is still "good law."

In concluding this section, it is important to note that a natural language keyword search is ***not*** a good mechanism for compiling a

Figure 6-6. Natural Language Search Option in OSCN

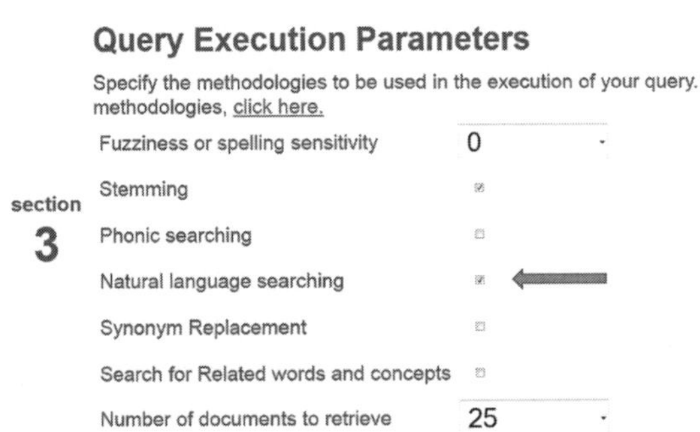

Source: Oklahoma State Court Network, www.oscn.net/applications/search.asp?simple =false.

comprehensive list of court opinions that discuss a specific legal concept. Since natural language search engines, by their very nature, only return what they determine to be the most relevant cases, the researcher may not see every case on-point. Also, since two judges may use alternative phrasing to describe a particular legal concept or subject, a natural language keyword search can miss one or more important cases because the search terms did not contain all possible variations. Furthermore, as discussed in Chapter 2 on Online Legal Research, natural language searching is best used for retrieving a few relevant documents that can then be used as a launching pad for further research.

III. Searching for Court Opinions by Subject Matter

Because the American legal system is based upon the principle of stare decisis, which requires lower courts to follow the legal rules established by higher courts, legal researchers must be able to locate court opinions that discuss a certain legal rule. However, this can often prove to be a difficult task with keyword searching alone because judges may use different words to describe the same concept. For example, consider the following question: What is a dog owner's liability when his dog bites and injures another person? A judge may describe the dog as a canine or an animal. In addition, other types of animal bites may also be relevant, such as cat bites. Because there are several ways to describe the legal concept, it may be difficult to capture all of the relevant court opinions using a keyword search. It is also not efficient to simply browse case reporters looking for relevant court opinions since reporters only publish court opinions in chronological order, not in subject order. Fortunately, legal publishers have created additional tools, called digests, to help researchers locate court opinions by subject.

A. West's American Digest and Key Number System

"Digests" are tools for locating court opinions by subject matter. The premier digest system in the United States is produced by West and is available in print and online via WestlawNext and Westlaw Classic. To create the digest, West employs attorney-editors who read published court opinions and create short summaries of each major point of law stated in each opinion.[8] These short summaries of individual legal rules are called headnotes. They are printed at the beginning of each court opinion published by West. Because many court opinions are dozens of pages long, headnotes make it easier and faster for researchers to determine whether a particular case is relevant to their client's issues. Headnotes also make it easier for researchers to determine which part of a court's opinion discusses a particular legal rule because each headnote number is indicated in the text of the opinion that supports the headnote. Note that headnotes are not part of the official court opinion and, therefore, should not be cited in any legal document. They are simply a tool designed to make researchers more efficient by summarizing the legal rules discussed in an opinion and by helping researchers to quickly find the parts of an opinion that are most relevant to the issue at hand.

After the headnotes are created, they are assigned to a specific "topic" and "key number" within West's Key Number System (also known as the Topic and Key Number System). "Topic" refers to the broad area of the law to which the headnote belongs, such as contracts, property, or torts. There are more than 400 topics in West's Key Number System ranging from abandoned property to zoning. "Key numbers" refer to specific points of law within each topic.

The Topic and Key Number System can be analogized to the subject arrangement of books in a library. Once a specific book is found on the library shelves, other books on the same topic can be found nearby. The same is true for the Topic and Key Number System in West's American Digests. Once a particular key number is identified as being relevant to a research project, headnotes from other cases that

---

8. Thomson Reuters, *Westlaw Research Fundamentals: How to Find Cases*, http://lscontent.westlaw.com/images/content/FindCases10.pdf.

also address that issue can be easily found nearby in the digest *regardless* of whether the cases use the same keywords to discuss the issue.

Note that each topic and key number on Westlaw is assigned a combination of numbers. Using the dog bite example above, the individual headnotes discussing injuries caused by animals are placed within the broad topic "Animals." Animals is assigned the topic number "28," and the individual headnotes on this issue would be assigned to key number 66.5, which discussed injuries caused by dogs specifically. Figure 6-7 shows how the Topic and Key Number System in WestlawNext is presented.

After clicking the link for key number "66.5 Injuries to persons—Dogs" within the topic "Animals," you are presented with a list of subtopics within this key number. By clicking on "(1) Duties and liabilities in general," you can examine sixteen headnotes that West has categorized under this subject. Figure 6-8 shows how the headnotes

Figure 6-7. Browsing the West Key Number System in WestlawNext

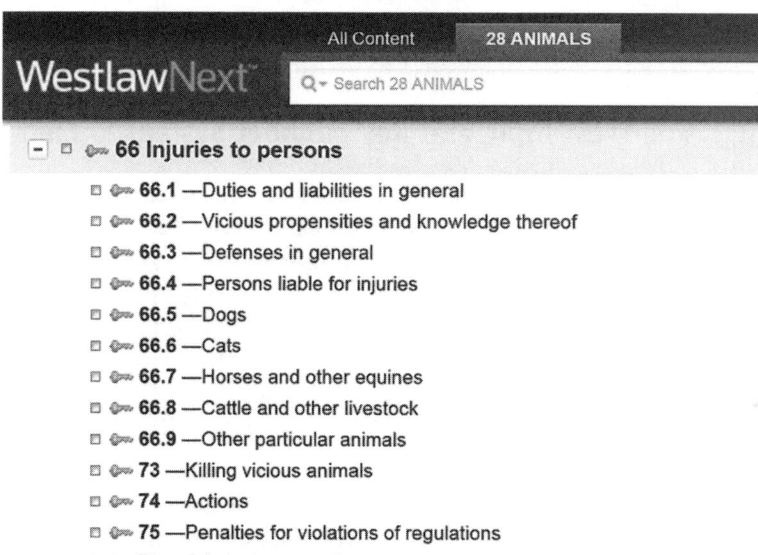

Reprinted with permission of Thomson Reuters.

Figure 6-8. Browsing to a Specific Topic and Key Number in WestlawNext

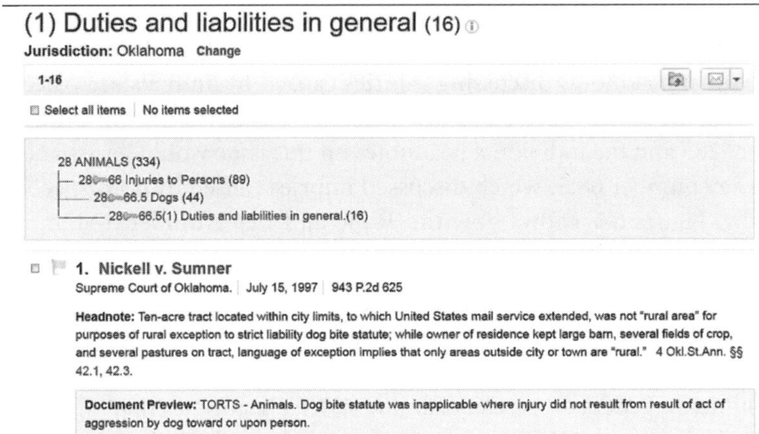

Reprinted with permission of Thomson Reuters.

from Oklahoma cases that discuss this specific issue are presented in WestlawNext.

B. Using West Topic and Key Number System to Find Cases by Subject

There are three ways that the digest can be used to find relevant cases by subject. The first and most common way to locate cases using the digest is to begin with one known case and use the headnotes from that opinion to find additional cases in the digest. Figure 6-9 demonstrates how the headnotes are presented in the Oklahoma case, *Hass v. Money*. If the *Hass* case was discovered through a secondary source, through a general natural language search of cases, or through a pleading from the opposing party, the headnotes in that case and the West Key Number System can be used to find related cases in Oklahoma. Assume, for example, that headnote 1 was relevant to your client's case. In Figure 6-9, on the right side of the screen, you can see the topic and key numbers to which this legal rule has been assigned in the digest.

Figure 6-9. Accessing the West Key Number System from the Headnote of a Case

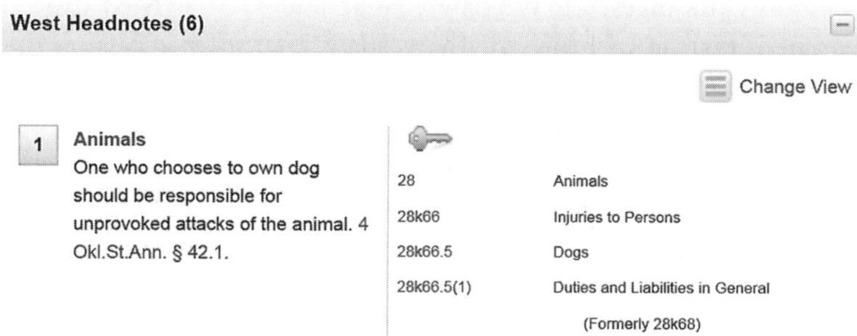

Reprinted with permission of Thomson Reuters.

By clicking on the link for "28k66.5(1) Duties and Liabilities in General," you can find other Oklahoma cases that discuss liability for injuries to persons caused by dogs. The results will be identical to those shown in Figure 6-8. After clicking the link for "28k66.5(1) Duties and Liabilities in General," you can specify a jurisdiction, such as Oklahoma state and federal cases, to limit the results. Cases from these courts would typically be the most important cases to an Oklahoma researcher since they are mandatory authority in this state. However, if you also wanted to find cases from courts outside Oklahoma, the jurisdiction could be changed to all states or specific states.

Second, the digest can be browsed in WestlawNext or Westlaw Classic. In WestlawNext, the digest is called the West Key Number System and can be accessed through the "Tools" tab on the home page. In Westlaw Classic, the "Key Numbers" link at the top of the screen provides options for searching and browsing the digest.

By simply drilling down through a series of increasingly specific menu listings, you can find all of the headnotes on a particular topic. Using the dog bite example, if you click on the broad topic "Animals," then browse to key number 66 on "Injuries to Persons," then click on key number 66.5 on "Dogs," and finally click on key number 66.5(1) on "Duties and Liabilities in general," you will be presented with 16 headnotes from Oklahoma cases that have been categorized under that very specific issue. The process is similar to clicking down through a very detailed outline of issues.

Finally, the digest on Westlaw Classic and WestlawNext can be searched, instead of browsed. In WestlawNext, after accessing the West Key Number System through the Tools tab, you will be presented with a search box at the top of the screen. You can enter a natural language search here, and WestlawNext will search only the text of the headnotes in the digest. For instance, you could search for "owner liability injury damages dog bite," and WestlawNext will run a natural language search in the digest. If you know the topic area you want to search, it is best to limit your search to that subject by checking the box next to the topic. In researching the dog bite example, you would check the box next to "28 Animals." Note that search results are organized by topic and key number. You can quickly skim the list to identify the topics and key numbers that contain the search results that are most relevant to your issue.

Searching in the digest on Westlaw Classic is somewhat different from searching the digest on WestlawNext. In Westlaw Classic, you begin searching the digest by clicking the "Key Numbers" link at the top of the screen. You are then presented with a "Search for Key Numbers" box, which searches the titles of the topics and key numbers only. After running a search for "dogs duties and liabilities in general," you will be presented with about 10 topics and key numbers that relate to that subject. Check the boxes to the left of those key numbers that you'd like to search in full text. Next, click the "Search Selected" button, and you will be presented with the headnotes from cases relating to that topic and key number.

C. Using West Digests in Print

Digests are also available in print format. The *Oklahoma Digest* includes all of the headnotes for Oklahoma state and federal court decisions. There are two ways to locate cases using a print digest. At the end of each digest set are volumes titled "Descriptive Word Index." Beginning with these volumes, you can find relevant cases in much the same way that you can browse the West Key Number System outline on WestlawNext. Begin by thinking of the broad topic that is being researched, such as Intellectual Property, and next browse the outline for increasingly narrower subtopics within Intellectual Property, such as Copyright and then Educational Use. The digest index will then provide a topic and key number that can be used to find related headnotes in the main digest volumes.

Another way to locate cases within a print digest is to begin with a known case. This process is much the same as the WestlawNext process described earlier. When you begin with a known, relevant case, the headnotes of that case will provide a topic and key number for each point of law. With specific topics and key numbers in hand, you can use the print digest to locate the headnotes from other cases that discuss that particular legal rule. To find the correct print volume, simply look at the range of topics and key numbers printed on the spine of each volume. Next, look at the top corner of each page to find the page where the headnotes for the specific key number in question are listed.

Many different digest sets cover the various state and federal courts. There is a digest for each state covering the state and federal court opinions that are mandatory authority in that state. In addition, regional digests correspond to the regional reporters. For instance, the *Pacific Digest* includes all of the headnotes from state court opinions reported in the *Pacific Reporter. West's Federal Practice Digest* includes headnotes from all reported federal courts, including district courts, appellate courts, and the U.S. Supreme Court. The *Decennial Digest* is the largest and most comprehensive digest. It includes the headnotes of all reported state and federal courts nationwide.

Finally, remember to check the pocket parts when working with a print digest. Print volumes of the digest are updated annually with paper supplements inserted into the back of each volume. The pocket parts include headnotes from all of the court opinions published after the hardbound volume was published. In some cases, the pocket part can include the most recent ten or even twenty years of case headnotes.

D. Finding Cases by Topic on Lexis Advance and Lexis

Both Lexis Advance and Lexis provide several methods for finding court opinions by subject. Like Westlaw, Lexis includes headnotes at the beginning of each published case. Unlike Westlaw, however, Lexis headnotes are key legal points of a case drawn directly from the language of the court by Lexis attorney-editors.[9] Also, instead of assigning headnotes to individual key numbers, Lexis uses a broad topical outline to organize headnotes by subject. This outline functions in much the same way as the West Topic and Key Number System. However, note that Lexis uses computer algorithms extensively to assign headnotes to topics. This is in contrast to Westlaw, which uses teams of attorney-editors to both write the headnotes and place them in the appropriate topic and key number.

Similar to Westlaw, the topic outline on Lexis Advance and Lexis can be accessed from the headnotes of a known case. Links to the topic outline are listed just above each headnote in a case. When clicking those links, you are taken to place in the topic outline where related cases, statutes, secondary sources, and other materials are organized. Figure 6-10 shows how LexisNexis headnotes and the topic outline are presented on Lexis Advance. Clicking the link for one of the topics shown below will allow you to retrieve other primary and secondary materials related to that topic.

9. *LexisNexis Headnotes Tutorial*, http://web.lexis.com/help/multimedia/hn2.textOnly.htm.

Figure 6-10. Headnotes and Topic Outline on Lexis Advance

LexisNexis® Headnotes ⊟Hide

Torts > Remedies > Damages > General Overview
Torts > ... > Types of Negligence Actions > Animal Owners > Ownership & Possession
Torts > Strict Liability > Harm Caused by Animals > General Overview
Torts > Strict Liability > Harm Caused by Animals > Defenses

HN1 In Oklahoma , the owners of any dog shall be liable for the full amount of any damages sustained when their dog, without provocation, bites or injures any person, while such person is in or on a place where he has a lawful right to be. Okla. Stat. tit. 4, § 42.1 (1991). Since amended effective Feb. 1, 1992, the statute reads as follows: the owner or owners of any dog shall be liable for damages to the full amount of any damages sustained when his dog, without provocation, bites or injures any person while such person is in or on a place where he has a lawful right to be. *Shepardize* - Narrow by this Headnote

In Lexis Advance, clicking the "Browse Topics" link in the top-right corner of the home page will also access the topic outline. The topic outline can be browsed and searched. You can drill down through progressively narrower subtopics until you reach a specific legal issue. At that point, you can search Lexis Advance to retrieve all of the documents relating to that issue. Lexis Advance will then return a search results screen with documents sorted by type—cases, statutes, secondary sources, etc. You can also search the topic outline. After clicking the Browse Topics link, you are presented with a search box that allows you to search the topic outline headings by keyword.

In Lexis, clicking on the drop-down menu for the "Search" tab presents options to search by topic or by headnote. From this point, the topic outline headings can be searched or browsed. Once you locate a relevant subtopic within the outline, either by searching or browsing, clicking the link for that subtopic will allow you to retrieve cases, statutes, secondary sources and other materials categorized within that narrow heading.

Two case-locating features that are unique to Lexis are "More Like This Headnote" and "More Like Selected Text." When viewing a case in Lexis, both of these options are available via links at the top of the case and at the end of each headnote. These search options can be used when you find a good, on-point case, and you want to find more cases like it.[10]

"More Like This" has two mechanisms for retrieving related cases: it can retrieve related cases based on citation patterns, called core cites, and based on keywords assigned to the case, called core terms. For either mechanism, the "More Like This" feature creates searches that include terms suggested by the researcher, the core cites or core terms, and other information that it gleans from the good, on-point case.[11]

The core cites mechanism examines the cases, statutes, regulations, and law review articles that are cited in cases. When core cites is selected within the "More Like This" feature, Lexis will retrieve cases that cite to the same cases, statutes, regulations, and law review articles as the case you are currently viewing.[12]

Lexis uses the core terms mechanism to search for cases with similar language patterns as the case currently displayed in Lexis.[13] When this option is selected, Lexis will present a list of core terms that can be selected by checking or unchecking the box next to each core term. Core terms are presented in the order of relevance assigned by Lexis.

Finally, if a portion of a case is especially relevant to your research, you can simply highlight the relevant text with your mouse and selected the "More Like Selected Text" feature. This feature will then automatically run a natural language search with the words from the selected text.

---

10. LexisNexis, *Search Tips: Using More Like This*, https://web.lexis.com/help/research/morelikethistips.asp.

11. *Id.*

12. LexisNexis, *More Like This*, http://support.lexisnexis.com/glossary/Record.asp?ARTICLEID=Glossary_More_Like_This.

13. *Id.*

IV. Unpublished Cases

Many court opinions are not published in reporters. Although unreported cases generally carry no precedential value, attorneys often review relevant unpublished opinions to gain insight on how the court may decide a particular issue.[14] In Oklahoma, unpublished cases can be searched and retrieved in the Oklahoma Public Legal Research System (OPLRS).[15] Unpublished state court opinions may not include headnotes or other editorial features present in published state court opinions. Summaries of unpublished court opinions are also published in the *Oklahoma Bar Journal.* Unpublished federal opinions can be found in West's *Federal Appendix* on Westlaw Classic and WestlawNext.

V. Citators and Case Law

No discussion of case law research can be complete without mentioning the important role that citators play in locating and determining the precedential value of cases. Citators like KeyCite on Westlaw, Shepard's on Lexis, and Citationizer on OSCN are tools that tell you whenever a later court opinion cites to the opinion you have in hand. Since courts cite to earlier opinions as they discuss the application of legal rules to the case in front of them, citators can be used to find related cases. Citators are discussed in detail in Chapter 11.

---

14. Note that Federal Rule of Appellate Procedure 32.1 prohibits courts from restricting the citation of unpublished opinions issued on or after January 1, 2007. *See* Fed. Rules of App. Proc. 32.1, http://www.law.cornell.edu/frap/Rule32_1. For a more detailed discussion of unpublished opinions, see Steven M. Barkan, Roy M. Merskey & Donald J. Dunn, *Fundamentals of Legal Research* 35 (9th ed. 2009).

15. Oklahoma Public Legal Research System, http://oklegal.onenet.net.

Chapter 7

Statutory Research

We all know of course that we cannot abolish all the evils in this world by statute or by the enforcement of statutes, nor can we prevent the inexorable law of nature which decrees that suffering shall follow vice....[1] —*Elihu Root*

I. Introduction

Statutes are legislative enactments. In Oklahoma, statutes are enacted by the bicameral Oklahoma State Legislature. Reflecting the historically independent nature of the Oklahoma people, Article 5 of the Oklahoma Constitution states, "[t]he Legislative authority of the State shall be vested in a Legislature, consisting of a Senate and a House of Representatives; but the people reserve to themselves the power to propose laws and amendments to the Constitution and to enact or reject the same at the polls independent of the Legislature, and also reserve power at their own option to approve or reject at the polls any act of the Legislature."

The Oklahoma Legislature, as a political body, may pass legislation in an attempt to address public policy concerns. Further, the Oklahoma Legislature may enact statutes to address emerging issues, to codify the law as reflected in court decisions (i.e. the common law), or to alter the common law. For instance, the Oklahoma Legislature in 2007 acted to address issues regarding immigration and employ-

1. Elihu Root, *Experiments in Government and the Essentials of the Constitution* 13–14 (1913).

ment. Occasionally, as has been the case with some state statutes addressing immigration issues, there is a conflict between the state statute and a federal statute. In such an event, the federal statute will preempt the state statute as long as Congress has the Constitutional authority to enact laws that govern the subject of the legislation.

Because statutory law governs many aspects of society, many projects will involve statutory research; as a result, an effective research strategy will normally entail a process to identify relevant statutory law. Additionally, statutory enactments may limit legal actions by prescribing a time frame in which a claim may be made. Such enactments are often referred to as statutes of limitations.[2] It is also important to remember that application of statutory law is often impacted by subsequent court rulings and regulations promulgated by administrative agencies. Therefore, statutory law research is almost always accompanied by case and administrative law research. Notwithstanding, reading and analyzing statutes involves different considerations than reading and analyzing judicial opinions.[3]

The focus of this chapter is an introduction to basic research of Oklahoma statutory law. In the process of creating Oklahoma statutory law, the legislature produces bills and other documentation of legislative action. This chapter will discuss the various resources of Oklahoma statutory law, including individual legislative enactments; enactments collected according to time of enactment, commonly referred to as session laws; and statutory codes, which are collections of statutes by topic. The chapter will also address the methods to research these resources. Chapter 8 will introduce methods to research Oklahoma legislative history.

---

2. The codified statutes placing such limitations on actions in Oklahoma are available at 12 O.S.2011, §91 et seq.

3. There is an entire branch of legal scholarship addressing the topic of interpretation and construction of legislation. And at least one leading text within this branch indicates that interpretation and construction of a statute are "interchangeable" terms. 2A N. Singer & N.J. Singer, *Sutherland Statutory Construction* §45.24 (7th ed. 2007). This topic is, however, beyond the scope of this chapter.

II. Legislative Enactments—Individual and Collections

A. Individual Enactment

1. *In Print*

An individual enactment is called a slip law; in Oklahoma, these are published as *Oklahoma Session Laws.* The enacted statutes are published by topic in the *Oklahoma Statutes.* As bills are passed during a legislative session, they are printed as a soft cover copy of the *Oklahoma Sessions Laws.* There will be several copies printed throughout the legislative session to include additional bills as they are passed by the legislature. A hardbound copy is printed within a few months after the legislature adjourns and contains all of the bills passed during the session. Until the annual supplement to the *Oklahoma Statutes* is printed, it is important to refer to the soft copies of the current *Oklahoma Session Laws* to determine the status of laws recently added, amended, or repealed.

2. *Available Online*

In addition to the print copies of individual enactments, bills passed during a legislative session are also available online. As will be discussed in greater detail in Chapter 8, the Legislative Service Bureau (LSB) provides access to the text and tracking information for bills. Further, session laws are also available on Westlaw, Lexis, and Bloomberg Law research services.

B. Codified Statutes

A subject arrangement of current statutes is routinely referred to as a code.[4] The official state code, *Oklahoma Statutes*, is published

4. "Technically, a code refers to statutory and non-statutory law reenacted by the legislature as positive law." Elyse H. Fox, *Legal Research Dictionary: From Advance Sheets to Pocket Parts* 24 (2d ed. 2006). Positive law is the "authoritative text of a statute. Unless the statute is reenacted by the legislature

under the "direction of the Oklahoma Supreme Court Justices"[5] by a commercial publisher.[6] West is the commercial publisher of the official editions of the *Oklahoma Statutes* in hardbound volumes that are updated each year with supplemental volumes.[7]

C. Session Laws

As illustrated in Figure 7-1, in the print session laws, each bill is given a heading corresponding to its subject matter and a chapter number that is chronologically assigned by the date the bill was approved by the Governor or filed with the Secretary of State. The print *Oklahoma Session Laws*, like the *Oklahoma Statutes*, serves as an official publication, although it is published by West. HeinOnline also provides electronic, image-based access to the *Oklahoma Session Laws*. Bloomberg Law, which designates the source for Oklahoma session laws as Oklahoma Acts, is another resource for the session laws. On Bloomberg Law session laws may be downloaded in a variety of formats including PDF, and the Bill Number is also displayed. (See Figure 7-2.)

From 1998 through the current legislative session session laws are also available to browse or to search via the Oklahoma State Court Network (OSCN).[8]

---

in code form ... the session law is the positive law and the code is prima facie evidence of the law." *Id.* at 71.

5. 75 O.S.2011, § 192.

6. "'Oklahoma Statutes 2011' and annual cumulative supplements thereto shall be compiled, codified, annotated, printed and published by a publisher selected by the Chief Clerk of the House of Representatives, from bids submitted for that purpose." 75 O.S.2011, § 191.

7. "Supplement—an addendum to the Oklahoma Statutes printed every year, with the exception of once every ten years when the Oklahoma Statutes are published in their entirety, with additions to or deletions from Oklahoma laws to bring them up to date and to correct any errors." Oklahoma State Senate, *Glossary of Terms*, http://www.oksenate.gov/legislation/glossary.html.

8. Oklahoma State Court Network, www.oscn.net.

Figure 7-1. Image of Print Oklahoma Session Laws Available from HeinOnline

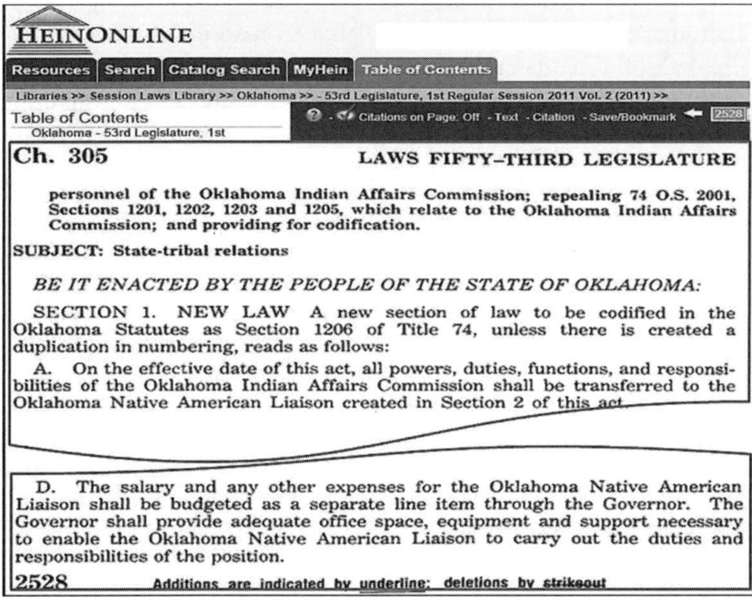

HEINONLINE

Resources | Search | Catalog Search | MyHein | Table of Contents

Libraries >> Session Laws Library >> Oklahoma >> - 53rd Legislature, 1st Regular Session 2011 Vol. 2 (2011) >>

Table of Contents
Oklahoma - 53rd Legislature, 1st

Citations on Page: Off - Text - Citation - Save/Bookmark 2528

Ch. 305 **LAWS FIFTY-THIRD LEGISLATURE**

personnel of the Oklahoma Indian Affairs Commission; repealing 74 O.S. 2001, Sections 1201, 1202, 1203 and 1205, which relate to the Oklahoma Indian Affairs Commission; and providing for codification.

SUBJECT: State-tribal relations

BE IT ENACTED BY THE PEOPLE OF THE STATE OF OKLAHOMA:

SECTION 1. NEW LAW A new section of law to be codified in the Oklahoma Statutes as Section 1206 of Title 74, unless there is created a duplication in numbering, reads as follows:

A. On the effective date of this act, all powers, duties, functions, and responsibilities of the Oklahoma Indian Affairs Commission shall be transferred to the Oklahoma Native American Liaison created in Section 2 of this act.

D. The salary and any other expenses for the Oklahoma Native American Liaison shall be budgeted as a separate line item through the Governor. The Governor shall provide adequate office space, equipment and support necessary to enable the Oklahoma Native American Liaison to carry out the duties and responsibilities of the position.

2528 Additions are indicated by underline; deletions by ~~strikeout~~

Source: HeinOnline. Reprinted with permission.

Figure 7-2. Oklahoma Acts on Bloomberg Law

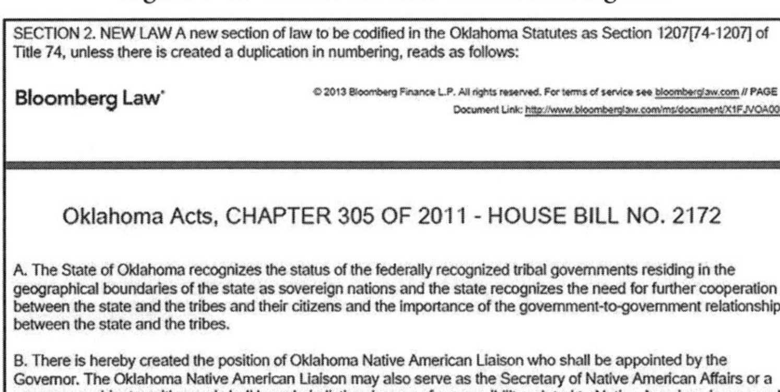

SECTION 2. NEW LAW A new section of law to be codified in the Oklahoma Statutes as Section 1207[74-1207] of Title 74, unless there is created a duplication in numbering, reads as follows:

Bloomberg Law

© 2013 Bloomberg Finance L.P. All rights reserved. For terms of service see bloomberglaw.com // PAGE 1
Document Link: http://www.bloomberglaw.com/ms/document/X1FJVOA003

Oklahoma Acts, CHAPTER 305 OF 2011 - HOUSE BILL NO. 2172

A. The State of Oklahoma recognizes the status of the federally recognized tribal governments residing in the geographical boundaries of the state as sovereign nations and the state recognizes the need for further cooperation between the state and the tribes and their citizens and the importance of the government-to-government relationship between the state and the tribes.

B. There is hereby created the position of Oklahoma Native American Liaison who shall be appointed by the Governor. The Oklahoma Native American Liaison may also serve as the Secretary of Native American Affairs or a successor cabinet position and shall have jurisdictional areas of responsibility related to Native American issues and

Source: Bloomberg Law BNA. Reprinted with permission.

D. Historical Statutory Compilations

Oklahoma Statutes is the current version of the official statutes of Oklahoma. However, prior to *Oklahoma Statutes* publication, Oklahoma had other code compilations. As indicated in the table in the appendix to this chapter, one of the earliest statutory compilations dates back to 1891 when Oklahoma was still a territory.

To read a statute's language in its earlier form, the researcher may consult one of these older codes. The publisher of *Oklahoma Statutes* has provided a conversion table that lists where in the new statutory compilation the old code section exists.[9] This table may also indicate if a code section has been repealed and therefore is not located in the newer version of the code. For earlier versions of the statute, a researcher may need to consult the index of these older codes to determine where that subject matter was treated.

E. Annotated Statutes

An annotated code is one in which the editors have added cross-references to related publications for each sections of the code. These annotations are located following the text and source notes of the code sections. These related publications include primary and secondary authority, such as judicial opinions, law review and journal articles, legal encyclopedia entries, and treatises. Researchers often find the selected judicial opinion annotations, referred to as notes of decisions, useful. For each case listed in the notes of decisions, the annotation contains a brief paragraph summarizing the case with a citation to the case.

Oklahoma Statutes Annotated (*OSA*) is a West publication. As illustrated in Figure 7-3, *OSA* references West-published secondary sources and topic and key number references included in *West's Analysis of American Law*, as discussed in Chapter 6.

---

9. In *Oklahoma Statutes 2011*, the conversion tables are located in Volume 9.

Figure 7-3. *Oklahoma Statutes Annotated* in Print with Citation

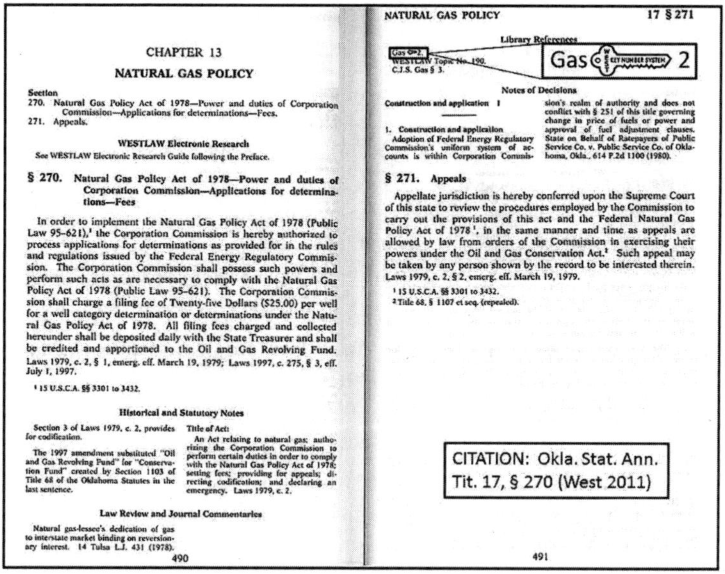

CHAPTER 13

NATURAL GAS POLICY

Section
270. Natural Gas Policy Act of 1978—Power and duties of Corporation Commission—Applications for determinations—Fees.
271. Appeals.

WESTLAW Electronic Research

See WESTLAW Electronic Research Guide following the Preface.

§ 270. Natural Gas Policy Act of 1978—Power and duties of Corporation Commission—Applications for determinations—Fees

In order to implement the Natural Gas Policy Act of 1978 (Public Law 95-621),[1] the Corporation Commission is hereby authorized to process applications for determinations as provided for in the rules and regulations issued by the Federal Energy Regulatory Commission. The Corporation Commission shall possess such powers and perform such acts as are necessary to comply with the Natural Gas Policy Act of 1978 (Public Law 95-621). The Corporation Commission shall charge a filing fee of Twenty-five Dollars ($25.00) per well for a well category determination or determinations under the Natural Gas Policy Act of 1978. All filing fees charged and collected hereunder shall be deposited daily with the State Treasurer and shall be credited and apportioned to the Oil and Gas Revolving Fund. Laws 1979, c. 2, § 1, emerg. eff. March 19, 1979; Laws 1997, c. 275, § 3, eff. July 1, 1997.

[1] 15 U.S.C.A. §§ 3301 to 3432.

Historical and Statutory Notes

Section 3 of Laws 1979, c. 2, provides for codification.

The 1997 amendment substituted "Oil and Gas Revolving Fund" for "Conservation Fund" created by Section 1103 of Title 68 of the Oklahoma Statutes in the last sentence.

Title of Act:

An Act relating to natural gas; authorizing the Corporation Commission to perform certain duties in order to comply with the Natural Gas Policy Act of 1978; setting fees; providing for appeals; directing codification; and declaring an emergency. Laws 1979, c. 2.

Law Review and Journal Commentaries

Natural gas-lessee's dedication of gas to interstate market binding on reversionary interest. 14 Tulsa L.J. 431 (1978).

490

NATURAL GAS POLICY 17 § 271

Library References

Gas ⚷2.
WESTLAW Topic No. 190.
C.J.S. Gas § 3.

Gas ⚷ KEY NUMBER SYSTEM 2

Notes of Decisions

Construction and application 1

1. Construction and application

Adoption of Federal Energy Regulatory Commission's uniform system of accounts is within Corporation Commission's realm of authority and does not conflict with § 251 of this title governing change in price of fuels or power and approval of fuel adjustment clauses. State on Behalf of Ratepayers of Public Service Co. v. Public Service Co. of Oklahoma, Okla., 614 P.2d 1100 (1980).

§ 271. Appeals

Appellate jurisdiction is hereby conferred upon the Supreme Court of this state to review the procedures employed by the Commission to carry out the provisions of this act and the Federal Natural Gas Policy Act of 1978[1], in the same manner and time as appeals are allowed by law from orders of the Commission in exercising their powers under the Oil and Gas Conservation Act.[2] Such appeal may be taken by any person shown by the record to be interested therein. Laws 1979, c. 2, § 2, emerg. eff. March 19, 1979.

[1] 15 U.S.C.A. §§ 3301 to 3432.
[2] Title 68, § 1107 et seq. (repealed).

CITATION: Okla. Stat. Ann. Tit. 17, § 270 (West 2011)

491

Reprinted with permission of Thomson Reuters.

III. Methods of Statutory Research

The most efficient manner to conduct research in Oklahoma's print statutes will be influenced by the type and amount of information available, as noted in Chapter 1. For example, researchers may gather the citation or popular name for the relevant statutory provision from reading a secondary source or from reviewing an applicable case. Because of the different types of information that may be initially available, there is not a single way to conduct statutory research. However, Table 7-1 suggests a process for conducting statutory research. The process will vary based on the information and resources available. Research can be conducted in either print or online materials, both of which will be covered in the following sections.

Table 7-1. Outline for Oklahoma Statutory Research

1. Generate a list of search terms.
2. Look up the terms in the index of the print *Oklahoma Statutes Annotated*. Alternatively, search the Oklahoma Statutes on the Oklahoma State Court Network (OSCN) or expand the titles on OSCN to browse the topics covered by sections within various titles on OSCN. Other online resources include the free website of the Oklahoma Legislature or a subscription database such as Fastcase, WestlawNext, Lexis Advance, or Bloomberg Law.
3. Locate and read the statutes. If using *Oklahoma Statutes Annotated* in print, check the pocket parts and supplemental pamphlets to ensure the currency of the statute.
4. Read annotations to find citations to cases and other resources that interpret, apply, or discuss the statute. In *Oklahoma Statutes Annotated*, the annotations follow the language of the statute. On OSCN, citing cases and Oklahoma Attorney General opinions appear in the "Citationizer Summary of Documents Citing This Document" section following the text of the statute.
5. Read and analyze the relevant cases and secondary sources discussing the statute.

A. Using Codes in Print

As mentioned above, after the Oklahoma Legislature enacts statutes, the statutes are arranged according to subject matter, a process known as codification. The official print publication of this collection of codified Oklahoma statutes is referred to by a title of the same name *Oklahoma Statutes* (O.S.). O.S. is divided into eighty-five parts, known as titles, which address specific topics and subject areas. When a new statute is enacted, it is added to a title containing other statutes on a similar subject. The statute is also assigned a section number that arranges the statute within the title. The West publication, *Oklahoma Statutes Annotated*, uses the same numbering system.

The simplest way to locate a code section is to have the citation. The citation includes the title number designated to that topic as well as the section number. The topics/titles are alphabetically arranged: Title 1 is Abstracting and Title 85 is Workers' Compensation. See Appendix A for additional examples.

Working without the citation to the statutory provision governing the issue, another approach is to use the multi-volume general index. Because state statutes are prepared by state legislators, many of whom are not attorneys, it is often helpful to conduct a keyword search of the print index. For example, a search of electronic resources for the key term "statute of limitations" may not produce results because the Oklahoma statutory provisions establishing the period of time within which a claim must be brought is referred to as a "limitation on action." Using the print index, a researcher familiar with the legal terminology will locate the provisions addressing statute of limitation issues.

Another approach to statutory research is to use the Popular Names Table located at the end of the set. Often, an act is given a short name or acquires a popular name through usage. This table indexes those names and provides a cross-reference to the appropriate section in the code.

B. Using Online Codes

Although many experienced researchers prefer to conduct state statutory research in print, it is also important to know how to effectively search online sources for Oklahoma statutory law. Oklahoma statutes can be located in numerous online sources. This section will concentrate on five sources: Bloomberg Law, Fastcase, the Oklahoma State Court Network (OSCN), Lexis products, and Westlaw products. Bloomberg Law and Fastcase provide the current code and prior codes, while the other sources provide access to more extensive collections of historical codes.[10]

1. Bloomberg Law

Oklahoma statutes may be located by selecting the "Legislative and Regulatory Tab" and following the "State Legislative Materials" link on the Bloomberg Law Service. The service then displays a map of the states, which allows you to select the state of interest. Alternatively, you may click the "Statutes and Regulations Link" under the "Getting Started" section. The system displays the options to view federal or individual state statutes. Figure 7-4 indicates the options for accessing the codified statutes. You can drill down into a particular code section using the browse function to access an expandable table of contents. In this way, the research method is similar to that of the print code. However, Bloomberg does not provide a popular names table or an alphabetical index. Rather than using an index, you may also locate statutes by conducting a keyword search. However, this alternative method may produce a greater number of irrelevant results than using an index. Similarly, Bloomberg Law does not provide a popular names table search but provides the option of searching the Oklahoma Statutes or Oklahoma Acts[11] for short titles that may have been assigned to an act. While only the current edition of Oklahoma Statutes may be searched, Oklahoma Acts searching covers the period of 1997 to present.

Notwithstanding that Bloomberg Law indicates that the Oklahoma Statutes search is a search of the current statutes, it is necessary to check the currency of the results. As shown in Figure 7-5, by scrolling over the currency icon, the system will indicate that the provision is current through a specific session of the legislature. In late 2012, the system indicated that provisions were current only through the 2010 Regular Session of the Fifty-Second Legislature.

---

10. Because Chapter 8 provides an introduction to the resources available from the Oklahoma Legislative Service Bureau (LSB), that resource will not be discussed here.

11. Oklahoma Acts is the designation Bloomberg Law makes for the collection of Oklahoma session laws.

Figure 7-4. Oklahoma Statutes on Bloomberg Law

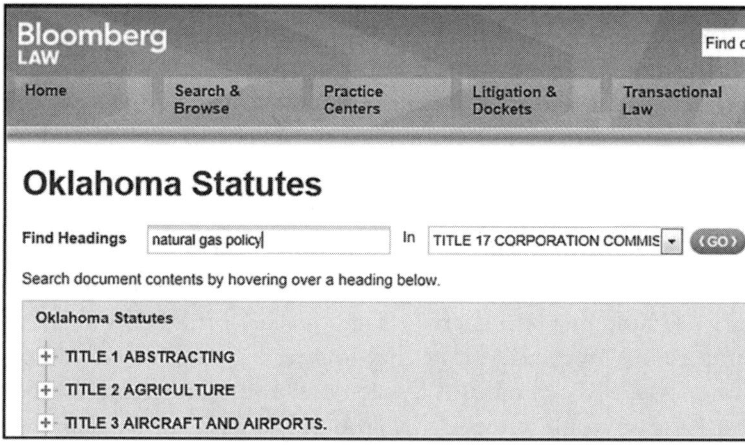

Source: Bloomberg Law BNA. Reprinted with permission.

Figure 7-5. Bloomberg Law Currency Information

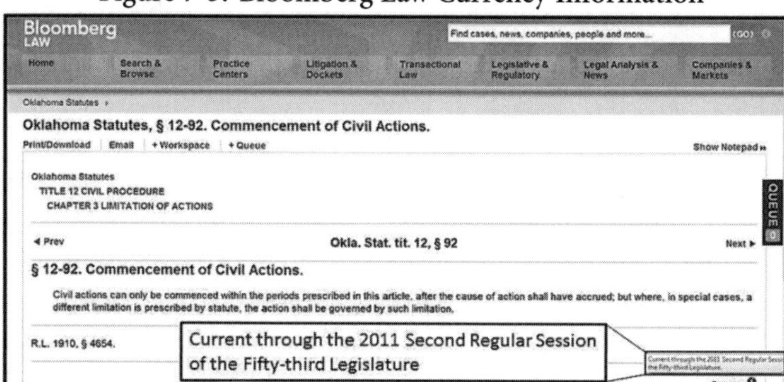

Source: Bloomberg Law BNA. Reprinted with permission.

2. Fastcase

Fastcase is the research service provided at no cost to members of the Oklahoma Bar.[12] Fastcase is also available for use by law students without cost at the law schools in Oklahoma. Further, Fastcase has developed apps to permit research via the iPhone, iPad, and Android phones.[13] This discussion will outline research of Fastcase for Oklahoma statutes via desktop rather than no cost apps.

According to its website, "Fastcase provides the law exactly as it comes from courts, legislatures, and agencies, without the extraordinary overhead that characterizes traditional legal research and its editorial gloss. We communicate that overhead savings directly to our subscribers."[14] Based on such a statement, a researcher would expect that Fastcase would provide a less robust, no frills service. However, like Bloomberg Law, Fastcase allows you to 1) retrieve a statutory provision by citation; 2) browse and drill down to a specific provision; and (3) conduct a keyword search of the Oklahoma Statutes. As indicated in Figure 7-6, Fastcase permits you to format the search as a natural language or a Boolean search. Despite the presence of this functionality, Fastcase does not allow searching within the table of contents.

3. Oklahoma State Court Network (OSCN)

OSCN's "quickcase" function provides easy access to statutes as well as cases when a citation is already known. Alternatively, Oklahoma Statutes on OSCN may be located by following the "Oklahoma Statutes Citationized" link under the "Legal Research" tab. Figure 7-7 shows that OSCN allows you to browse the expandable contents of the statutes or to search the entire collection of statutes or individual titles. However, searching only the table of contents is not possible.

---

12. Members of the Oklahoma Bar may access Fastcase by signing in through the Oklahoma Bar Association website at http://www.okbar.org. No cost Fastcase access may also be available to members of other bar associations. See Fastcase, Bar Association Subscribers (in italics), http://www.fastcase.com/barmembers/.

13. Fastcase, *Fastcase Launches First Legal Research App For Android*, http://www.fastcase.com/fastcase-launches-first-legal-research-app-for-android/.

14. Fastcase, *What is Fastcase?*, http://www.fastcase.com/whatisfastcase/.

Figure 7-6. Fastcase Statutory Research Interface

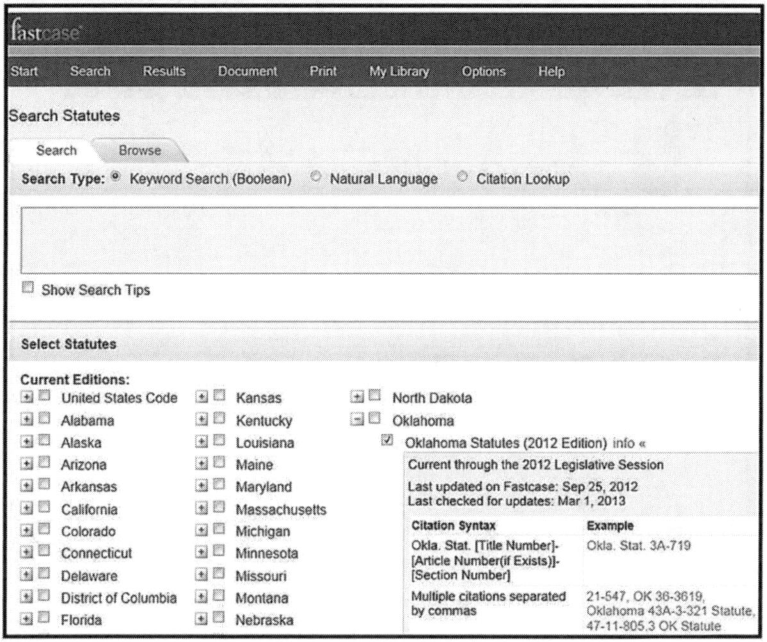

Source: Fastcase. Reprinted with permission.

OSCN also provides an advanced search function. The advanced search function, as indicated in Figure 7-8, includes Boolean and natural language searching as well as special field searching for statutes only. The field searching allows you to limit results using time restrictions, including "effective on or before," "superseded on or before," or other options, such as "act name." Using the special field functionality on OSCN, the researcher may search for statutes effective or superseded from 1890–2006.

4. *Statutes on Lexis and Lexis Advance*

a. *Get a Document with a Citation on Lexis*

As with print resources, Lexis allows you to efficiently retrieve a statutory provision with a citation. The "Get a Document" function

Figure 7-7. Oklahoma Statutes Citationized on OSCN

Source: Oklahoma State Court Network, www.oscn.net/applications/oscn/index.asp?ftdb=stokst&level=1.

retrieves the document by citation. For those researchers unfamiliar with the proper citation format, Lexis provides assistance through the "citation format" link, which allows you to locate the proper format by searching an alphabetical list of publications. Unfortunately, the "Get a Document" function is currently not available when using Lexis Advance.

b. Keyword Searching for Statutes on Lexis and Lexis Advance

Researchers often choose to begin their search for statutes with a keyword search. Keyword searching is most effective when limiting a search to databases containing the most relevant documents. On Lexis, the current Oklahoma Statutes file is OKCD. When searching this database, natural language searching and terms and connectors searching are available. Additionally, terms and connectors searching within the file's segment (often referred to as field) is an included feature. It is often helpful to search within the Section or Heading

Figure 7-8. Advanced Search Function on OSCN

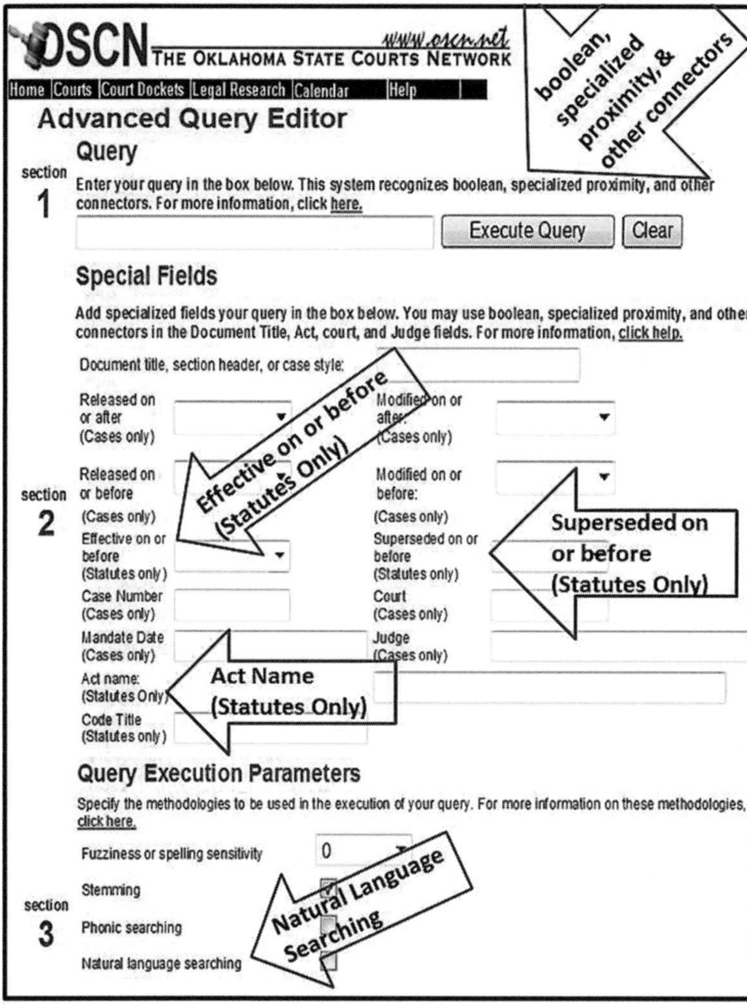

Source: Oklahoma State Court Network, www.oscn.net/applications/oscn/search.asp?simple=false.

field for fact unique terms related to the issue being researched. For instance, to locate a statute on sanctioning mixed martial arts activities, you might construct a search such as "SECTION(sanction-

Figure 7-9. Lexis Advance Browse Sources

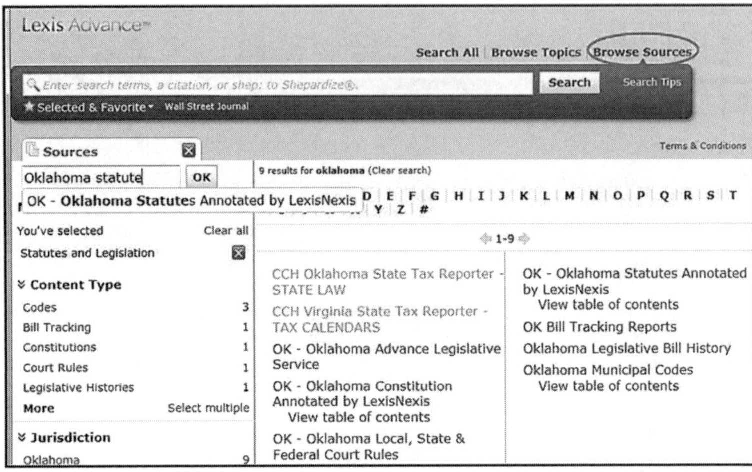

ing) and mixed martial arts." Lexis also provides access to the table of contents for the code; permitting you to search the table of contents, drill down to a particular section, or search within a particular title.

As Figure 7-9 illustrates, the July 2012 release for Lexis Advance included the functionality to browse for sources. You may use the browse sources function to access "Oklahoma Statutes Annotated by LexisNexis" and then search or browse the expandable table of contents for a specific applicable provision. Alternatively, you may perform a natural language search or terms and connectors search using the "all in one" search box. However, when conducting a terms and connectors search, Lexis Advance does not currently permit segment searching. Even so, inclusion of a "W/SEG" Connector in the search tips for Lexis Advance suggests that segment searching will be included in future releases.

Whether conducting a natural language search or a terms and connectors search when using the "all in one" search box of Lexis Ad-

Figure 7-10. Using Filtering in Lexis Advance

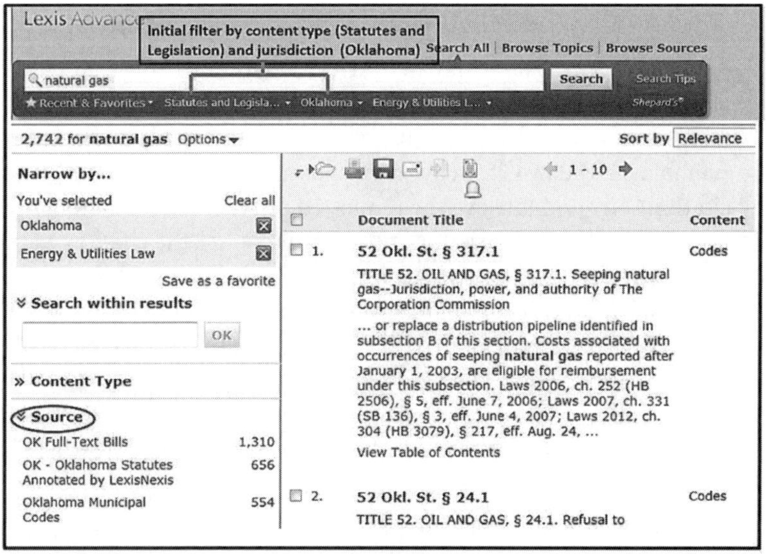

vance, researchers should apply the "Statutes and Legislation" content type filter and the Oklahoma "jurisdiction" filter to limit the search to the most relevant results. In contrast to a search of the "Oklahoma Statutes Annotated by LexisNexis," the "all in one" search on Lexis Advance, even with the "Statutes and Legislation" content type filter applied, produces results that include bills, court rules, and other resources in addition to statutes. As a result, additional time will be required to sift through the results. Alternatively, as indicated in Figure 7-10, when conducting an "all in one" search, you may select to further "narrow by" source the results. Such an action will help to ensure you are reviewing the most relevant resources.

5. *Statutes on Westlaw and WestlawNext*

a. *Find by Citation on Westlaw Classic and WestlawNext*

A statutory provision may be retrieved with a citation on either Westlaw or WestlawNext. Retrieving a document with a citation on Westlaw is not complicated. On either the law school or the Oklahoma tab on Westlaw Classic, you may insert the citation in the "Find by citation" box and retrieve the requested provision. The system operates to locate the statute without the need to enter the citation using only one precise format. For instance, the system would locate the proper statute even if the searcher "incorrectly" entered "10 OK ST ANN 40.7" rather than the correctly formatted, "10 Okl. St. Ann. § 40.7" Westlaw citation (10 represents the title number and 40.7 the section number). Retrieving a statute by citation using the "Find and Print" function accessed through the link at the top of the display is also possible.

Retrieving a statute with a citation on WestlawNext is also not a difficult task; however, unlike the Westlaw Classic system, WestlawNext may be unable to locate a statute if the citation is incorrectly entered. Using the incorrect "10 OK ST ANN 40.7" citation in either the main single search box or in the citation field of an advanced search produces no results. It is more effective to select Oklahoma as the jurisdiction and simply enter the section number "40.7" in the search box. Entering "40.7" with the set jurisdiction produces results that list the correct section within Title 10 of the Oklahoma Statutes. Alternatively, as illustrated in Figure 7-11, using the Oklahoma Statutes Find Template, which is linked below the "Tools and Resources" heading, a researcher will be prompted to enter the proper title and section number.

b. *Keyword Searching for Statutes on Westlaw Classic and WestlawNext*

While inexperienced researchers often choose to begin their search for statutes with a keyword search, this may not be the most effective means of research. Using a secondary source, which discusses the research topic and identifies the applicable statutory provisions, may be more effective. Thus, if you are unfamiliar with a research topic and

Figure 7-11. Oklahoma Statutes Find Template on WestlawNext

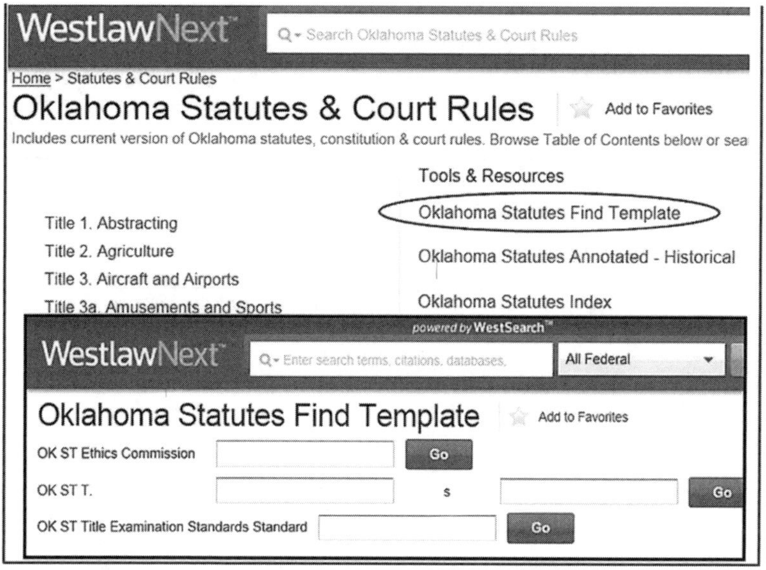

Reprinted with permission of Thomson Reuters.

would like to use keyword searching, you may find it useful not to limit the keyword search to Oklahoma Statutes but rather to perform the keyword search and then browse secondary sources to identify the key statutory provisions. Even so, it is possible to perform a keyword search of only Oklahoma Statutes in both Westlaw Classic and WestlawNext.

On Westlaw Classic, you may enter the database designator "OK-ST-ANN" in the "Search for a database" box on the Law School Tab to be directed to search function for Oklahoma Statutes Annotated. You then have the option of using a natural language or a terms and connectors search of the database. Additionally, you also have the option of browsing the linked Table of Contents or a Statutes Index to assist in identifying the applicable statutes.

Figure 7-12. Scope and Functions of Oklahoma Statutes on WestlawNext

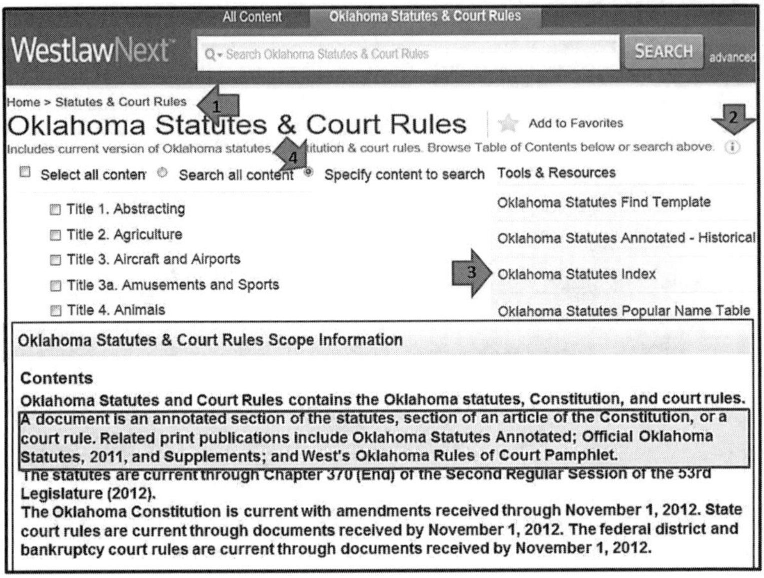

Reprinted with permission of Thomson Reuters.

As the breadcrumb trail[15] designated by arrow 1 in Figure 7-12 indicates, on WestlawNext you may select the "Statutes & Court Rules" link on the "All Content" tab and then select Oklahoma to limit searching to "Current Oklahoma statutes, constitution, and court rules."

Selecting the information button, as indicated by arrow 2 in Figure 7-12, will display scope information about the coverage of resources being searched.

15. A breadcrumb trail is "a series of hyperlinks displayed at the top of a web page, indicating the page's position in the overall structure" of the website or database. *Oxford Dictionary of English* (3d ed. 2010).

Figure 7-13. Statutory Annotation Information, including Content & Analysis Tab, on WestlawNext

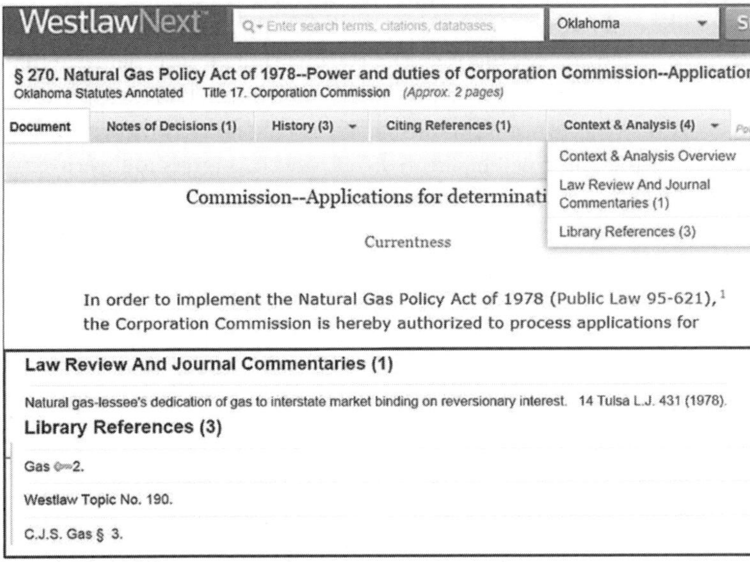

Reprinted with permission of Thomson Reuters.

You may conduct a basic search using the search box, or you may select to conduct an advanced search, including Boolean terms and connectors. Similar to searching in Westlaw Classic, you may also use the statutes index to locate provisions on a specific topic. The link to the statutes index is included under the "Tools and Resources" heading, as shown by arrow 3 of Figure 7-12. Further, you may limit a search to specific titles by selecting the "Specify content to search" (arrow 4 of Figure 7-12) option and then clicking on the box preceding the title number and alphabetical topic.

Researchers using Westlaw Classic's "OK-ST-ANN" database and WestlawNext to locate the Oklahoma statutes are obtaining results included in the *Oklahoma Statutes Annotated* in print. The "annotations" on WestlawNext, unlike the annotations in the print OSA and on Westlaw Classic, do not follow the text of the statutes; instead, the annotations are linked via the tabs across the top of the display. (See Figure 7-13.)

IV. Federal Statutory Research

As indicated in the introduction to this chapter a federal statute will routinely preempt a conflicting state statute; thus, it is imperative that a researcher also be familiar with federal statutory research. Given the focus of this chapter on Oklahoma statutory research, however, the coverage of this topic will be limited. Yet, since Congress follows a similar model of enacting and publishing legislation, initially publishing enactments as session laws and later codifying the statutes into arrangements by subject, federal statutory research can be conducted in a manner similar to the procedures described previously in this chapter.

A. Slip Laws

The federal slip laws are not published in permanent print volumes. Instead individual enactments may be found online via several free government sources, including THOMAS[16] and the Federal Digital System.[17] Public laws can also be accessed using commercial databases, including WestlawNext, Lexis Advance, and Bloomberg Law.

B. Session Laws/*Statutes at Large*

At the completion of the Congressional session, the federal statutes are bound in chronological order in an official government publication, the *Statutes at Large*. A law is available in *Statutes at Large* from one to two years after it is enacted. As a result, researchers often look to commercial publications of federal statutes before publication of the official session laws.

In print, *LexisNexis Advance* is published monthly and is available for use until the *United States Code Service*, discussed below, is pub-

16. The address is http://thomas.loc.gov/home/thomas.php.

17. Private and Public Laws are available for browsing on the Federal Digital System, http://www.gpo.gov/fdsys/browse/collection.action?collectionCode=PLAW.

lished. Thomson Reuters publishes the *United States Code Congressional and Administrative News* (*USCCAN*). *USCCAN* pamphlets, which are also issued monthly, are subsequently bound into hardback volumes.[18] In addition to the session laws, *USCCAN* may also include some legislative history documents.

C. Codified Statutes

The *United States Code* is composed of fifty-one titles. These titles are further subdivided into sections. A reference to a federal statute requires both the title and the section (e.g., 42 U.S.C. § 2991b-2). The *United States Code* is published in an official series with the same name, *United States Code (USC)*, and is updated annually with cumulative bound supplements and reissued in bound volumes every six years. Codified federal statutes are accessible via a number of electronically available sources, including the Legal Information Institute.[19] However, many electronic resources do not provide an official version of federal statutes. An official version of the code is available online through the Office of the Law Revision Counsel of the U.S. House of Representatives.[20] The Office of the Law Revisions Counsel's website also contains a link to another no cost online resource, the Federal Digital System (FDsys), which provides access to an online version of the *USC*.

D. Annotated Code Sources

Because the *USC* may be several months to years out of date and because the *USC* does not include annotations, despite citation rules instructing legal writers to cite to it,[21] the *USC* may be of limited value

18. *USCCAN* is also available on Westlaw Classic and WestlawNext.

19. A researcher may access the *United States Code* maintained by the Legal Information Institute by browsing titles or by searching at http://www.law.cornell.edu/uscode/text.

20. U.S. House of Representatives, Office of the Law Revision Counsel, *United States Code*, http://uscodebeta.house.gov.

21. *The Bluebook: A Uniform System of Citation*, Rule 12.2 at 112, 114 (19th ed. 2010).

to researchers. Instead, researchers may find commercially published annotated code sources more useful because they are updated more frequently and contain additional useful information in the form of case annotations and library references. The commercially published annotated codes are West's *United States Code Annotated* (*USCA*) and LexisNexis's *United States Code Service* (*USCS*). Both are available online and in print. While the two commercially annotated code resources are similar, there are some differences. For example, the *USCS* may reference secondary sources traditionally published by Mathew Bender, a popular legal publisher acquired by the parent company of LexisNexis, while the *USCA* will reference secondary sources published by publishers affiliated with Thomson Reuters. Because of such differences, researchers may find it useful to review federal statutory provisions in both sources.

V. Appendix 7 State of Oklahoma & Oklahoma and Indian Territory Statutory Compilations[22]

Oklahoma Statutes, 2011: Comprising All Laws of a General and Permanent Nature Including Laws and Amendments Passed by the First Regular Session of the Fifty-Third Legislature, 2011; Edited and Published Under the Direction of the Justices of the Supreme Court. St. Paul, MN: West Pub. Co., 2011.

Oklahoma Statutes, 2001: Comprising All Laws of a General and Permanent Nature Including Laws and Amendments Passed by the First Regular and First Extraordinary Sessions of the Forty-Eighth Legislature, 2001. Edited and Published Under the Direction of the Justices of the Supreme Court. St. Paul, MN: West Pub. Co., 2001.

22. Updated and modified information from American Association of Law Libraries, Pub. No. 3–78, *State Documents Bibliography: Oklahoma* 23–25 (2009).

Oklahoma Statutes, 1991: Comprising All Laws of a General and Permanent Nature Including Laws and Amendments Passed by the First Extraordinary and First Regular Sessions of the Forty-Third Legislature, 1991. Edited and Published Under the Direction of the Justices of the Supreme Court. St. Paul, MN: West Pub. Co., 1991.

Oklahoma Statutes, 1981: Comprising All Laws of a General and Permanent Nature Including Laws and Amendments Passed by the First Regular and First Extraordinary Sessions of the Thirty-Eighth Legislature, 1981. Edited and Published Under the Direction of the Justices of the Supreme Court. St. Paul, MN: West Pub. Co., 1981.

Oklahoma Statutes, 1971: Comprising All Laws of a General and Permanent Nature Including Laws and Amendments Passed by the First Regular Session of the Thirty-Third Legislature, 1971. Edited and Published Under the Direction of the Justices of the Supreme Court. St. Paul, MN: West Pub. Co., 1971.

Oklahoma Statutes, 1961: Comprising All Laws of a General and Permanent Nature Including Laws and Amendments Passed by the Regular Session of the Twenty-Eighth Legislature, 1961. Edited and Published Under the Direction of the Justices of the Supreme Court. St. Paul, MN: West Pub. Co., 1961.

Oklahoma Statutes, 1951: Compromising All Laws of a General and Permanent Nature Including Laws and Amendments Passed by the Regular Sessions of the Twenty-Third Legislature, 1951. Edited and Published Under the Direction of the Justices of the Supreme Court. St. Paul, MN: West Pub. Co., 1951.

Oklahoma Statutes, 1941: Comprising All Laws of a General and Permanent Nature Including Laws and Amendments Passed by the First Regular Sessions of the Eighteenth Legislature, 1941. Edited and Published Under the Direction of the Justices of the Supreme Court pursuant to Act of May 9, 1941, Laws 1941. St. Paul, MN: West Pub. Co., 1942.

Oklahoma Statutes, 1931: Compiled and Annotated by Frank O. Eagin and C. W. Van Eaton, Approved by Oklahoma Code Commission; William H. Murray, Governor, Chairman … [and others] Oklahoma City, OK: Harlow Pub. Co., 1931–32.

Compiled Statutes of Oklahoma, 1921: Annotated by Clinton Orrin Bunn, Under the Provisions of Chapter 125, Session Laws of Oklahoma, 1921; Supervised and Approved by the Code Commission, Consisting of Hon. John B. Harrison ; Hon. Thomas H. Doyle, and the Attorney General of the State of Oklahoma, by R.E. Wood, Assistant Attorney General. Session Laws of Oklahoma, 1921 Ardmore, OK: Bunn Pub. Co., 1922.

Revised Laws of Oklahoma, 1910: Being a Compilation, Classification and Revision of All General Laws of the State of Oklahoma in Force and Effect on the 25th Day of February 1911. St. Paul, MN: The Pioneer Co., 1912.

The Compiled Laws of Oklahoma, 1909, a Compilation of All the Laws of a General Nature Now in Force, Including the Session Laws of 1909, Being Correct Copies of the Enrolled Bills. Kansas City, MO: Pipes-Reed Book Co., 1909.

General Statutes of Oklahoma 1908; a Compilation of All the Laws of a General Nature Including the Session Laws of 1907, Annotated to Volume 18 Oklahoma Reports, 96 Pacific Reporter, 76 Kansas Reports and 150 California Reports. Kansas City, MO: Pipes-Reed Book Co., 1908.

Wilson's Revised and Annotated Statutes of Oklahoma, 1903. Revised and Annotated by W.F. Wilson. Guthrie, OK: The State Capital Company, 1903.

Annotated Statutes of the Indian Territory, Embracing All Laws of a General and Permanent Character in Force at the Close of the Second Session of the Fifty-Fifth Congress. St. Paul, MN: West Publishing Co., 1899.

Morgan's Digest of Oklahoma Statutes and Supreme Court Decisions. Perry, OK: D.T. Morgan, 1897.

The Statutes of Oklahoma, 1893. Being a Compilation of All the Laws Now in Force in the Territory of Oklahoma. Guthrie, OK: State Capital Printing Co., 1893.

The Statutes of Oklahoma, 1890. Guthrie, OK: State Capital Printing Co., 1890.

Chapter 8

Legislative Process and Legislative History Research

I. Introduction

Legislative history may help an advocate interpret a statute that is vague or ambiguous, or help an attorney develop an argument supporting the application of a statute in a particular manner. Legislative history may document both the process a bill passed through to become a statute as well as the substantive modifications and debate occurring during this process. Thus, legislative history material may yield valuable information about the intent of the legislature in enacting and amending a statute or proposing a bill. However, because Oklahoma legislative history has traditionally focused on procedural aspects of legislation, its usefulness in determining legislative intent has been limited. As a result, commercial firms specializing in legislative history research have not developed in Oklahoma and, while more substantive legislative history materials are becoming available, advocates and attorneys continue to find it necessary to conduct their own legislative history research. This chapter provides an overview of the Oklahoma legislative process and resources available in Oklahoma legislative history research. The section following this introduction attempts to define legislative history in Oklahoma. The next section describes the Oklahoma legislative process. The chapter concludes with discussion of the research resources available and the use of these resources in compiling a legislative history and tracking a bill.

II. Defining Legislative History and Its Use in Oklahoma Courts

A. Defining Legislative History in Oklahoma

According to the Glossary of Legislative Terms compiled by the Staff of the Oklahoma House of Representatives and available on the Oklahoma Legislature website, legislative history is "[i]nformation on the background of legislation that may be used to determine 'intent.' In Oklahoma, legislative history is chronological."[1] What is meant by the statement that legislative history is chronological is somewhat unclear. It appears to mean that legislative history in Oklahoma is procedural rather than substantive. As described by the Tenth Circuit in the 1988 case of *Miller v. Commissioner of Internal Revenue*, "Oklahoma legislative history does not include debates, committee reports, or other documentation necessary to shed light on a statute's underlying purpose...."[2] In reality, Oklahoma legislative history does contain committee reports. However, the committee reports do not provide substantive analysis of the proposed legislation; instead, committee reports in Oklahoma provide only limited information regarding the committee's recommendations.[3] (See Figure 8-1.)

B. Use of Legislative History in Oklahoma Courts

Although limited substantive legislative history is available, the Oklahoma Supreme Court has acknowledged that legislative history may be considered in determining the proper interpretation of a

1. Oklahoma House of Representatives, *Glossary of Legislative Terms*, http://www.okhouse.gov/Information/GlossaryOfTerms.aspx.

2. *Wilson v. Al McCord Inc.*, 858 F.2d 1469, 1477 (10th Cir. 1988).

3. "[Oklahoma] Committee Reports [c]onsist of: (1) 'do pass,' (2) 'do pass as amended,' (3) 'do pass committee substitute,' (4) 'do not pass,' and (5) 'report progress.' Conference committee reports are just another version of the bill." *William H. Manz, Guide to State Legislation, Legislative History, and Administrative Materials* 327 (7th ed. 2008).

Figure 8-1. House of Representatives Committee Report

OKLAHOMA HOUSE OF REPRESENTATIVES
COMMITTEE REPORT

4/6/2011 8:51:10 AM

TRANSPORTATION COMMITTEE

SB200

By: Denney of the House

Halligan of the Senate

Title: Special license plates; providing for Ovarian Cancer Awareness plates. Effective date.

Coauthored By:

Recommendation: DO PASS AS AMENDED BY CS

Amendments:

1. Committee Substitute Attached

_______________ Chr.
Representative T.W. Shannon

YEAS: 19

Brown, Hall, Lockhart, Richardson, Cockroft, Hardin, Martin,, Sc, Roberts,, S., Farley, Joyner, McPeak, Shannon, Faught, Kouplen, Murphey, Wright, Grau, Liebmann, Proctor

NAYS: 0

CONSTITUTIONAL PRIVILEGE:

Req. No. 7453 Page 1

Source: Oklahoma State Legislature, www.oklegislature.gov.

statute. The Oklahoma Supreme Court has broadly defined the sources it will look to when construing a statute. For example, in *Atlantic Refining Co. v. Oklahoma Tax Commission*, point four of the syllabus prepared by the Court states,

> [C]ourts, in construing a statute, may...recur to the history of the time when the act was passed; and this is frequently necessary, in order to ascertain the reason as well as the meaning of particular provisions....[T]he history of the times during which a law was enacted tends strongly to disclose the reasons for the act and therefore the evils sought to be remedied....[T]he courts will take judicial notice of the facts of contemporaneous history, the prior state of the law, the particular abuse or defect which the act was meant to remedy and will then apply the language of the act to such state of affairs.[4]

III. Oklahoma Legislature and the Legislative Process

A. Oklahoma Legislature

Like other states,[5] Oklahoma has a bicameral legislature consisting of two chambers, the State Senate, composed of 48 members, and the House of Representatives, composed of 101 members.[6] Regular sessions of the Legislature convene annually at noon on the first Monday in February. Regular sessions must be adjourned by 5:00 p.m. on the last Friday in May every year. The Oklahoma Legislature is in ses-

---

4. *Atlantic Refining Co. v. Okla. Tax Comm'n*, 360 P.2d 826 (Okla. 1959). Notwithstanding the broad nature of this statement, in determining when it is appropriate to use the legislative history, the Oklahoma Supreme Court has indicated ambiguity may be a precondition for resort to legislative history as evidence of legislative intent. *See, e.g.*, *Pure Oil Co. v. Cornish*, 52 P.2d 832, 834 (Okla. 1935); *In re Martin's Estate*, 80 P.2d 561 (1938); *State ex rel. Rucker v. Tapp*, 380 P.2d 260 (Okla. 1963). *But cf. Surety Bail Bondsmen of Okla., Inc. v. Ins. Comm'r*, 243 P.3d 1177 (Okla. 2010).

5. Okla. House of Reps. Office of Comm. Staff, *Oklahoma House of Representatives Legislative Manual* 1 (13th rev. ed., 2010), http://www.okhouse.gov/Documents/LegislativeManual2010.pdf.

6. Paula George, *The Oklahoma Legislature, in Oklahoma Almanac 2009–2010*, at 99 (Connie G. Armstrong ed., 2010).

sion Monday through Thursday. Extraordinary sessions may be called by the governor or by the Legislature itself.[7]

The two years between general elections represent a "Legislature." Legislatures are identified by consecutive numbers.[8] For example, the Legislature elected in November 2010 is Oklahoma's Fifty-third Legislature. The 2011 session is the first session and the 2012 session will be the second session of the Fifty-third Legislature. Legislation originating in the Senate of the Fifty-third Legislature is numbered consecutively beginning with "1" and legislation originating in the House of Representatives is numbered beginning with "1001."[9]

B. Legislative Process

The Oklahoma legislative process is governed by Article V of the Oklahoma Constitution. In accordance with Article V of the Oklahoma Constitution,

> [e]very bill shall be read on three different days in each House, and no bill shall become a law unless, on its final passage, it be read at length, and no law shall be passed unless upon a vote of a majority of all the members elected to each house in favor of such law; and the question, upon final passage, shall be taken upon its last reading, and the yeas and nays shall be entered upon the journal.[10]

Table 8-1 illustrates in further detail the Oklahoma legislative process. Additionally, thorough discussions of the Oklahoma legislative process are available via the Oklahoma Legislature website[11] and the *Oklahoma Legislative Manual.*

---

7. *Id.*
8. *Id.* at 100.
9. *Id.* at 99.
10. Okla. Const. art. V, § 34.
11. *Oklahoma House of Representatives Legislative Manual, supra* note 5.

Table 8-1. Steps in Oklahoma Lawmaking Process Documentation

Process	Documentation
The author of the bill introduces the bill and the bill proceeds through a first and second reading.* In most cases the first and second readings are by title only.	Introduced Bill (initial version and subsequent vesions) Journal Entry
The bill is assigned to a committee for consideration, is returned from the committee with recommendation, and is placed on the General Order or Consent Calendar.	Committee Report** Journal Entry
The bill is advanced for the third reading, debate, and final vote. If the measure does pass, the measure and all amendments are engrossed, signed by the presiding officer, and forwarded to the other chamber of the legislature.	Video Recordings of Floor Proceedings (Current) Select Audio Recordings of Proceedings (Past) Voting Records Journal Entry
Once received by the other chamber, the bill will follow a process similar to that followed by the initial chamber.	Introduced Bill Committee Report Video Recordings of Floor Proceedings (Current) Select Audio Recordings of Proceedings (Past) Voting Records Journal Entries

Table 8-1. Steps in Oklahoma Lawmaking Process Documentation (*continued*)

If the bill is amended, the author of the bill in the first chamber may determine that the amendments are acceptable and move to have the amendments accepted. There is then a fourth reading and vote.	Amended Version of the Bill Journal Entry
If the amendments are not accepted, a conference may be called. The conference committee must act on the engrossed amendments by accepting or rejecting each engrossed amendment from the second chamber.	Conference Committee Report Journal Entry
The report first goes to the house of origin where it may be accepted or rejected. If accepted, the report is forwarded to the second house. If the second chamber accepts the report, the measure is enrolled and forwarded to the governor.	Video Recording of Floor Proceedings Voting records Journal Entries

* Bills must be filed prior to introduction. As provided in the Fifty-Third Legislature Oklahoma Senate Rule 5-2, bills may be prefiled beginning November 15 on odd-numbered years and ending at the time of sine die adjournment of the Second Session.

** The committee rarely makes a "do not pass" recommendation because it could enable the bill to advance to the floor where, inconsistent with the committee's evaluation, it could be approved. For that reason, a "report progress" motion is used to designate committee opposition and retain the committee's control of the measure. *See* Okla. State House of Reps., *The Course of Bills in Becoming Law*, http://www.okhouse.gov/Information/CourseOfBills.aspx; Okla. State House of Reps., *How an Idea Becomes a Law* and *The Path of a New Law in Oklahoma*, http://www.okhouse.gov/Information/FlowCharts.aspx.

IV. Locating Oklahoma Legislative History Materials

This section summarizes some of the primary sources of Oklahoma legislative history materials and provides an outline of the materials that are available. In Oklahoma, the primary sources of legislative history include bill chronologies, House and Senate journals, committee reports, floor debates, and other miscellaneous sources, such as Governor's messages and news sources.[13]

A. Bill Chronologies

Bill chronologies, reflecting the procedural nature of legislative history in Oklahoma, are perhaps the most prominent source of legislative history. Bill chronologies are available in print in the bound House and Senate journals. Bill chronologies are also available in the *Journal Record Legislative Reporter* (formerly *Oklahoma Legislative Reporter)* Final Wrap Up. Additionally, as illustrated in Figure 8-2, bill chronologies may be accessed at no charge via the Oklahoma Legislative Service Bureau Bill Tracking Reports website.[14] Westlaw and Lexis bill tracking databases also provide bill chronology information.

B. House and Senate Journals

Oklahoma House and Senate journals, as illustrated in Figure 8-3, contain the record of daily legislative activities. They are published in summary form that does not contain the full text of documents or a verbatim report of legislative debate. Oklahoma House and Senate journals are maintained by the Archives Division of the Oklahoma Department of Libraries. A significant number of county, public, and academic law libraries in Oklahoma also maintain print copies of the journals. House journals since 1999 and Senate journals since 2003 are also available on the Oklahoma Legislature website.[15] Westlaw Classic has House journals from the Second Regular Session of the 47th Legislature (2000) to the present

13. Manz, *supra* note 3, provides a detailed outline of primary sources of Oklahoma legislative history sources, at 327–28.

14. *Oklahoma Legislative Service Bureau Bill Tracking Reports*, http://www.oklegislature.gov/AdvancedSearchForm.aspx.

15. Okla. House of Reps., *House Journals*, http://www.okhouse.gov/Legislation/Leg_Journals.aspx; *Okla. State Senate*, *Oklahoma Senate Journals*, http://www.oksenate.gov/publications/journals.html.

Figure 8-2. Bill Chronology Available on the Oklahoma Legislative Service Bureau Website

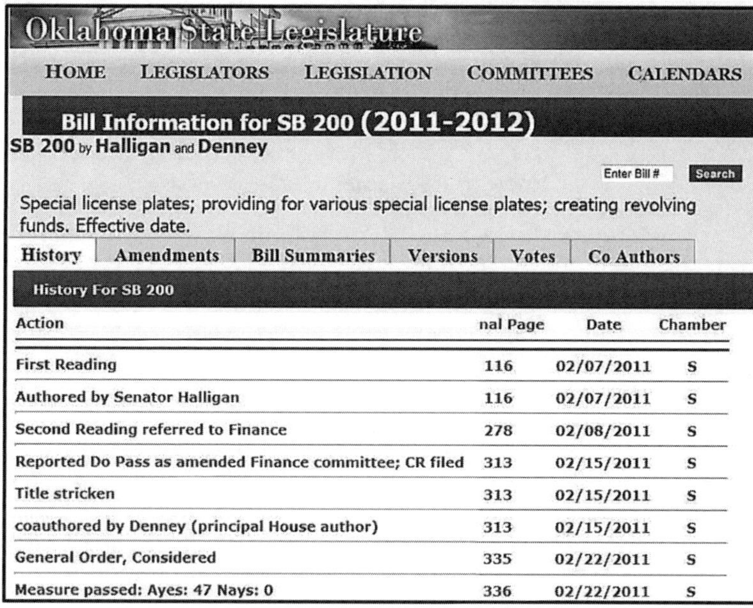

Oklahoma State Legislature

HOME LEGISLATORS LEGISLATION COMMITTEES CALENDARS

Bill Information for SB 200 (2011-2012)

SB 200 by **Halligan** and **Denney**

Enter Bill # Search

Special license plates; providing for various special license plates; creating revolving funds. Effective date.

History | Amendments | Bill Summaries | Versions | Votes | Co Authors

History For SB 200

Action	nal Page	Date	Chamber
First Reading	116	02/07/2011	S
Authored by Senator Halligan	116	02/07/2011	S
Second Reading referred to Finance	278	02/08/2011	S
Reported Do Pass as amended Finance committee; CR filed	313	02/15/2011	S
Title stricken	313	02/15/2011	S
coauthored by Denney (principal House author)	313	02/15/2011	S
General Order, Considered	335	02/22/2011	S
Measure passed: Ayes: 47 Nays: 0	336	02/22/2011	S

Source: Reprinted with permission of Thomson Reuters.

and Senate journals from the 49th Legislature (2003) to the present in the OK-LH-JRNLS database. Journals are available on WestlawNext, too.

Legislative History→Oklahoma Legislative History→Oklahoma Legislative History: Journals is one research trail that will display the advanced search function for Oklahoma House and Senate journals on WestlawNext. Searching using the bill number or topic as a search term, as well as adding a date restriction may be an effective means of locating the desired entry in the *Oklahoma House Journal*. Additionally, on WestlawNext, the journal entries are available in either a text or a PDF format. Use of the PDF format permits easier page number identification for citation purposes.

Figure 8-3. Searching for House of Representative Journals on WestlawNext

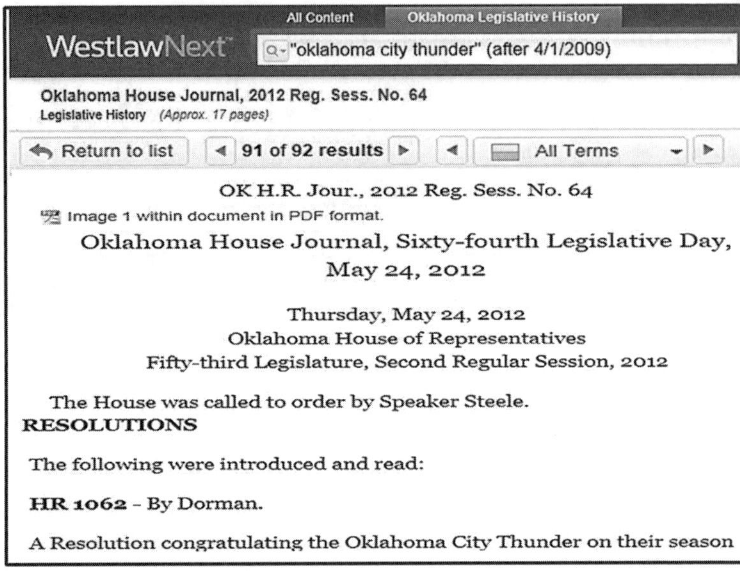

Source: Reprinted with permission of Thomson Reuters.

C. Bills Files—Bill Text

"The official bill files contain every form of a bill from its introduction to final action."[16] Since 1989, the Clerks of House of Representatives and the Senate Records Office have been charged with keeping the bill files for the respective chambers of the Oklahoma Legislature. For years prior to 1989, the bill files are maintained by Archives Division of the Oklahoma Department of Libraries.[17] Unfortunately, due to space restrictions, bill files maintained by the Senate Records and the Clerk of the House of Representatives are located in an off-site storage facility with limited hours. Therefore, some ad-

16. Okla. Dep't of Libs., *Resources Regarding Oklahoma's Legislative Measures*, http://www.odl.state.ok.us/lawinfo/billinfo.htm.

17. *Id.*

vanced planning is needed to obtain access original bill files for legislation since 1989. There are, however, some alternative sources of the text of bills. Oklahoma City University Law Library maintains Oklahoma Senate and House bills in print for the period 1986-2000.[18] Additionally, the Oklahoma Legislature's website provides a "Versions" tab that provides access to introduced and amended bill text. Bill texts are available electronically on this source from 1993 through the current Legislature. Lexis Advance, as the display in Figure 8-4 shows, also provides access to all "versions of Oklahoma Bills."

Figure 8-4. Oklahoma Bill Versions available on Lexis Advance

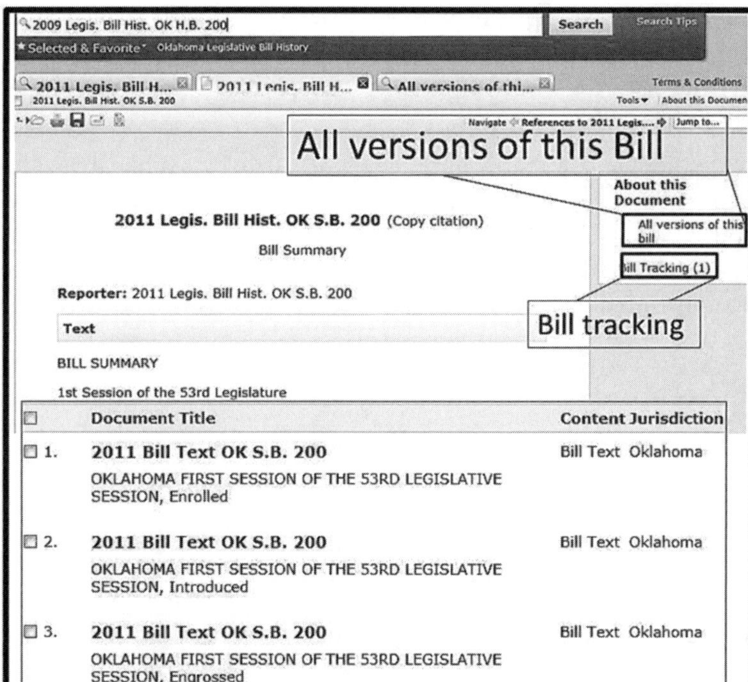

18. According to the library catalog, the University of Tulsa's Mabee Legal Information Center maintains microfiche for Oklahoma House Bills from 1981 to 1988 and Oklahoma Senate Bills for the period 1979 to 1988.

D. Committee Reports

Print copies of committee reports are maintained in the bill files. Requests for access to bill files for legislation introduced after 1988 may be made to the respective chambers of the Legislature. Print committee reports documenting limited committee action taken prior to 1989 are maintained by the Archives Division of the Oklahoma Department of Libraries.[19] Since 2003, committee reports have also become available electronically at no cost through the Oklahoma Legislative Service Bureau's (OLSB) Bill Tracking Reports Website.[20] As the scope note in Figure 8-5 shows, Committee Reports are also available in the Lexis Oklahoma Legislative Bill History database (OKLH). Westlaw Classic provides access to committee reports in the Oklahoma Legislative History Reports (OK-LH-REP) database. Committee reports can also be retrieved from WestlawNext.

Despite the fact that committee reports may be readily accessible, their value in establishing legislative intent may be minimal; as previously noted and as illustrated in Figure 8-1, Oklahoma committee reports do not contain substantive analysis, but consist of the limited recommendations, including "do pass," "do pass as amended," or "do not pass."

E. Floor Debates, Proceedings and Votes

When the Oklahoma Senate is in session, video of live floor debates is available on the Oklahoma Legislature's website under the video tab.[21] Access to audio tapes of Senate sessions from 1971 to 1986 are available from the Archives Division of the Oklahoma Libraries, and access to taped audio sessions since 1987 are available from the

19. *See* Okla. Dep't of Libs., *supra* note 16. Note also that bill files, while accessible through the respective chamber offices, are maintained offsite and requests to review the files may involve significant delay.

20. Okla. Legis. Serv. Bureau, *Bill Tracking Reports Website*, http://www.oklegislature.gov/AdvancedSearchForm.aspx.

21. Okla. State Senate, *Senate Audio and Video*, http://www.oksenate.gov/news/listen.htm.

Senate.[22] Podcasts and archived audio clips may also be accessed from the Senate website. Similarly, limited audio files from the Oklahoma House of Representative are available from the House of Representative website.[23] Enhanced video functionality for select floor proceedings for both the Oklahoma House of Representatives and Senate became available in 2011.[24]

F. Other Documents

1. Fiscal Impact Statements

Rule 5-8 of the Rules of the Oklahoma Senate states, "[n]o amendment, bill or resolution which creates a direct fiscal impact on state tax revenues shall be considered by the Senate or any committee thereof unless such amendment, bill or resolution is accompanied by documentation of the fiscal impact of such amendment, bill or resolution."[25] Fiscal impact statements may be useful in determining the legislative intent supporting a particular measure. Fiscal impact statements are available electronically on the Oklahoma Legislative Service Bureau website. On the OLSB site, fiscal impact statements, if required, are linked on the Bill Summaries Tab for specific proposed or enacted legislative measures. Additionally, as noted in the source information (Figure 8-5) Oklahoma legislative bill history materials on Lexis Advance, the equivalent to the Okla-

---

22. While tapes may be accessed, listening to the tapes is virtually impossible because the equipment to play the tapes is not available.

23. Okla. House of Reps., *Audio Archives*, http://www.okhouse.gov/OkhouseMedia/AudioArchive.aspx.

24. Michael McNutt, *Video Service to Offer Feeds of House Action*, Oklahoman, July 27, 2010, at 16A. A similar story, *Oklahoma House of Representatives Signs with New Video Provider*, is available from the same author at http://www.newsok.com/article/3479795.

25. Rules of the Oklahoma Senate: Fifty-third Legislature R.5-8B, H.R. 1003, 53d Leg., Reg. Sess. (Okla. 2011), http://www.oksenate.gov/publications/senate_journals/sj2011/sj20110104.pdf. Rule 7.12 of the 50th Legislature imposed a similar requirement for fiscal analysis. Okla. H.R. Jour., 2005 Reg. Sess. No. 2, (Feb. 7, 2005), http://www.okhouse.gov/Journals/HJ2005/2005%20hleg%20day%202.rtf.

Figure 8-5. Source Information for Oklahoma Legislative Bill History on Lexis Advance

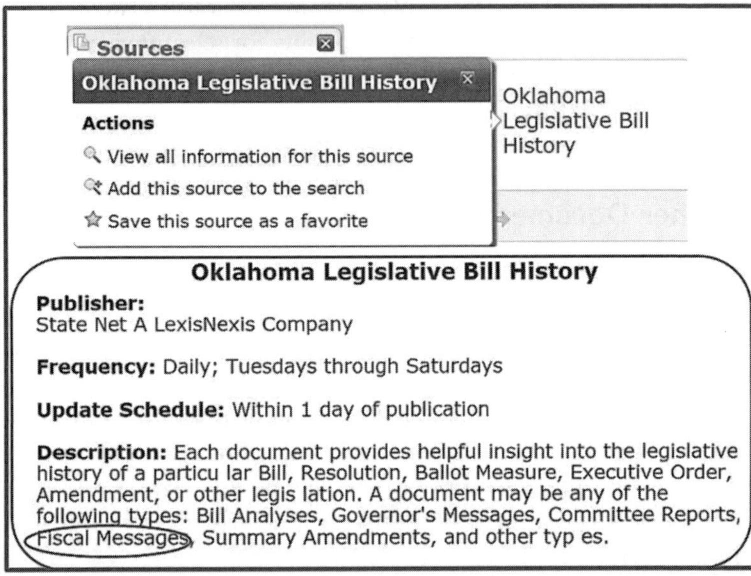

homa Legislative History (OKLH) database in Lexis, is intended to include fiscal messages; however, a search of the database for fiscal impact information produced limited relevant results.

2. Gubernatorial Action on Measures

Proposed legislation may, of course, result in political debate. This debate includes not only legislators but also state officials, including the Governor. As a result, gubernatorial action on a legislative measure, like Presidential Signing Statements in the federal system, may also provide insight as to the intent of the legislation or at least how the Governor interpreted the legislative direction encompassed in the legislation. From 2004 to 2010, messages from the Governor were available on the Governor's Legislative Bill Tracker.[26] Although, the legislative tracker is no longer available on the Governor's website,[27] messages may be accessed as part of the enrolled legislation via the Secretary of State's Office.[28] Veto messages are also published in the House and Senate journals. WestlawNext, Westlaw Classic, Lexis, and Lexis Advance provide access to these messages. The database designator for the Oklahoma Legislative Bill History database, including Governor's Messages, on Lexis is OKLH and in Westlaw Classic the database designator is OK-LH-MSG. Oklahoma gubernatorial messages may be accessed on WestlawNext using the research trail: Home→Legislative History →Oklahoma Legislative History→Oklahoma Legislative History: Governor Messages. Following this process and searching for the terms "governor's message" and the topic being researched produces results including both the text and press releases about gubernatorial messages. Figure 8-6 demonstrates an alternative method of accessing gubernatorial messages related to legislation, as well as journals and committee reports, through the legislative history materials tab available from the session laws on WestlawNext.

3. *New and Other Unofficial Legislative Information Sources*

Unofficial information about a bill may appear in a number of sources, including state news sources; however, these sources are not normally indexed. Some of these sources are described in this section.

The *Journal Record* is a legal and business newspaper for Oklahoma that frequently contains articles about pending legislation. An online fee-based subscription version of the *Journal Record,*

---

26. Okla. Gov. Brad Henry, *Legislative Tracker*, continues to be available via the Internet Archive's capture of the webpage at http://web.archive.org/web/20070524110155/http://www.governor.state.ok.us/billtrack/index.php.

27. Okla. Gov. Marry Fallin, http://www.ok.gov/governor/.

28. Okla. Sec. of State, *Enrolled Legislation*, https://www.sos.ok.gov/gov/legislation.aspx.

Figure 8-6. Legislative History Materials Tab on WestlawNext

Source: Reprinted with permission of Thomson Reuters.

which contains an archive may be accessed at http://www.journal-record.com/. The *Journal Record* is also available via Lexis and Westlaw.

The *Journal Record Legislative Report* (*JRLR*) provides legislative news coverage. Because there is no index to the *Journal Record Legislative Report*, to find information concerning particular legislation, use the House and Senate journals to locate the dates upon which action regarding the legislation took place; then browse the daily editions of the *JRLR* issued for that period. An archive of the *JRLR*, beginning with the February 5, 2003 edition, is also available electronically.[29] The *JRLR* is also available on Lexis.

29. *Journal Record Legislative Report*, http://www.okstatewatch.com/www/ok/index.htm.

V. Researching the Legislative History of Codified Laws

As may be evident from the previous section of this chapter, legislative history materials are most easily accessed if you know the bill number of the enacted law and the legislative session in which the law was enacted. Because codified law may have been created or modified by several separate legislative enactments, researching the legislative history of a codified law requires the identification of the bill number and legislative session information for each enactment affecting the codified law. What follows is a description of the means of locating this information using print or electronic resources.

A. Identifying the Relevant Session Law

Examine the code section in the *Oklahoma Statutes* or *Oklahoma Statutes Annotated*, as discussed in Chapter 7. Immediately following the text of the section, the historical data information provides one or more citations to chapters and sections in the *Oklahoma Sessions Laws* for a specific year. The first citation listed in the historical data is the original enactment that created the code section. When using the print edition of the *Oklahoma Statutes*, check the annual supplemental volumes for references to session laws reflecting recent amendments to the code section. Similarly, if using *Oklahoma Statutes Annotated* in print, check the pocket parts and supplemental pamphlet for references to session laws reflecting recent amendments to code sections.

Codified Oklahoma statutes are also available electronically on a number of electronic resources, including the Oklahoma State Courts Network (OSCN), Westlaw Classic, WestlawNext, Lexis, and Lexis Advance. As shown in Figure 8-7, Bloomberg Law provides links to session laws for statutes enacted after 1997. OSCN also provides historical data information. The historical data on OSCN is hyperlinked to superseded codified statutory sections; in contrast, WestlawNext, in the "credits" data, links to Oklahoma session laws.

Figure 8-7. Bloomberg Law Link to Session Laws

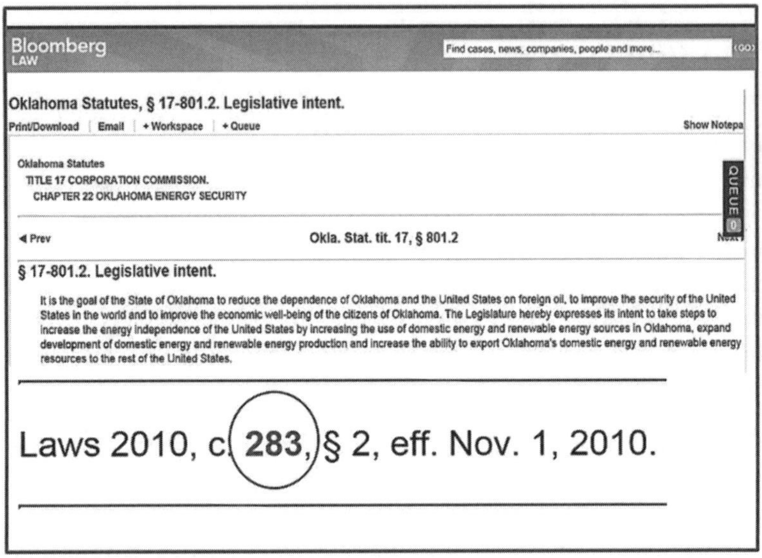

Source: Bloomberg Law BNA. Reprinted with permission.

In addition to historical data, *Oklahoma Statutes Annotated* contains historical and statutory notes for many code sections. While the historical notes do not provide specific information about bill numbers, the notes often outline changes in the language of the statute. Information regarding these changes can be useful for legislative history analysis.

B. Identify the Bill Number for Each Session Law

You can find the text of each session law listed in the historical data line by consulting *Oklahoma Session Laws* for the year cited. *Oklahoma Session Laws* may be accessed in print, and image-based session laws are available electronically on HeinOnline. Text, rather than image-based, session laws are also available electronically on OSCN as well as Westlaw and Lexis systems. The bill number will be

Figure 8-8. Bill Number Designation Available on OSCN Session Laws

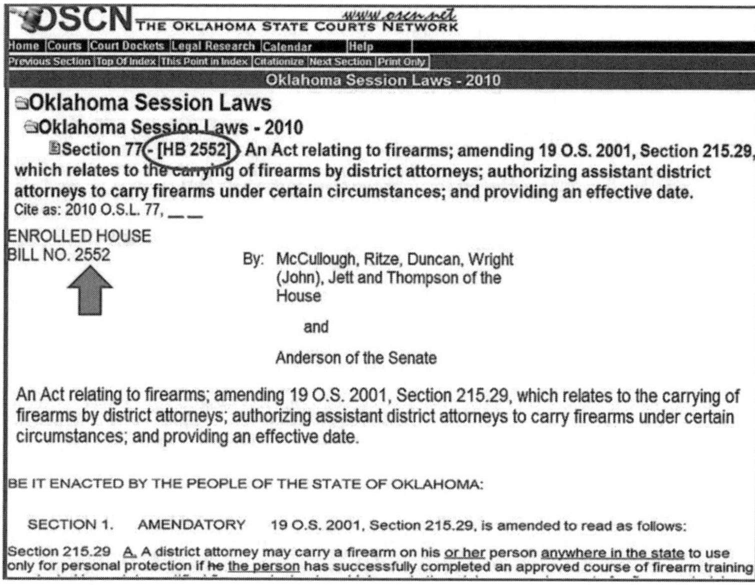

OSCN THE OKLAHOMA STATE COURTS NETWORK www.oscn.net

Home | Courts | Court Dockets | Legal Research | Calendar | Help

Previous Section | Top Of Index | This Point in Index | Citationize | Next Section | Print Only

Oklahoma Session Laws - 2010

Oklahoma Session Laws

Oklahoma Session Laws - 2010

Section 77 - [HB 2552] An Act relating to firearms; amending 19 O.S. 2001, Section 215.29, which relates to the carrying of firearms by district attorneys; authorizing assistant district attorneys to carry firearms under certain circumstances; and providing an effective date.

Cite as: 2010 O.S.L. 77, __

ENROLLED HOUSE BILL NO. 2552

By: McCullough, Ritze, Duncan, Wright (John), Jett and Thompson of the House

and

Anderson of the Senate

An Act relating to firearms; amending 19 O.S. 2001, Section 215.29, which relates to the carrying of firearms by district attorneys; authorizing assistant district attorneys to carry firearms under certain circumstances; and providing an effective date.

BE IT ENACTED BY THE PEOPLE OF THE STATE OF OKLAHOMA:

SECTION 1. AMENDATORY 19 O.S. 2001, Section 215.29, is amended to read as follows:

Section 215.29 A. A district attorney may carry a firearm on his or her person anywhere in the state to use only for personal protection if he the person has successfully completed an approved course of firearm training

Source: Oklahoma State Court Network, www.oscn.net.

preceded by H.B. for House Bills and S.B. for Senate Bills and as shown in Figure 8-8 appears at the beginning of each law. Once you have identified the bill number and legislative session information for each enactment affecting the codified law, you can use the resources outlined previously in this chapter to research the legislative history for the codified law.

VI. Tracking Bills

Until this point, this chapter has focused on legislative history of bills that have been considered in previous legislative sessions and have become law. Bill tracking generally refers to research into legislative activity regarding bills in the current legislative session. Bill tracking may be useful for lobbying, following committee activity on proposed legislation related to your practice areas, and tracing amendments and changes to bill text. Additionally, bill tracking may be useful to develop information about bills previously considered but not passed into law. Bill tracking is most efficient if you know a bill number. Finding a bill number is not difficult, however, since information about all pending bills is accessible online.

A. Using the Oklahoma Legislature System

Locating information about a pending bill, which may subsequently constitute the legislative history material for that bill, can be accomplished through the Oklahoma Legislative Service Bureau's Bill Tracking Reports website as described earlier in this chapter. It is also possible to register for a free account to receive email notifications regarding any actions on the pending bill from the Legislature via the Legislative Electronic Notification System (LENS).[30] (See Figure 8-9.)

Figure 8-9. Setup Page for Notifications from the Legislative Electronic Notification System (LENS)

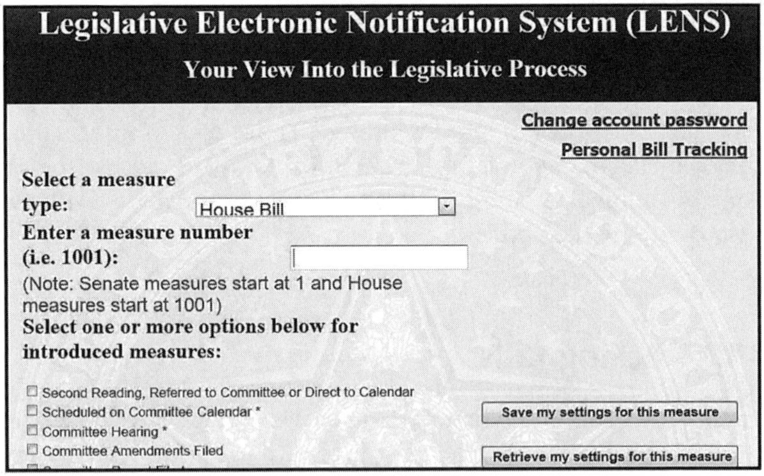

Source: Oklahoma State Legislature, www.oklegislature.gov.

30. Okla. Legis. Serv. Bureau, *Legislative Electronic Notification System*, http://newlsb.lsb.state.ok.us/EBillTrack/logon2.aspx.

B. Using WestlawNext and LexisNexis

Westlaw Classic offers bill tracking in the OK-BILLS database. Bill tracking email notifications are available via Westlaw. The OK-BILLS-OLD database archives bill summaries and full text bills from past regular and special legislative sessions beginning in 2005. Bills tracking information is included regardless of whether a bill was passed into law. Statutes and Court Rules→Oklahoma→Tools and Resources: Oklahoma Bill Tracking is the research trail to access the Oklahoma bill tracking feature on WestlawNext.

Lexis offers the text of bills for the current legislative session and bill tracking information, including summaries, status, and a chronological list of actions taken, in the OKBILL file. The alert function can also be utilized to set up notifications regarding actions on current bills.

VII. Conclusions Regarding Oklahoma Legislative History Research

In Oklahoma, legislative history can be particularly difficult to research.[31] Additional sources of substantive legislative history materials continue to become accessible; however, Oklahoma legislative history information has traditionally reflected the procedural components of the legislative process. Although print and electronic, free and subscription sources are making more accessible the limited legislative history materials that may evidence legislative intent, the most productive means of beginning legislative history research may simply be to try to speak to the legislator who authored and introduced the legislation.

31. See Darla Jackson, *Legislative History: A Guide for the State of Oklahoma*, 30 Leg. Ref. Servs. Q. 119, 120 (Jan–June 2011), http://www.tandfonline.com/doi/pdf/10.1080/0270319X.2011.585327, for a discussion of how the confidential nature of Oklahoma legislators' communications may have, in part, limited the availability of legislative history sources.

VIII. Federal Legislative History Research

A chart comparing Oklahoma and federal sources of legislative history appears in Table 8-2. Similar to the situation in Oklahoma, a vast amount of legislative material is available from government websites. THOMAS, the Library of Congress website at http://thomas.loc.gov, provides bill summaries and status, committee reports, and the *Congressional Record*, a resource recording debate in the House and Senate.[32] The Government Printing Office's Federal Digital System (FDsys) at http://www.gpo.gov/fdsys/ contains bills, selected hearings and reports, and the *Congressional Record.*

A. Federal Legislative Process and Publication

Researching federal legislative history involves a process similar to researching Oklahoma legislative history. When a federal statute is enacted, it is assigned a *public law number.* This number is in the form Pub. L. No. 103-3, where the numerals before the hyphen are the number of the Congress in which the law was enacted and the numerals after the hyphen are assigned chronologically as bills are enacted. The public law number given above is for the *Family Medical Leave Act* (FMLA), which was passed in 1993 during the 103rd Congress.

The new statute is later published as a session law in *Statutes at Large,* which is the federal counterpart of *Oklahoma Session Laws.* Session laws are designated by volume and page in *Statutes at Large.* For example, 107 Stat. 7 is the citation in the *Statutes at Large* for FMLA. West also publishes *United States Code Congressional and Administrative News* (*USCCAN*), a commercial version of the session laws containing select legislative history documents. Finally, the new statute is codified with statutes on similar topics in the *United States*

---

32. Congress.gov, which is in its initial beta phase, will eventually replace the Library of Congress's existing congressional information site, Thomas.gov. *About Congress.gov*, http://beta.congress.gov/about.

Code (USC). The citation or the first section of the FMLA is 29 U.S.C. § 2601.

As with Oklahoma legislative history, the most effective method of conducting federal legislative history research is through the use of the codified citation. If you do not have a citation for the codified statute, use finding tools such as the index or popular names table of an annotated code to locate the citation. With a codified statute citation, you can find the session law citation and public law number, which will lead to the legislative history documents discussed below.

B. Sources of Federal Legislative History

1. Committee Reports and Hearings

Committee reports are considered perhaps the most persuasive authority regarding legislative intent. Unlike Oklahoma's committee reports, which are brief and contain little substantive information, Congressional committee reports are often lengthy documents containing committee analysis of the bill and the reasons for enacting the legislation. Additionally, committee reports may also reflect the views of committee members who disagree with the reasons stated by the majority. Further, congressional hearing materials, including transcripts from the proceedings and documents such as prepared testimony and exhibits, provide evidence of congressional intent. Some committee reports are included in the Legislative History volumes of *USCCAN*.

2. Floor Debates

Congressional floor debates are published in the *Congressional Record*. While floor debates can provide some evidence of congressional intent, because members of Congress can amend their remarks and even submit written statements that are published in transcript form as if they were delivered on the floor, be cautious when considering these debates.

Table 8-2. Comparison of Oklahoma and Federal Legislative History Sources

Action	Oklahoma Sources	Federal Sources
Committee Work	Committee reports provide little evidence of legislative intent. Oklahoma committee reports do not contain substantive analysis, but consist of the limited recommendations, including "do pass," "do pass as amended," or "do not pass."	Reports written by committees are the most persuasive form of legislative history. Transcripts of hearings and other documents may also be available.
Debate	*Senate Journal* and *House Journal* reflect the occurrence, but do not contain the statements of Senators and House Members. Audio and video of floor proceeding are available from a variety of sources, including the video tab of the Oklahoma Legislative Service Bureau website.	The *Congressional Record* publishes the statements of Senators and House Members during debate.
Session Law	*Oklahoma Session Laws*	*Statutes at Large* (official); *United States Code Congressional and Administrative News*
Codified Law	*Oklahoma Statutes* (official) *Oklahoma Statutes Annotated*	*United States Code* (official); *United States Code Annotated;* *United States Code Service*

3. Compiled Legislative History

As stated previously, due to the nature of Oklahoma legislative history materials, commercial firms specializing in legislative history research have not been established in Oklahoma. In contrast, numerous sources of compiled legislative history for certain federal statutes have developed. Two often cited sources that reference compiled legislative histories of major federal statutes are Sources of Compiled Legislative Histories[33] and *Federal Legislative Histories: An Annotated Bibliography and Index to Officially Published Sources.*[34] *USCCAN* also provides some compiled legislative history documents.

4. Online Sources for Federal Legislative History

The sites noted earlier in this chapter provide useful information for legislative history research. THOMAS, the Library of Congress site, provides bill summaries and status, committee reports, and the *Congressional Record.* The Government Printing Office's Federal Digital System contains bills, selected hearings, and reports, as well as the *Congressional Record.* Federal legislative history is also available through resources available from Lexis and Westlaw.

---

33. Nancy P. Johnson, *Sources of Compiled Legislative Histories: A Bibliography of Government Documents, Periodical Articles, and Books, 1st Congress–110th Congress* (2d ed. 2012) (available in print at most academic libraries and may also be available electronically through HeinOnline).

34. Bernard D. Reams, *Federal Legislative Histories: An Annotated Bibliography and Index to Officially Published Sources* (1994) (obviously somewhat dated).

Chapter 9

Oklahoma Administrative Law

Our government has recently unleashed the greatest avalanche of regulations in peacetime history; and wherever we examine their workings we see that they are using a sledgehammer to miss a nut.—Christopher Booker[1]

I. Introduction

Whether or not you share Mr. Booker's sentiments regarding the effectiveness of the increasing number of regulatory provisions, research regarding these provisions is essential.[2] Oklahoma administrative law research encompasses research concerning the rules and decisions of Oklahoma governmental executive agencies. Often, the

1. Quoted in Antony Jay, *The Oxford Dictionary of Political Quotations* 52 (1996); similarly stated in Christopher Booker, *The Regulatory Crisis of the 1990s—The Problem...*, Economic Affairs 21 (June 1994).

2. Whether conducting research regarding personal legal issues or practicing as an attorney, it is only in very rare cases that research does not include some component of administrative law research. "Few attorneys are going to be very far into their practice before they are called upon to represent a client whose driver's license is being revoked, who has an industrial injury, who is being fined for not maintaining a sanitary restaurant or who is being pursued for child support by the Oklahoma Department of Human Services." Gary E. Payne, *A Primer on Administrative Law in Oklahoma*, 79 Okla. B.J. 39 (Jan. 12, 2008).

issuance of rules (also routinely referred to as regulations)[3] and decisions by an agency is referenced as an agency action. Agency actions include aspects of all three functions of government. Agencies write rules and regulations that interpret and apply statutes in areas of the agency's competence. These rules and regulations are similar in form to statutes and, like statutes, are a source of primary authority. Agencies also carry out executive functions such as issuing licenses and conducting inspections to ensure that laws are being followed. Further, an agency may perform quasi-judicial functions by holding hearings and issuing administrative decisions involving application of the agency's rules and regulations.

The overarching legislation that governs agency actions in Oklahoma is the Oklahoma Administrative Procedures Act (OAPA).

The Oklahoma Administrative Procedures Act (OAPA) is composed of two articles. Article I of the act relates to "agency filing and publication requirements for rules."[4] Article II of the act addresses "agency notice and hearing requirements for individual proceedings."[5] Because the Oklahoma legislature relied upon the National Conference of Commissioners on Uniform State Laws (NCCUSL) Model State Administrative Procedure Act[6] and the Revised Model State Administrative Procedure Act,[7] as well as the Federal Administrative Procedure Act[8] for guidance in drafting OAPA,[9] authority from jurisdictions that have adopted similar provisions of the NCCUSL model

3. *State v. Freeman*, 370 P.2d 307 (Okla. 1962) (discussing the meaning of the terms "rules and regulations" as referenced in 75 O.S. 1961, § 250.

4. 75 O.S.2011, § 250.1.

5. *Id.*

6. *55th Conference Handbook of the National Conference of Commissioners on Uniform State Laws and Proceedings of the Annual Conference Meeting* 197 (1946).

7. Model State Administrative Procedure Act, Revised 1961 Act, 15 U.L.A. 174 (2000).

8. Pub. L. No. 79–404, 60 Stat. 237 (1946) (codified as amended in scattered sections of 5 U.S.C.).

9. Michael P. Cox, *The Oklahoma Administrative Procedures Act: Fifteen Years of Interpretation*, 31 Okla. L. Rev. 886 (1978).

laws may be persuasive when there is no Oklahoma authority on provisions of OAPA.

Agency, as defined by OAPA, "includes but is not limited to any constitutionally or statutorily created state board, bureau, commission, office, authority, public trust in which the state is a beneficiary, or interstate commission, except: a. the Legislature or any branch, committee or officer thereof, and b. the courts."[10] The constitutional and statutory provisions that create the agencies establish the power and duties of the agencies. Each agency has only that authority established by the Oklahoma Constitution or statutory provisions, often referred to as the enabling act. Thus, one prominent basis for challenging an agency action is that the action exceeded the authority established in the enabling act. As a result, the first step in Oklahoma administrative law research may be to locate the statutory or congressional provision creating the agency or granting the agency the power to act. The process for researching Oklahoma administrative law is outlined in Table 9-1.

Table 9-1. Outline of Oklahoma Administrative Law Research Strategy

1. Locate the statutory or constitutional provision creating the agency or granting the agency authority to act. Use of the annotated code (including the Oklahoma Constitution) will assist in determining whether there is authority indicating that the agency acted within the grant of power.
2. Locate the text of relevant rules in the *Oklahoma Administrative Code.*
3. Update rules using the *Oklahoma Register* to locate recent changes or proposed changes. Citator tools may assist in locating entries in the *Oklahoma Register.*
4. Locate agency and judicial decisions applying rules in similar circumstances or opinions of the Attorney General regarding applicable rules.

10. 75 O.S.2011, § 250.3.

II. Locating Statutory or Constitutional Provisions Creating an Agency or Granting an Agency Authority to Act

Following the guidance in Chapters 4 and 7, you should be able to locate the constitutional and statutory provisions creating an agency or granting it the power to act. However, there are some tools that may expedite your research. One such tool is the listing of Oklahoma agencies, boards, and commissions prepared by the Oklahoma Department of Libraries.[11] Not only does this source provide a listing of agencies, boards, and commissions, it also provides, as illustrated in Figure 9-1, information regarding the mission and responsibilities of these bodies as well as a reference to constitutional and statutory authority.

Figure 9-1. Oklahoma Agencies, Boards, and Commissions

Corporation Commission, Oklahoma

(Constitution, Article 9 § 15; 17 O.S. § 1 et seq.)

Agency Code 185 (IA)
Jim Thorpe Building, 2101 N Lincoln Boulevard PO Box 52000, Oklahoma City 73152-2000
405/521-2211, FAX 405/522-1623, TDD 405/521-3513 www.occeweb.com

Consumer Services:
Pollution Complaint/Royalty Owner Information Hot line 800/522-0034
Public Utility Complaints 800/522-8154

Commissioners— Bob Anthony 405/521-2261, Patrice Douglas 405/521-2264 405/521-2267.

Administration Lori Wrotenbery, Director, 405/521-2307;
Administrative Proceedings Division, Michael Decker, 405/521-2241
Consumer Services Division, Kim Dobbins, Acting Director, 405/522-0478
Information Technology Division, Michelle Smith, Director, 405/521-4520

Source: Oklahoma Department of Libaries and Thomson Reuters, www.odl.state.ok.us/sginfo/abc.pdf.

11. Oklahoma Department of Libraries, *ABC: Oklahoma Agencies Boards, and Commissions* (2012), http://www.odl.state.ok.us/sginfo/abc/abc.pdf (link for the download is also available at Oklahoma Department of Libraries, *ABC: Oklahoma State Agencies, Boards, and Commissions*, http://www.odl.state.ok.us/sginfo/abc/index.htm).

Another tool that may be of use is the agency website. The Oklahoma Government Website Information Act[12] requires each state agency to post the following material on its website:

1. Any administrative rules adopted pursuant to the Administrative Procedures Act, which the public body uses to operate;
2. Any proposed administrative rules submitted by the public body pursuant to the Administrative Procedures Act;
3. Any statutes [affecting] the public body and its operations; and
4. Any statutes the public may find useful in interacting with the public body.[13]

In compliance with this provision, agencies have posted the authority on their websites; however, the location of this information on the website varies by agency and may not be readily apparent. For instance, the Department of Labor's website details the Oklahoma Constitutional and statutory provisions on the "Legal References" page,[14] which is linked under the "Transparency" tab of the agency's main page.[15]

Finally, commercially prepared materials, such as West's Oklahoma Law Finder,[16] a topical guide to the content of Oklahoma West publications including state and federal statutes (see Figure 9-2), also lists the constitutional and statutory provisions concerning various Oklahoma agencies.

III. Locating Administrative Rules

As stated in the introduction, Oklahoma administrative agencies promulgate rules implementing Oklahoma constitutional and statu-

---

12. 74 O.S.2011, § 3106.3 et seq.
13. *Id.*
14. Okla. Dep't of Lab. Comm'r, *Transparency—Legal References*, http://www.ok.gov/odol/Transparency/Legal_References/index.html.
15. Okla. Dep't of Lab. Comm'r, *Homepage*, http://www.ok.gov/odol/.
16. Thomson Reuters, *Westlaw Store—West's Oklahoma Law Finder, 2012 ed.*, http://store.westlaw.com/wests-oklahoma-law-finder-2012/181045/22063940/productdetail.

Figure 9-2. *West's Oklahoma Law Finder*

CORPORATION COMMISSION

Generally
Okl. Const. Art. 9 § 15 et seq.
17 O.S.A. § 1 et seq.

Appeal and review
Generally
6 OK Appellate Practice (Ellis & Muchmore) § 21:1 et seq.
Civil procedure
Title 12, Ch. 15, App. 2

Compensation
74 O.S.A. § 250.4 et seq.

Gratuities
17 O.S.A. § 48

Lobbying
74 O.S.A. § 4249 et seq.

Motor vehicle enforcement section
Powers and duties, transfer
47 O.S.A. § 1166

Powers and duties
Okl. Const. Art. 9 § 18

Source: Reprinted with permission of Thomson Reuters.

tory authority. Like the constitutional and statutory authority they implement, these agency rules are primary authority. In accordance with the OAPA, notice of rules adopted by a covered state agency to govern the agency's enforcement or administration of legislation must be included in the *Oklahoma Register*.[17] In 1990, by legislative

17. 75 O.S.2011, § 303.

action, the responsibility for publishing the *Oklahoma Register* and the *Oklahoma Administrative Code* and "otherwise implementing the provisions of Article I of the Administrative Procedures Act" was transferred from the Department of Libraries to the Office of Administrative Rules.[18] The *Oklahoma Administrative Code* (OAC) is the resource in which researchers locate agency administrative rules.

The *Code* is organized into six major divisions as described below:

(1) Titles. Each Title identifies an administrative agency, except for Title 1 which includes executive orders.

(2) Chapters. Each Chapter identifies a major area of regulatory control within an agency's authority. Each Chapter identifies a group of Sections which are:

> (A) related to the same major agency program or legally-designated regulatory power;
>
> (B) dependent on a common set of definitions; or
>
> (C) independent of another Chapter in meaning or effect.

(3) Subchapters. Each Subchapter identifies a group of Sections related to the same general subject within a Chapter. The use of Subchapters is optional.

(4) Parts. Each Part identifies a group of Sections related to the same subject within a Subchapter. The use of Parts is optional.

(5) Sections. Each Section identifies a specific agency statement within a Chapter, Subchapter, or Part. Each Section is considered to be a single "rule."

(6) Appendices. Each Appendix identifies a graphic....[19]

For example, 165:20-5-32 refers to the Oklahoma Corporation Commission regulation in Title 165 Chapter 20, Subchapter 5, Part 7, Section 32 on pipeline construction and consumer safety and the

---

18. 75 O.S.2011, § 250.9 (noting amendment by Laws 1990, c. 300, § 5, eff. July 1, 1991).

19. Okla. Admin. Code § 655:10-3-10 (2011).

notice requirements for pipeline construction. Note that the "Part" is not indicated in the citation.

A. *Oklahoma Administrative Code* in Print

Full editions of the OAC are published approximately every five years. While the Office of Administrative Rules, the office responsible for the publishing the rules, was created earlier, the first edition of the OAC was published in 1996 and another full edition was published in 2001 and 2006. The 2011 edition of the OAC consists of nineteen volumes, inclusive of its comprehensive subject index. The OAC is updated annually in the form of a multi-volume cumulative supplement.[20]

B. *Oklahoma Administrative Code* Available Electronically

1. *Secretary of State's Website*

The current Oklahoma administrative rules and regulations are available electronically via the Oklahoma Secretary of State's website.[21] However, the online version is not acknowledged as an official version of the administrative code.[22] Additionally, while the website of the Secretary of State provides access from 2001 forward for the *Oklahoma Register*,[23] only the current version of the OAC is available.

---

20. Okla. Sec. of State, Office of Admin. Rules, *Homepage*, https://www.sos.ok.gov/oar/default.aspx.

21. Okla. Sec. of State, Office of Admin. Rules, *ONLINE Oklahoma Administrative Code and Register*, https://www.sos.ok.gov/oar/onlineRegister.aspx.

22. "The online OAC is unofficial and contains rules and executive orders as they appear in the database that is used to produce the official OAC ... The official OAC is published annually in paper and on CDRom, and is available from the Office of Administrative Rules." Okla. Sec. of State, Office of Admin. Rules, *ONLINE Oklahoma Administrative Code and Register*, https://www.sos.ok.gov/oar/onlineRegister.aspx.

23. Okla. Sec. of State, Office of Admin. Rules, *View Register*, https://www.sos.ok.gov/oar/online/viewRegisters.aspx.

Figure 9-3. Oklahoma Regulation on WestlawNext

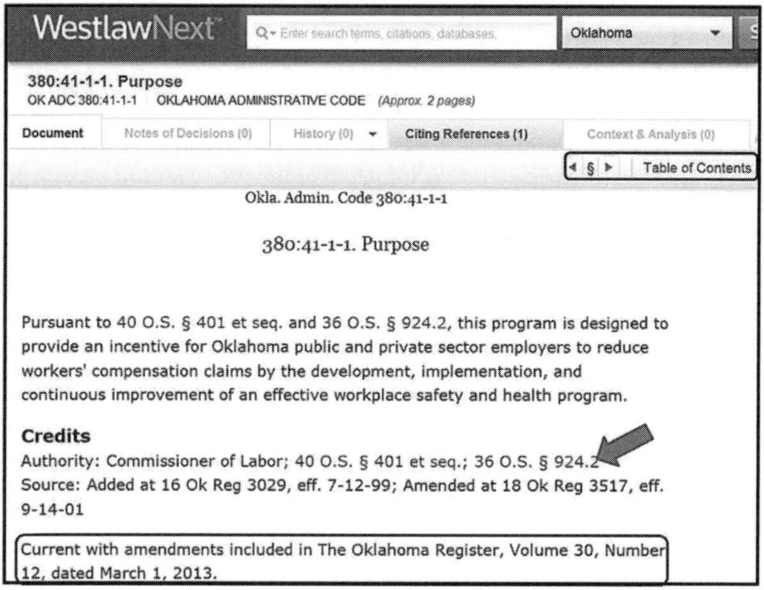

Source: Reprinted with permission of Thomson Reuters.

The no-cost online code can be browsed or the researcher can conduct a basic keyword search of the code.

2. *Westlaw Classic and WestlawNext*

The *Oklahoma Administrative Code* is also available on Westlaw Classic and WestlawNext. As illustrated in Figure 9-3, the Oklahoma Regulations Scope Information indicates that WestlawNext contains current regulations; however, the note also indicates that the regulations are from the 2006 edition of the *Oklahoma Administrative Code*, plus amendments, additions, and revocations since its publication. This is somewhat confusing given, as previously indicated, that the 2011 edition of the OAC has been published. However, once a section is opened (see Figure 9-3) in WestlawNext, the currency information is displayed as a date.

Westlaw Classic and WestlawNext also provide access to historical administrative regulations from 2001 and forward. Historical regulations are accessible on WestlawNext by clicking on the "Oklahoma Historical Regulations" link under Tools and Resources (upper right of the display) when the researcher has accessed Oklahoma Regulations. The database designator for the OAC on Westlaw Classic is OK-ADC and the historical code is OK-ADC plus the two digit year indicator. The designator for the 2001 Oklahoma Administrative Code would be OK-ADC01.

Further, WestlawNext provides not only the current text of the regulation, but also a number of other features to assist in research. For instance, as indicated by the arrow in Figure 9-3, WestlawNext provides authority information, including enabling statutory authority for many regulations. Contextual understanding is also facilitated by WestlawNext's table of contents and browsing tools, which allow for easy viewing of surrounding regulations dealing with a similar topic.

3. Lexis and Lexis Advance

The OAC is also available on Lexis and Lexis Advance. On Lexis, the file name for the OAC is OKCADMN. Be aware of the need to check the currency of the OAC on Lexis. In 2013, the scope note for the OKCADMN reflected that the data was only current through the 2011 Supplement as applicable on December 26, 2012. Historical Oklahoma regulations are available on Lexis in the Oklahoma Administrative Code Archives files from 2004 forward. The file designator for these files is OKAD plus the two-digit year indicator. In Lexis Advance, neither archive files nor scope notes are available. However, as evidenced in Figure 9-4, once a regulation is located and opened for display, the text indicates the currency of the document. Additionally, one helpful feature of Lexis Advance is the chapter authority information. As discussed above, it is essential to be able to identify the enabling statutory and constitutional authority for an agency action. The chapter authority function in Lexis Advance provides this information. This information is not displayed in the free online source from the Secretary of State.

Figure 9-4. Oklahoma Regulation on Lexis Advance

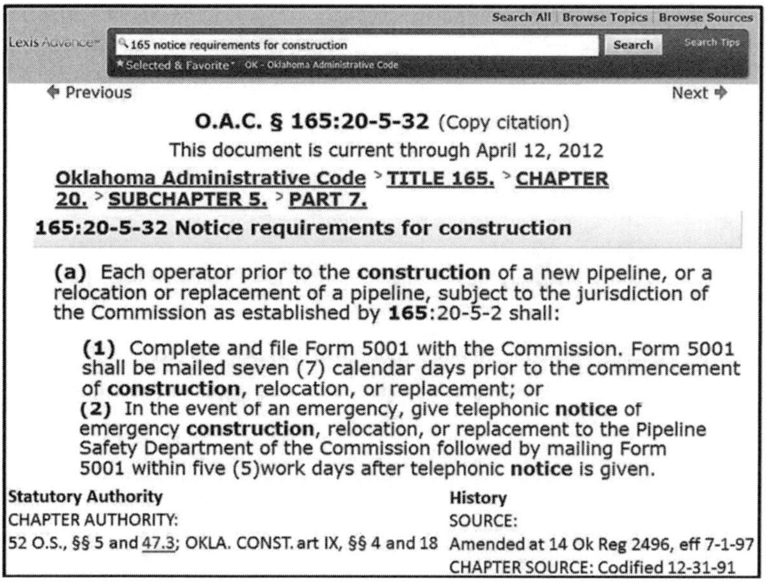

4. *Bloomberg Law*

The OAC may be accessed using several methods on Bloomberg Law. Perhaps the least complex is using the "Statutes and Regulations" Link from the Home page. The OAC is then accessible by selecting the link to that resource in the listing of state materials. It should be noted, however, that Bloomberg Law cautions researchers regarding the accuracy and currency of the OAC via its "Message to Users" (indicated by the arrow in Figure 9-5). The primary theme of the message, as indicated in the lower portion of Figure 9-5, is the OAC on Bloomberg is not the official code. Bloomberg Law acknowledges that the official code is the print edition published by the Oklahoma Secretary of State.

Figure 9-5. *Oklahoma Administrative Code* on Bloomberg Law

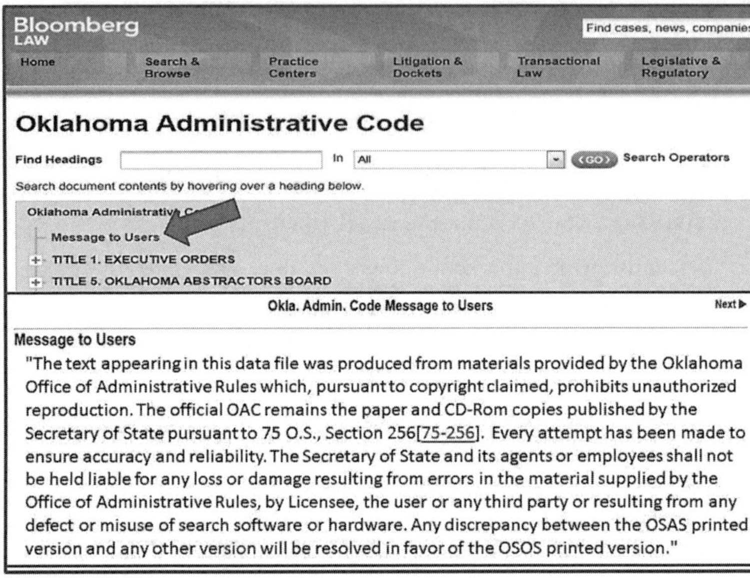

Source: Bloomberg Law BNA. Reprinted with permission.

Similar to Westlaw, Bloomberg Law states that the currency of the code is through an older annual supplement. As a result, the currency of the unofficial OAC on Bloomberg Law may also be of concern. However, close examination of the currency information confirms that the OAC is being updated with reference to recent issues of the *Oklahoma Register* (see Figure 9-6).

Perhaps the most efficient means of accessing Oklahoma regulations on a particular topic on Bloomberg Law is through use of the "Practice Centers." The practice centers facilitate research of both primary and secondary sources in a particular area of the law. For instance, when you enter the Labor and Employment Law Center, links to "Laws & Regulations" as well as "Books & Treatises" are available. Selecting the "Laws & Regulations" option allows the researcher to select "State Laws & Regulations" on related topics.

Figure 9-6. Accuracy and Currency of Oklahoma Regulations on Bloomberg Law

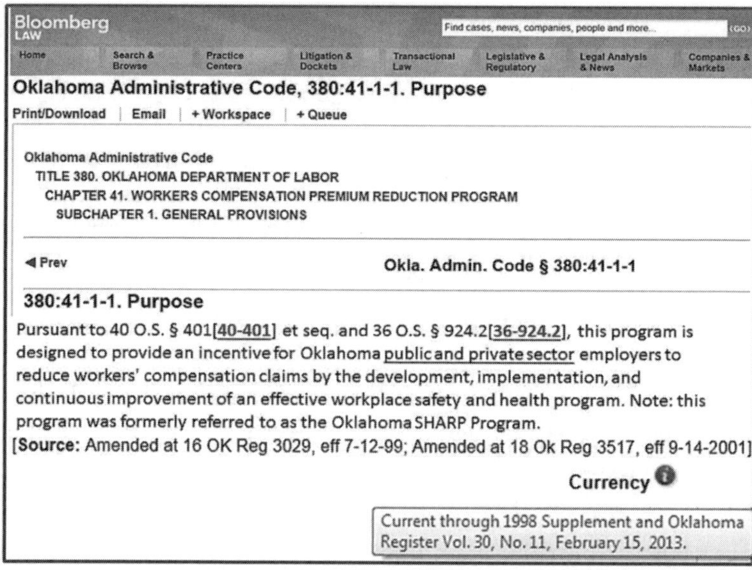

Source: Bloomberg Law BNA. Reprinted with permission.

IV. Updating Rules

A. The *Oklahoma Register*

As discussed above, it is sometimes unclear if the rules accessed are the most recent rules or if there have been changes. Because the OAPA requires proposed and adopted rules to be published in the *Oklahoma Register*, the *Oklahoma Register* is the primary source used to ensure that legal professionals are not citing to legal authority that is not current. Previously designated as the *Oklahoma Gazette*, this semi-monthly publication originated in 1962 and its name was modified by statute in 1983.[24] Publication of the *Oklahoma Register*, as de-

24. 75 O.S.2011, § 255, http://www.oscn.net/applications/oscn/DeliverDocument.asp?CiteID=93496 (noting amendment by Laws 1983, HB 1158, c. 76, §1, eff. Nov. 1, 1983).

tailed above, is the responsibility of the Secretary of State's Office of Administrative Rules. Included in the *Oklahoma Register* are:

- Notices of intended rulemaking (comment periods and public-hearings)
- Notices of continued or cancelled comment periods or public hearings
- Notices of the adoption and submission of proposed rules for gubernatorial and legislative review
- Notices of gubernatorial approval/disapproval of rules
- Notices of legislative disapproval of rules
- Notices of withdrawn rules
- Recently enacted emergency and preemptive rules (after approval by the Governor)
- Finally adopted permanent rules (after gubernatorial/legislative review) that will become effective at least 10 days after publication
- Recently issued executive orders.[25]

As indicated previously, editions of the OAC are published every five years. During the periods between publication of OAC editions, annual cumulative supplements are published. The *Oklahoma Register* allows for updating of rules by providing access to changes occurring after the publication of the OAC and the annual supplement.

> Between the annual OAC publications, the semi-monthly issues of The Oklahoma Register serve as supplementation to the OAC. At any given point in time, therefore, current rules can be found by checking the latest full edition of the OAC and the latest annual supplement (if any), and by checking emergency, permanent, and preemptive rule updates promulgated in issues of the Register after the August 15 closing date for the last annual OAC publication (i.e., edition or annual supplement).[26]

---

25. Okla. Sec. of State, Office of Admin. Rules, *Order Form*, https://www.sos.ok.gov/forms/oar/ordfrm1.pdf.

26. *Id.*

The *Oklahoma Register* is available from a number of sources.[27] An online version is linked from the website of the Oklahoma Secretary of State.[28] However, it should be noted that the online version is "unofficial and is updated [only] after each official issue is published."[29] The official print *Oklahoma Register* is available for order,[30] or WorldCat[31] may be used to locate the print edition at state depository libraries. The *Oklahoma Register* is also available on Lexis and Lexis Advance. Westlaw Classic and WestlawNext do not provide access to the *Oklahoma Register* but do provide an Oklahoma Regulation Tracking function for tracking pending and recently adopted rules. On Westlaw Classic, the database designator to use for the tracking function is OK-REGTRK. As illustrated in Figure 9-3, the tracking function can be performed on WestlawNext by clicking on the "Oklahoma Regulation Tracking" link under Tools and Resources.

In addition to facilitating research of new and modified rules, the *Oklahoma Register* also provides notices of proposed rules and notifies the public of the process for submitting comments regarding the proposed rule. Practicing attorneys and business concerns often monitor and prepare comments on proposed rules affecting their clients or industry. Prior to preparing the comments, they often desire to review the comments (if any) made by competing concerns. While the U.S. federal rule-making system provides a central electronic repository for submitting and searching for comments made on proposed

---

27. For a quick summary of the various sources for the *Oklahoma Register*, see Lisa Goodman & Stephanie Marshall, *State Administrative Law: Don't Let It Scare You!*, http://www.docstoc.com/docs/2172818/SWALL—-Administrative-Law-Presentation at 8.

28. Okla. Sec. of State, Office of Admin. Rules, *ONLINE Oklahoma Administrative Code and Register*, *supra* note 21.

29. *Id.*

30. Okla. Sec. of State, Office of Admin. Rules, *Order Form*, *supra* note 25.

31. Online Computer Library Center, Inc., *WorldCat, Oklahoma Register*, http://www.worldcat.org/title/oklahoma-register/oclc/10187453&referer=brief_results.

agency rules,[32] there is no such central electronic repository for comments submitted concerning proposed rules in Oklahoma. However, select high profile agencies, such as the Oklahoma Corporation Commission, do have database systems that allow access to comments on proposed agency actions.[33]

Note that agency adoption of a rule is not the final step in the permanent rule-making process. Rather, agency adopted rules must be submitted to both the Governor and the Oklahoma Legislature.[34] Only after this process is complete will a rule be promulgated in the *Oklahoma Register*.

You may find that locating secondary sources, including news items, regarding gubernatorial and legislative consideration of agency rules may assist you in locating references to proposed rules in the *Oklahoma Register*. For instance, the Oklahoma State Newsroom will allow you to search for news related to legislative or gubernatorial statements or press releases addressing regulations issued by specific agencies. The newsroom also allows you to search for news articles by specific agency such as the Corporation Commission.[35] Additionally, both Westlaw and Lexis allow you to set up alerts for news sources and the Oklahoma Register or Regulation Tracking. Unfortunately, no alert function is currently available from the online *Oklahoma Register* available from the Secretary of State.

---

32. Federal eRulemaking Portal—"regulations.gov," http://www.regulations.gov.

33. Oklahoma Corporation Commission, *OAP Orders and Case Files Database Search*, http://imaging.occeweb.com/imaging/OAP.aspx.

34. Okla. Sec. of State, Office of Admin. Rules, *Oklahoma's Permanent Rulemaking Process: An Overview for Regulated Agencies and the Regulated Public* (Jan. 7, 2010), https://www.sos.ok.gov/forms/oar/procss_per.pdf.

35. State of Okla., *Newsroom*, http://www.ok.gov/portal/newsroom.php.

Figure 9-7. Updating Regulations Using KeyCite on WestlawNext

Source: Reprinted with permission of Thomson Reuters.

B. Using KeyCite to Update Rules

When you access a provision of the administrative code on Westlaw Classic and WestlawNext, the system displays a KeyCite indicator to advise you if a proposed regulation would modify the existing regulation. As suggested in Figure 9-7, WestlawNext displays the indicator twice to ensure that the researcher is aware of possible modifications. When the researcher clicks the red or yellow flag indicator, the system provides a link to the text of the emergency or proposed regulation in the *Oklahoma Register* (see arrow 1 of Figure 9-7). Further, as emphasized by Arrow 2 of Figure 9-7, WestlawNext allows the researcher to set up a KeyCite Alert, which is discussed in more depth in Chapter 11 on citators. The KeyCite Alert prompts the system to notify the researcher if further modifications are proposed or become final.

Unfortunately, Shepard's citation tool and Bloomberg Law do not currently provide the same updating features for Oklahoma regulations as are provided by Westlaw. Perhaps this function will be added in the future.

V. Locating Agency and Judicial Decisions or Opinions of the Attorney General Regarding Application of the Rule

A. Agency Decisions and Determinations

While the Oklahoma Government Website Information Act requires Oklahoma agencies to post statutory and administrative rule information on the agency website, there is no requirement that agencies post agency administrative decisions on their websites. As a result, locating agency decisions can be challenging. The OAC has not been annotated by commercial vendors,[36] making research for administrative agency decisions more difficult. Notwithstanding, there are several resources that may be used to locate Oklahoma agency decisions. Although a majority of the Oklahoma agencies do not yet post all agency decisions to their websites, some administrative agencies do provide access to some or all of their decisions and determinations through the agency website. For example, the Oklahoma Corporation Commission provides access to not only its decisions but also submitted background documents concerning "hot topic" cases from its home page.[37] Additionally, the Corporation Commission provides access to databases containing scanned images of agency determinations and case files. Locating documents regarding a specific case can be a challenge for those unfamiliar with the database because well-constructed searches may require the user to be familiar with the

36. This lack of state annotations is unlike the availability of annotations for the *Code of Federal Regulations*, which West initially annotated through the development of the Regulations Plus service on Westlaw Classic.

37. Oklahoma Corporation Commission, *Homepage*, http://www.occweb.com.

codes for specific case type, docket codes, or the case number.[38] However, with the planned implementation of an electronic filing system, it is anticipated that location of such documents will become easier.[39]

Westlaw and Lexis services also provide access to some agency decisions. For example, Westlaw provides access to Oklahoma Corporation Commission decisions that have appeared in the West Public Utilities Reporter through the Oklahoma Public Utilities Reports database (OK-PUR) beginning in 1955. WestlawNext also provides access to select resources containing Oklahoma agency decisions. Further, Lexis's Oklahoma Agencies & Attorney General Opinions, Combined database (OKAGEN) provides access to select Oklahoma Attorney General opinions, Oklahoma Securities Commission decisions and interpretive opinions, and Oklahoma Tax Commission orders. Unfortunately, Bloomberg Law does not yet provide access to a robust collection of Oklahoma administrative agency decisions.

Some agency decisions are also available from the no-cost Oklahoma Public Legal Research System (OPLRS). OPLRS is a service provided by the University of Oklahoma College of Law, which allows for the searching of Department of Labor and Oklahoma Merit Protection Commission Decisions, as well as rules from these bodies and some judicial opinions.

B. Judicial Decisions

Courts generally require that the individual challenging the agency action has exhausted his administrative remedies prior to initiating a suit.[40] However, judicial review of agency action is not uncommon.

---

38. Oklahoma Corporation Commission, OAP Orders and Case Files Database Search, *supra* note 33.

39. Telephone Conversation with Teryl Williams, Attorney with the Oklahoma Corporation Commission (Mar. 23, 2012).

40. There are exceptions to the requirement for exhaustion of administrative remedies. "[E]xhaustion of administrative remedies is a prerequisite for resort to the courts. However, this doctrine will not bar court action if an administrative remedy is unavailable, ineffective or would be futile." *Daffin v. State ex rel. Okla. Dep't of Mines*, 251 P.3d 741, 745 (Okla. 2011).

Because the *Oklahoma Administrative Code* is not an annotated resource, and because a commercial publisher has not developed an annotated version of the OAC, other traditional case law research methods, which are outlined in previous chapters, should be followed to locate judicial decisions involving agency actions.

C. Opinions of the Attorney General

The Attorney General issues advisory opinions at the request of other state bodies. These opinions may interpret regulations and can serve as persuasive authority when a party is challenging an agency action or rule. Published opinions of the Attorney General are, of course, more persuasive than unpublished opinions.[41]

Opinions of the Attorney General may be located in various formats depending upon the date that the opinion was issued. The Oklahoma Attorney General's website[42] suggests a number of sources of the opinions. Recent opinions of the Attorney General (i.e., select opinions issued during the last calendar year) are accessible through a link on the website. While the opinions are accessible, they are not included in a searchable database on the website. However, the website does link to several sources which permit searching. One such source is the Oklahoma State Court Network (OSCN).[43] On OSCN, Opinions of the Attorney General are available from 1977 to the present and may be searched or browsed.

Another source providing electronic access to Opinions of the Attorney General from 1948 to present is the Oklahoma Public Legal Research System (OPLRS),[44] which also provides access to select ad-

41. "'Unpublished Opinions' from Assistant Attorneys Generals in the Attorney General's office may be informative. They do not have the force and effect of official Attorney General Opinions." Okla. Office of the Atty. Gen., *Attorney General Legal Opinions*, http://www.oag.ok.gov/oagweb.nsf/opinions.html.

42. *Id.*

43. Oklahoma State Court Network, *Oklahoma Attorney General's Opinions Index*, http://www.oscn.net/applications/oscn/index.asp?ftdb=STOKAG&level=1.

44. Oklahoma Public Legal Research System, http://oklegal.onenet.net/.

ministrative agency decisions. OPLRS also provides access to unpublished opinions from the Assistant Attorney Generals from 1969 to present. Opinions of the Attorney General are also accessible in Westlaw Classic and WestlawNext as well as Lexis and Lexis Advance.

VI. Concluding Remarks on Oklahoma Administrative Law Research

As Gary Payne, the then Chief Administrative Law Judge of the Oklahoma State Department of Health, wrote in 2008, "It is important to note that the rules and regulations of state agencies are not static. Attorneys should check for revisions of agency rules the same way as they should check for statutory changes.... the rules regulating state agencies are not monolithic. Every agency has unique rules."[45] Thus, while the resources mentioned in this chapter will assist with administrative law research in Oklahoma, researchers may also want to consult with a knowledgeable practitioner experienced in the rules of a specific agency.

VII. Federal Administrative Law Research[46]

Because the Oklahoma legislature modeled, in part, the legislation establishing procedures for state administrative agencies on federal law, federal agencies function similarly to Oklahoma agencies. As a result, only brief coverage of federal administrative law research is included in this section.

Federal regulations are included in the *Code of Federal Regulations* (CFR), which is published by the Government Printing Office (GPO). The CFR codifies regulations issued by federal agencies. Like regula-

45. Payne, *supra* note 2, at 43.

46. Portions of this section are based on materials authored by Suzanne E. Rowe, editor of the Carolina Academic Press Legal Research Series, and are used with permission.

tions in the OAC, regulations in the CFR are organized by agency and subject. While the fifty titles of the CFR roughly correspond to the titles of the United States Code (USC), there are a number of exceptions. For instance, Title 11 of the USC addresses bankruptcy while the same title in the CFR deals with federal elections.

CFR volumes arc updated annually, with specific titles updated each quarter (e.g., Titles 1 through 16 are updated as of January 1; Titles 17 and 27 are updated as of April 1).[47] However, as is often the case with official government publication, CFR updates may become available only months after their scheduled release. Each year, the CFR volume's covers are printed using a different color, which makes it easy to tell whether a print volume has been updated.

Federal regulations are available online via the Federal Digital System (FDsys)[48] and on Westlaw Classic, WestlawNext, Lexis, Lexis Advance, and Bloomberg Law. While the text on FDsys is only as current as the print versions, the text on the commercial services is more up to date. Additionally, the Electronic Code of Federal Regulations (e-CFR),[49] similar to commercially provided CFR versions, is not official but is updated on a regular (almost daily) basis.

There are several methods by which you can locate a regulation addressing a particular subject. Of course, the method you use may be influenced by your level of knowledge about the law on that topic and the resources available to you. First, you can look up your research terms or the relevant agency's name in the general index, and then read the regulation referenced. However, it may be more efficient to begin your research by looking at an annotated statutory code, which will often contain cross-references to relevant regulations. Starting your research in a secondary source may also lead you directly to relevant regulations.

New regulations and proposed changes to existing regulations are published first in the *Federal Register*, the federal equivalent of the

---

47. *Code of Federal Regulations*, http://www.gpo.gov/fdsys/browse/collectionCfr.action?collectionCode=CFR.

48. *Id.*

49. U.S. Gov't Printing Off., *Electronic Code of Federal Regulation*, http://ecfr.gpoaccess.gov/cgi/t/text/text-idx?c=ecfr&tpl=%2Findex.tpl.

Oklahoma Register. In addition to providing the text of new and proposed regulations, the *Federal Register* also contains notices of hearings, responses to public comments on proposed regulations, and helpful tables and indexes. With the exception of federal holidays, the *Federal Register* is published every weekday. Because it has continuous pagination throughout the year, it is not uncommon for the *Federal Register* to include in excess of 80,000 pages for a single volume. An online version of the *Federal Register* is available on FDsys[50] and a "web edition," commonly referred to as Federal Register 2.0, is also "published" online.[51] Additionally, the *Federal Register* is available via the online research providers, including Westlaw Classic, WestlawNext, Lexis, Lexis Advance, and Bloomberg Law.[52]

Updating a federal regulation in print or using FDsys requires a somewhat complex procedure involving the use of a resource entitled the List of Sections Affected (LSA). An in-depth treatment of this process is beyond the scope of this coverage. Additionally, because the procedure is somewhat complex and time-consuming, most researchers use the e-CFR or a commercial service such as KeyCite or Shepard's to assist in updating regulations.

Federal agencies, like Oklahoma agencies, carry out quasi-judicial functions and decide administrative cases that arise under the agency's regulations. Some of these decisions are published in government reporters specific to each agency and some are also reported in commercial publications. Westlaw Classic, WestlawNext, Lexis, and Lexis Advance have databases containing decisions of select federal agencies. Bloomberg Law also provides access to select federal agencies decisions, including the decisions of the Securities and Exchange Commission. The website for the agency may also allow a researcher to ac-

---

50. *Federal Register*, http://www.gpo.gov/fdsys/browse/collection.action?collectionCode=FR.

51. *Federal Register*, https://www.federalregister.gov/. *Federal Register 2.0* also allows a researcher to subscribe to feeds of federal register entries on a particular topic.

52. It is not readily apparent on the Bloomberg Law home page how to search the *Federal Register*. Clicking on the "Legislative and Regulatory" tab displays this option.

cess the agency's decisions. The University of Virginia Library hosts a useful site, which provides deep links to federal agency decision and other agency actions.[53]

53. U. of Va. Lib., *Gov't Info. Resources, Administrative Decisions*, http://guides.lib.virginia.edu/administrative_decisions.

Chapter 10

Researching Tribal Law

I. Introduction

Those familiar with Oklahoma and United States history are aware of significant contributions of Native Americans to Oklahoma. In fact, Oklahoma means "Red People" in the Choctaw language.[1] Given this history, it is not surprising that 39 tribal governments are present in Oklahoma.[2] Additionally, the Native American population of over 390,000 comprises approximately eight percent of Oklahoma's total

1. Muriel H Wright, *Contributions of the Indian People to Oklahoma*, 14 Chron. of Okla. 156 (1936), http://digital.library.okstate.edu/chronicles/v014/v014p156.html.

2. Okla. Indian Affairs Comm'n, *Oklahoma Indian Nations Information Handbook*, http://web.archive.org/web/20120721013924/http://www.ok.gov/oiac/documents/FY07.2006-07%20WEB%20EDITION2.pdf. Thirty-eight of the tribes in Oklahoma are federally recognized. Okla. Indian Affairs Comm'n, *2011 Oklahoma Indian Nations Pictorial Directory*, http://www.digitalprairie.ok.gov/cdm/fullbrowser/collection/stgovpub/id/20794/rv/compoundobject/cpd/5215. A listing of the tribes located in Oklahoma and links to the tribal websites is available from several sources, including Oklahoma Indian Affairs Commission, *Tribal Nations*, http://web.archive.org/web/20120522030226/http://www.ok.gov/oiac/Tribal_Nations/index.html and American Indian Cultural Center and Museum, *Oklahoma Tribes*, http://www.theamericanindiancenter.org/oklahoma-tribes/. Several of the cites in this footnote are to archived resources of the Oklahoma Indian Affairs Commission (OAIC). 74 O.S.2011, § 1206–1207 established the Oklahoma Native American Liason (OKNAL) position, to be appointed by the Governor, and transferred the responsibilites of the OIAC to the OKNAL. However,

population;[3] this ranks Oklahoma as the state with the third highest population of Native Americans.[4] Thus, it is difficult to practice real estate, probate, family, and other types of law without touching on issues of either tribal or federal Native American law. Further, non-natives often become involved in state and tribal issues involving taxation, gaming, and other commercial ventures due to the nature of tribal economic development.

Researchers and practitioners must be aware of the distinction between federal Indian law and tribal law. Federal Indian law addresses the status of tribes and the relationship of the tribes to the U.S. federal government. Federal Indian law primarily includes matters addressed by treaties between the federal government and various tribes, federal statutes, federal administrative law, federal executive orders, and federal case law. In contrast, tribal law is the law that tribes, as sovereign bodies, use to govern tribal operations and members. Of course, there are times when federal Indian law and tribal law overlap; however, the primary focus of this chapter is not federal Indian law, but tribal law.

According to one well known text, tribal law has three major sources: "contemporary legal documents, traditions and oral law, and academic studies."[5] This chapter will discuss each of these sources, but it will do so using other terminology and in a different order. Academic studies are addressed as part of the discussion of secondary sources. Contemporary legal documents are discussed in the context of tribal constitutions, codes, and case law. Finally, traditions and oral law are included in the section on customary law.

OKNAL has not yet established a web presence containing links to information and documents.

3. U.S. Census Bureau, *State and Country Quick Facts, Oklahoma,* http://quickfacts.census.gov/qfd/states/40000.html.

4. U.S. Census Bureau, *State Rankings—Statistical Abstract of the United States, American Indian, Alaska Native Population Alone, Number—July 2008*, http://www.census.gov/compendia/statab/2011/ranks/rank13.html.

5. Justin B. Richland & Sarah Deer, *Introduction to Tribal Legal Studies* 9 (2d ed. 2010).

II. Secondary Sources

A. Legal Research Guides

Those unfamiliar with tribal law research may find that a research guide, which may go beyond the information provided in this chapter, is a useful tool. The University of Tulsa Law Library has several guides on tribal and Native American law issues.[6] The University of Oklahoma Law Library provides an Annotated Bibliography of Federal and Tribal Law.[7] Oklahoma City University Law Library has a general guide on researching Native American law and has a topic specific guide on researching the intellectual property rights of indigenous peoples.[8] If you are researching at one of these institutions, a guide prepared by the staff at that institution will be most helpful because that guide will address the resources available via the specific library. Additional guides on tribal law issues may be located using Cornell University Law Library's Legal Research Engine.[9] Finally, *Basic Indian Law Research Tips—Tribal Law*, a guide prepared by David Selden and posted on the Native American Rights Fund website, is a useful resource.[10]

---

6. University of Tulsa Mabee Legal Information Center, *Native American LibGuides*, http://mlic.utulsa.libguides.com/cat.php?cid=31819.

7. Marilyn Nicely, *Annotated Bibliography of Federal and Tribal Law: Print and Internet Sources*, http://thorpe.ou.edu/guide/IndianLawResearchGuide.pdf.

8. Amanda Burdick-Brown, *Native American Law*, http://law.okcu.libguides.com/content.php?pid=147779; Andrew Knife Chief, Okla. City U. L. Lib., *Intellectual Property Rights of Indigenous People*, http://law.okcu.libguides.com/content.php?pid=318609.

9. Cornell U. L. Lib., *Legal Research Engine Home*, http://library.lawschool.cornell.edu/WhatWeDo/ResearchGuides/Legal-Research-Engine.cfm. (Site routinely undergoes maintenence and may be unavailable for some time.)

10. David Selden, *Basic Indian Law Research Tips—Tribal Law*, http://www.narf.org/nill/resources/tribal_law_research_2012.pdf.

B. Treatises, Deskbooks, Study Aids, and Text

1. Cohen's Handbook of Federal Indian Law

Cohen's Handbook of Federal Indian Law,[11] often referred to as simply Cohen, is perhaps the most prominent source in Native American law. While the title indicates a focus on federal Indian law, tribal law topics are also addressed in this resource. However, various editions of the book, which was originally published in 1941, differ in their tone and approach[12] and vary widely on the topic of tribal sovereignty. In Chapter 4 of the 2012 edition, entitled Indian Tribal Governments, there is treatment of tribal law as addressed in treaties, tribal constitutions, customary and common law, as well as legislative, administrative, and judicial tribal law. Cohen is also available via Lexis,[13] Lexis Advance, and LexisNexis Academic, which is accessible at many main campus academic libraries as well as at academic law libraries. The 1945 printing of the first edition of Cohen is available at no cost via the Native American Constitution and Law Digitization Project coordinated by the University of Oklahoma Law Library and the National Indian Law Library of the Native American Rights Fund.[14]

2. American Indian Law Deskbook

The *American Indian Law Deskbook*,[15] in its fourth edition, is the work of the Conference Of Western Attorneys General (CWAG) and is the "product of effort from many individual in CWAG-affiliated states."[16]

---

11. *Cohen's Handbook of Federal Indian Law* (Nell Jessup Newton et al. eds., 2005).

12. *Id.* at xi.

13. *Cohen's Handbook of Federal Indian Law* (Nell Jessup Newton et al. eds., 2012) (available at LEXIS, 2NDARY, COHEN).

14. Felix H. Cohen, *Handbook of Federal Indian Law* (1945), http://thorpe.ou.edu/cohen.html.

15. *American Indian Law Deskbook* (Clay Smith et al. eds., 4th ed. 2008).

16. *Id.* at xxii. Oklahoma is an associate member state of the CWAG, and as such would qualify as a "CWAG-affiliated state"; however, Oklahoma is not a full member of CWAG and the deskbook has not traditionally included

Figure 10-1. *Cohen's Handbook of Federal Indian Law* on Lexis Advance

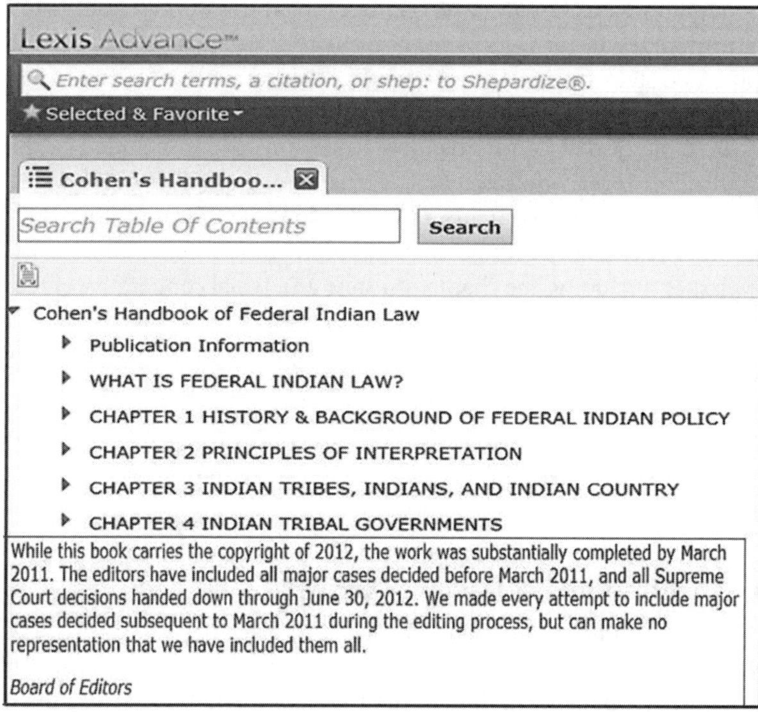

Although a deskbook is traditionally a "quick and dirty ready reference to the most important points of law in a given area,"[17] the *American Indian Law Deskbook* is designed to be a "comprehensive

---

a chapter drafted by an Oklahoma representative. Conference of Western Attorney Generals, *Members*, http://www.cwagweb.org/members.html.

17. Tim Pleasant & Deena Degenova, *Book Review*, 50 Am. J. Legal Hist. 108, 109 (2008–2010) (reviewing *American Indian Law Deskbook*).

and objective treatise."[18] The Deskbook has a different focus than Cohen. While Cohen focuses "on the federal aspects of Indian law, the Deskbook, although covering much of the same essential background material, turns its primary focus to relationships between the tribes and state and local governments."[19] Although this focus is broad enough to include coverage of some tribal law related issues, review of the table of cases and table of statutes and codes included in the publication reveals no reference to tribal court cases or tribal codes. Even so, the table of contents and index to the publication does suggest that particular sections of the book include discussion of tribal law issues, including the chapter on state and tribal cooperative agreements.

The *American Indian Law Deskbook* is not currently available electronically via traditional database providers such as Westlaw or Lexis. The title is available electronically at some libraries, including Oklahoma State University Library, but currently no law libraries in Oklahoma do not provide access to the electronic version.

3. American Indian Law in a Nutshell

American Indian Law in a Nutshell[20] is, as indicated, part of the Nutshell series published by West and, like other books in that series, is a study guide with the purpose of setting forth "in succinct form the essentials of the very complex body of federal Indian Law...."[21] In its fifth edition, the focus of this title is federal Native American law; however, it does include some discussion of tribal law in the chapter on Indian tribal governments.[22] Additionally, ths title addresses de-

---

18. *Id.* (citing the foreword of the *American Indian Law Deskbook*, 4th ed. 2008).

19. *Id.* at 108.

20. William C. Canby, Jr., *American Indian Law in a Nutshell* (5th ed. 2009). William Canby has been praised for his service as a professor of Indian Law at Arizona State University and is a Justice on the U.S. Ninth Circuit Court of Appeals. Alan A. Matheson, *Judge William C. Canby, Jr.: A Tribute*, 33 Ariz. St. L.J. 1 (2001).

21. Canby, *supra* note 20, at III.

22. *Id.* at 65–75.

terminations of circumstances when tribal law, as opposed to state or federal law, governs.[23] The index at the end of the book may provide assistance in locating those sections that address issues related to tribal law. This title is also one of the few nutshells available electronically via Westlaw.[24] The electronic format allows a search for content discussing tribal law.

4. Tribal Legal Studies

Introduction to Tribal Legal Studies,[25] now in its second edition, is described in the foreword, as a text developed to support the curricula of courses intended to "make students more aware of legal and cultural issues necessary for them to understand and serve the interest of their Native communities and governments."[26] The book is organized into a lesson format that discusses federal, state, and tribal legal issues. Because this title was developed as a teaching tool, it is an excellent source for those unfamiliar with tribal law issues.

Tribal Criminal Law and Procedure,[27] the second book in the Tribal Legal Studies series, discusses tribal criminal law and procedure from a tribal perspective by referencing tribal statutory law, tribal case law, and the cultural values. The authors discuss topics including the

---

23. "Although the subject of 'Indian Law' legitimately might be thought to include the internal law that each tribe applies to its own affairs and members, that is neither the common definition nor the one used here. Instead, that body of law is separately referred to as 'tribal law,' and it may range from oral tradition to entire codes borrowed nearly intact from non-Indian sources. No attempt will be made in this volume to set forth the content of the various bodies of tribal law. Instead, the concern will be to determine when tribal law (rather than state or federal law) governs a particular situation." *Id.* at 3.

24. Access is limited to those institutional users subscribing to other Native American law resources or to the study aid collections available through the Law School Exchange.

25. Justin B. Richland & Sarah Deer, *Introduction to Tribal Legal Studies* (2d ed. 2010).

26. *Id.* at vii.

27. Carrie E. Garrow & Sarah Deer, *Tribal Criminal Law and Procedure* (2004).

structures and practices of tribal justice systems, and compare of traditional tribal justice with Anglo-American law and jurisdictions,covering elements of criminal law and procedure, and alternative sentencing. Because this title was originally published in 2004, some of the information, specifically that on jurisdiction, may be somewhat dated; however, the title is an excellent introductory source.

C. Law Reviews and Journals

Some law reviews and journals may prove helpful in researching tribal law. *Tribal Law Journal* is an "on-line forum" hosted by the University of New Mexico School of Law.[28] The stated purpose of the journal is to provide "native peoples, practitioners, and law students an opportunity to contribute their work to the discussion relating to internal indigenous law. Contributions include, but are not limited to, tribal court case comments, reflections on tribal systems, the development of tribal law, the value of tribal law, interviews, and teachings."[29]

The *American Indian Law Review*, a student-edited law review addressing federal, state, and tribal Native American issues, is a publication of the University of Oklahoma. The *American Indian Law Review* is available electronically via HeinOnline (1973–present), Westlaw Classic and WestlawNext (select coverage 1983–1992, full coverage 1993–present) and Lexis and Lexis Advance (1997–present).

As described in Chapter 3, articles on tribal law may also be located using the various electronic indexes, including LegalTrac and the Index to Legal Periodicals.

---

28. University of New Mexico School of Law, *Tribal Law Journal*, http://tlj.unm.edu/.

29. *Id.*

D. Other Sources

1. Sovereignty Symposium

Useful secondary sources unique to Oklahoma include the publications of the Sovereignty Symposium. The Sovereignty Symposium was established in 1988 by the Oklahoma Supreme Court along with other partners. Presenters at the annual Symposium have included a U.S. Supreme Court Justice, Oklahoma Attorney Generals, tribal leaders, law professors, and governmental officials. The Sovereignty Symposium publication is provided each year to participants. Copies are also made available for sale to law schools. Recent materials have been distributed electronically via compact disk. Scanned copies of older materials can be accessed via compact disk; however, the materials are not available via the web or traditional commercial legal information providers. Recently, Oklahoma City University Law Library included information from the table of contents of the Symposium publications in its electronic library catalog and shared this information with OCLC. Thus, the table of contents of the Symposium publication are available via worldcat.org.[30]

2. Oklahoma Indian Legal Services

Other resources unique to Oklahoma are the publications of Oklahoma Indian Legal Services (OILS). OILS is a nonprofit legal aid organization, which provides legal services to low income Native Americans residing in Oklahoma. OILS publications include the *Guide to Pro Se Form Pleadings Available in Tribal Courts*, which provides a listing of contact information for tribal court clerks and the types of forms available from each of the included tribal courts.[31] OILS also published *The Indian Child Welfare Act: Case and Analysis*.[32] This publication includes case annotations organized by

30. Online Computer Lib. Ctr., Inc., *WorldCat*, http://www.worldcat.org/.

31. Okla. Indian Leg. Servs., *Guide to Pro Se Form Pleadings Available in Tribal Courts*, http://thorpe.ou.edu/OILS/court.html.

32. C. Steven Hager, *The Indian Child Welfare Act: Case and Analysis*:

the ICWA's individual sections as well as a collection of forms to assist attorneys and laypersons with the basic procedures required by the Act.

E. Sources for Locating Other Secondary Sources

Practitioners and other researchers may identify other helpful resources by reviewing a legal research guide or searching the online catalogs of law libraries located in Oklahoma, including the catalogs of the three law school libraries.[33] Unfortunately there is not an Oklahoma tribal court handbook,[34] but a variety of information is available on tribal websites.[35]

CD-ROM (Colline W. Meek ed., 15th ed. 2011). The upcoming edition will consider the U.S. Supreme Court case of *Adoptive Couple v. Baby Girl*, 133 S. Ct. 1521 (2013). *See* Okla. Indian Leg. Servs., *The Indian Child Welfare Act: Case and Analysis*, http://www.oilsonline.org/http_www.oilsonline.org/The_Indian_Child_Welfare_Act.html.

33. Okla. City U. Sch. of Law, *Law Library Catalog*, http://lawlibdb.okcu.edu/vwebv/searchBasic?sk=lawdb; U. of Okla. College of L., *Law Library, Search Catalogs, Search OU Law Library Catalog*, http://catalog.lib.ou.edu/uhtbin/cgisirsi/x/0/0/57/49?user_id=LAWSEARCH; Univ. of Tulsa College of L., *Library Catalog*, http://www.utulsa.edu/academics/colleges/college-of-law/Library/MLIC/Library%20Catalog.aspx.

34. There are handbooks for other states. The Indian Law Section of the State Bar of New Mexico maintains an electronic handbook authored by the University of New Mexico Tribal Law Journal. U. of N.M. Sch. of L., *Tribal Law Journal, Tribal Law Handbook*, http://tlj.unm.edu/handbook/index.php.

35. For example, the Court Rules and information about application for admission to the Cherokee Nation Bar Association is available on the tribe's website. Cherokee Nation of Okla., *Judicial Branch*, http://www.cherokeecourts.org/Home.aspx.

III. Tribal Constitutions, Codes, Treaties, and Compacts

A. Tribal Constitutions and Codes

Tribal constitutions and codes may be difficult to research because some tribes do not distribute their documents in the same manner that the states make legislation available.[36] Many tribes, consistent with the Indian Reorganization Act of 1934 (IRA), did organize and adopt constitutions to gain access to Congressional grants for tribes to "borrow funds for economic development and form tribal corporations."[37] Although Oklahoma tribes were not covered by the *IRA*, the Oklahoma Indian Welfare Act had similar provisions regarding organization for Oklahoma tribes[38] that likely influenced tribes to develop constitutions and codes and affected the availability of these legal documents.

One source of tribal constitutions and codes is the tribal websites of individual tribes. The Cherokee Nation, for example, makes the tribal constitution available electronically via its website;[39] however, the document is difficult to locate on the tribal website. In contrast, the link to the Legislative Research Center of the Cherokee Nation is readily apparent on the website. Further, the Legislative Research Center[40] provides a robust search tool to assist with the location of particular Cherokee legislation.

---

36. Selden & Martens, *supra* note 10, at 1, noting "unlike many state and federal codes, these documents generally are not published in print or electronically. Only approximately six tribal codes and constitutions can be purchased directly from commercial publishers."

37. Lindsay G. Robertson, *Native Americans and the Law: Native Americans Under Current United States Law*, http://thorpe.ou.edu/guide/robertson.html.

38. *Id.*

39. Constitution of the Cherokee Nation (rev. ed. 2006), www.cherokee.org/Portals/0/Documents/2011/4/308011999-2005-CN-CONSTITUTION.pdf.

40. Council of the Cherokee Nation, *Legislative Research Center*, http://

While tribes such as the Cherokee do make their "contemporary legal documents," such as the constitution and legislation or code, available, many other tribes do not. To assist in making such documents available, the Native American Rights Fund (NARF) makes available, via its Tribal Law Gateway, a Tribal Code and Constitutions Directory. The directory provides links to electronically available codes and constitutions and also provides contact information for the tribes.[41] Some of the links provided on the directory are to the Native American Constitution and Law Digitization Project, a joint project of the University of Oklahoma Law Library and the National Indian Law Library of NARF.[42]

An additional source of tribal constitutions, codes, and court rules is subscription based databases. Lexis and Lexis Advance currently provide access to some Montana tribal documents, but Lexis will be of limited use to those researching Oklahoma tribal issues. Similarly, while Westlaw Classic and WestlawNext provide access to documents of several tribes located in various geographic locations, few of the tribal constitutions and codes are from Oklahoma tribes.

B. Treaties

In contrast to tribal codes and ordinances, treaties affecting tribes may be easier to locate. One print resource for treaties is the *United States Statutes at Large*. Volume 7 of the *Statutes at Large* contains "Treaties Between the United States and the Indian Tribes." The *Statutes at Large* set is available electronically via HeinOnline, a subscription database provider. HeinOnline's *Treaties and Agreements Library* also contains the multi-volume work *Indian Affairs: Laws and Treaties*, compiled by Charles Kappler, who at the time of compilation was serving as the Clerk to the Senate Committee on Indian Affairs. Kapplar's compilation is also available via the digital library of

---

cherokee.legistar.com/Legislation.aspx.

41. Native American Rights Fund, *Tribal Law Gateway Home, Code & Constitution Directory*, http://www.narf.org/nill/triballaw/index.htm.

42. Native American Rights Fund and University of Oklahoma Law Library, *Native American Constitution and Law Digitization Project*, http://thorpe.ou.edu/.

Oklahoma State University[43] at no cost. Further, treaties affecting a specific tribe may be available via the tribe's website. For example, the Choctaw Nation of Oklahoma provides electronic access to treaties in the History section its website.[44]

Tribes often enter into agreements with states, counties, and other political entities regarding various topics.[45] The website of the Oklahoma Indian Affairs Commission indicates that there are compacts and agreements between Oklahoma political entities and tribes regarding cross-deputization, gaming, assistance to needy families, taxation on tobacco and motor fuel sales, and issuance of motor vehicle tags.[46] These compacts and agreements must be reviewed and ratified by the Joint Committee on State Tribal Relations and filed with the Secretary of State.[47] However, these agreements are not currently

---

43. Charles J. Kappler, *Indian Affairs: Laws and Treaties* (1904), http://digital.library.okstate.edu/kappler/index.htm.

44. Choctaw Nation of Oklahoma, *History*, http://www.choctawnation.com/history/.

45. However, to prevent overreaching by other governmental bodies in particular circumstances, by statute, some compacts must be approved by the Secretary of the Interior. Canby, *supra* note 20, at 353. Tribal constitutions may also impose procedural requirements for approval of such agreements. "It is important to determine which tribal entity will be signing the agreement and whether that entity … has authority to do so. Even though many tribes are organized under the Indian Reorganization Act, it is not safe to assume that any one tribe is organized like another … consult the tribe's constitution and ordinances to ensure that necessary authorization can be obtained under tribal law." [reference omitted] *American Indian Law Deskbook*, *supra* note 15, at 624.

46. Oklahoma Indian Affairs Commission, *Compacts, Contracts & Agreements*, http://web.archive.org/web/20120721012034/http://www.ok.gov/oiac/Compacts,_Contracts,_and_Agreements/index.html. In May 2011, the responsibilities of the Oklahoma Indian Affairs Commission were transferred to the Oklahoma Native American Liaison position. This position will be filled by appointment of the Governor. 2011 Okla. Laws 305, http://www.oscn.net/applications/oscn/DeliverDocument.asp?CiteID=462338. As a result, it is anticipated that this listing of compacts may become the responsibility of an alternative Oklahoma Agency.

47. 74 O.S.2002, § 1221, http://www.oscn.net/applications/oscn/DeliverDocument.asp?CiteID=102616.

available electronically via the website of the Oklahoma Secretary of State. Some of the compacts are available electronically from the National Congress of American Indians.[48]

IV. Tribal Case Law

Tribal case law is available in several print reporters. In addition, some websites provide online access. In general, Westlaw Classic and WestlawNext provide more coverage, but even that is limited. Currently, Lexis and Lexis Advance provide very little coverage of tribal case law.

A. *American Tribal Law Reporter*

Perhaps the most prominent of the print reporters is the *American Tribal Law Reporter* (ATLR). The *American Tribal Law Reporter* is published by West, and it includes the editorial enhancements of West's reporters, including synopsis, digest, and topic and key numbers, described in Chapter 6. The ATLR includes decisions of the appellate and supreme courts of several tribes, and some decisions from the federal courts of appeals and the United States Supreme Court on issues relevant to tribal law.[49]

The term "several" in the description should indicate that coverage is certainly not exhaustive. For example, review of the Table of Cases Arranged by Tribe in Volume 8 of the ATLR, published in 2010, discloses that cases from only ten tribes are reported. Further, none of the ten tribes with cases reported are tribes located in Oklahoma.

---

48. National Congress of American Indians, *Index of Agreements*, http://www.ncai.org/ncai/resource/agreements/. Gaming Compacts listed by state are also available. National Congress of American Indians, *Tribal-State Relations, Gaming Compacts*, http://web.archive.org/web/20120312220709/http://ncai.org/Gaming-Compacts.103.0.html.

49. Thomson Reuters, *West Store, West American Tribal Law Reporter*, http://west.thomson.com/productdetail/154534/40785196/productdetail.aspx.

The scope note for the ATLR in WestlawNext, Figure 10-2, discloses that the opinions of only two Oklahoma tribes, the Cherokee Nation of Oklahoma and the Sac and Fox Tribe, are included in the online ATLR. Additionally, the coverage of decisions of particular tribal courts in the ATLR may be significantly delayed. While the ATLR is more current when searched electronically, tribal decisions from several of the included tribes are nonetheless delayed.

B. *Indian Law Reporter*

Another prominent print reporter containing reports of tribal cases is the *Indian Law Reporter* (ILR), which is published by the American Indian Lawyer's Training Program. This multi-volume looseleaf contains primarily cases from federal courts addressing federal Indian law issues. However, there is a tab in each volume in which tribal court decisions are reported. While the ILR does not provide the editorial enhancements of the West reporters, it does include a table of cases and a topical index for each volume. The table of cases is not arranged by tribe, but the list does indicate which cases are reported in the tribal law tab. Additionally, the National Indian Law Library (NILL) has developed a cumulative index for all tribal court opinions included in the ILR. The cumulative index is available from NILL upon request.[50]

C. *Oklahoma Tribal Courts Reports*

A unique resource collecting Oklahoma tribal case law is the *Oklahoma Tribal Court Reports* (OTCR). The OTCR was initially published in 1994 by the Native American Legal Resource Center at Oklahoma City University. Although the initial publication was in 1994, as evidenced by the Index of Cases Reported (chronologically) in Volume 1 of the OTCR, there are case opinions dating from as far back

50. Native American Rights Fund, *Tribal Law Gateway Home, Tribal Court Opinion Research*, http://www.narf.org/nill/triballaw/court.htm.

Figure 10-2. *American Tribal Law Reporter* on WestlawNext

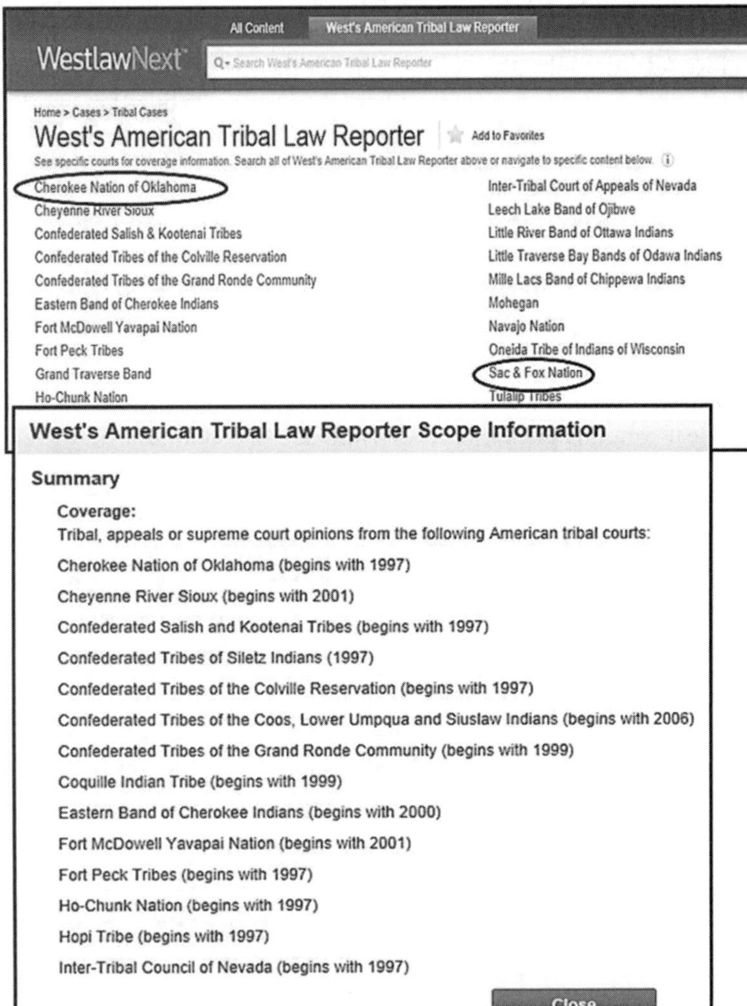

Source: Reprinted with permission of Thomson Reuters.

as 1979. The most recent volume of the OTCR, Volume 9, was published in 2008 and covers cases from 2000–2006. The OTCR is edited by Dennis Arrow, a professor at the Oklahoma City University School of Law and the Associate Director of the Native American Legal Resource Center.[51]

While the OTCR provides complete opinions, as acknowledged by the editor, it is "an 'unofficial' case law reporter, and the authoritative texts are the original opinions and orders filed with the clerks of Oklahoma's tribal and C.F.R. courts."[52]

Although the OTCR is available on Westlaw Classic and WestlawNext, it is not part of the West National Reporter System described in Chapter 6. Thus, the OTCR does not have many of the editorial enhancements of West reporters. Arrow has, however, provided some enhancements. For instance, each volume of the OTCR contains four indexes of cases reported. These indexes list cases alphabetically by party, alphabetically by tribe, chronologically, and by case number. Additionally, Arrow has provided headnotes for each case. The structure of the headnote system is original and is dissimilar to the Lexis or West headnote structure. The headnote structure is set forth in the blue appendix pages in each print volume.

Unfortunately, the headnote system may be of limited value in locating cases with similar headnotes because only volume 1 of the OTCR contains a digest following the headnote structure. Of course, a keyword search for headnote terms can be conducted when researching the OTCR on Westlaw systems. Figure 10-3 shows an excerpt of a case reported in the OTCR with the headnotes highlighted on WestlawNext.

Further, Arrow provides richly detailed introductions to each print volume of the OTCR. Because it outlines the progression of tribal law first in the United States and then in Oklahoma, the Introduction in Volume 1 may be of particular interest to those unfamiliar with tribal law. Unfortunately, Westlaw Classic and WestlawNext do not provide

---

51. Professor Arrow has also served as Associate Justice of the Supreme Court of the Cheyenne and Arapaho Tribes since 1995. Dennis Arrow, *Introduction*, 9 Okla. Tribal Ct. Rpt. VII (2008).

52. *Id.* at VI. CFR courts, also known as Courts of Indian Offenses, are courts operated by the Department of Interior, Bureau of Indian Affairs, on select reservations. These courts operate under federal regulations contained in Volume 25 of the *Code of Federal Regulations*; and as a result are often referred to as "CFR" courts.

access to the introductory materials. Additionally, West does not make the PDF image based format of the OTCR available for download, as it does with other reporters.

Although some enhancements are not available on Westlaw Classic or WestlawNext, using the OTCR on these commercial services does allow for use of KeyCite. This citator resource, discussed in Chapter 11, identifies inconsistent later decisions and identifies further cases and secondary sources citing and discussing the case. However, because only selected tribal cases are included on Westlaw and because reporting may be delayed, use of KeyCite does not assure that a subsequent unreported case has not negatively treated a previous decision.

Also of note is the fact that the OTCR, similar to the ATLR, is not included in the Westlaw subscription of most academic institutions. As a result, unless an academic law library has purchased access to the OTCR as an addition to its usual subscription, the resource may not be available for use electronically.

D. Other Online Sources

The Tribal Court Clearinghouse provides a no-cost search engine locate tribal case law. Moreover, the Tribal Court Clearinghouse has partnered with VersusLaw, a commercial database provider,[53] to provide access to the opinions, memoranda, and orders of 21tribal courts.[54] While the Tribal Court Clearinghouse and VersusLaw currently provide access to a collection of documents for a number of tribes, none of these tribes are located in Oklahoma. Yet, as the Clearinghouse continues to develop, a researcher may find this resource has begun to include Oklahoma tribes.

53. While VersusLaw is a commercial database provider, law students and law school faculty and staff may register for free use of the resource. VersusLaw, *Law School Program*, http://www.versuslaw.com/lawschool/lawschoolinfo.aspx.

54. Tribal L. & Policy Inst., *Tribal Court Clearinghouse*, Tribal Court Decisions, Twenty-One Tribal Courts, http://www.tribal-institute.org/list_elements/Tribal_Courts.htm.

Figure 10-3. OTCR on WestlawNext

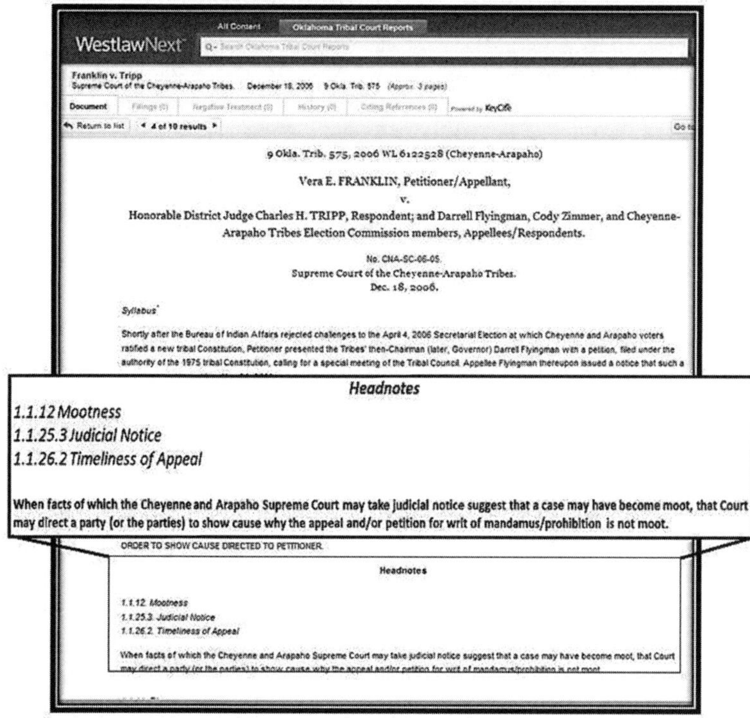

Source: Reprinted with permission of Thomson Reuters.

E. Tribal Websites

Finally, some tribal court opinions may be located on tribal websites. While currently the tribal courts of many tribes in Oklahoma do not routinely post opinions to the web or provide a systematic means of searching for opinions,[55] there are efforts to increase the

55. For example, the Cherokee Nation does provide free access to tribal court decisions. Users must register to access the opinions. The opinions or decisions are not searchable but are instead listed in chronological order by year in which the case was originally filed. Cherokee Nation of Oklahoma, Judicial Branch, *Announcements*, http://www.cherokeecourts.org/.

availability of tribal resources via existing governmental web resources. Further, the *Tribal Courts Directory of the National Tribal Justice Resource Center* (NTJRC),[56] a project of National American Indian Court Judges Association, which was "revitalized" in 2012, may be helpful in locating tribal court websites when a researcher is working to locate tribal court opinions.

V. Customary Law

Prior to this point in the chapter, the focus has been on the "contemporary legal documents" and "academic studies" available in tribal law research. Custom and tradition also comprise a vital source of tribal law. This part of the chapter will deal with sources that may be consulted to assist in establishing custom and tradition.

Oral societies, including Native American tribal societies, often pass along their customary practices and law as part of their oral traditions. The elder members of the tribe, who were raised within these traditions and have personal experience with the customs of the tribe[57] serve as the best sources of customary law. However, some non-legal materials may also assist as sources to establish custom.

Non-legal materials may include "written treatises on custom"; however, "courts will look at such texts cautiously because the works of 'anthropologists, ethnologists and other commentators' on custom often are inaccurate as only tribal members make the 'most accurate commentators on themselves.'"[58] While these texts may be viewed with caution by tribal courts, their information may nonetheless be valuable. This value is reflected in the fact that many Native Ameri-

56. Nat'l Am. Indian Ct. Judges Ass'n, *Tribal Courts Directory of the Nat'l Tribal Justice Resource Ctr.*, http://www.naicja.org/directory.

57. Richland & Deer, *supra* note 25, at 129.

58. Ezra Rosser, *Customary Law: The Way Things Were, Codified*, 8 Tribal Law Journal 18, 26 (2007/2008), http://tlj.unm.edu/volumes/018/8tlj18-ROSSER.pdf citing *In re Estate of Apachee*, 4 Nav. R. 178, 180 (W.R. Dist. Ct. Oct. 11, 1983).

can law collections, including those at the three academic law libraries in Oklahoma, include such resources. Use the catalogs of these libraries to locate selected texts.

Another resource that might be helpful in establishing the observations of community members is tribal newspapers. Often these publications include stories about and by community members. Additionally, the publications may include feedback, such as letters to the editor, regarding coverage of events and issues. Some tribes provide access to current news publications on their websites; however, many tribal newspapers are not available electronically. One source of Oklahoma tribal newspapers is the Oklahoma Historical Society's collection of Oklahoma newspapers. This collection contains Native American tribal newspapers as well as newspapers from towns and cities in Oklahoma. The newspaper catalog of the Oklahoma Historical Society provides information regarding whether particular newspapers are included in the collection.[59]

VI. Research Strategy in Tribal Law Research

The first step in a research strategy may be to consult secondary sources, such as those discussed in this chapter and identified in various research guides on tribal law research. If the secondary sources cite to tribal constitutions and codes, try to use an annotated versions of these resources. However, as previously noted, there are few commercially available print or annotated versions of tribal law sources.

If the consulted secondary sources do not cite to primary legal resources, research of primary sources may be available electronically via tribal websites, commercial databases, and no-cost collections of digitized materials, such as those provided by the Native American Constitutions and Law Digitization Project. Free resources are often selected because of cost concerns, but the substantial time investment required

59. Okla. Historical Socy., Research Ctr., *Archive Collection, Online Catalog, Newspaper Catalog*, http://okhistory.cuadra.com/starweb3/microfilm/servlet.starweb3?path=microfilm/microfilm.public.web.

to use these resources may offset the cost of commercial databases, which facilitate searching by providing editorial enhancements. Further, use of commercial databases may facilitate additional research by providing a citator function. However, as noted throughout the chapter, materials from all tribes may not be available in commercial sources.

Finally, consider how customary law and tradition may affect interpretation of written law. Research must be conducted into the customary law and traditions of the tribe and the issue of whether tribal law applies a hierarchy of law that gives priority to custom and tradition or to "subsequently [tribally] written law."[60]

VII. Conclusion

Tribal law can be particularly difficult to research. Contemporary legal documents may exist, but may not be routinely distributed.[61] Other important sources of law such as customs and traditions may be passed through generations orally. Effective research of tribal law requires creative use of legal and non-legal resources in a variety of print and electronic resources.

---

60. Rosser, *supra* note 58, at 24 (citing *Marino v. Mashantucket Pequot Gaming Enter.*, No. MPTC-CV-97-104, ¶20 Mashantucket Pequot Ct. Jan. 6, 2000).

61. One requirement for the exercising expanded tribal jurisdiction contained in the Violence Against Women Reauthorization Act of 2013, Pub. L. No. 113-4, § 904 127 Stat 54, 122 (2013) and the tribal Law and Order Act of 2010, Pub. L. No. 111-211, §234, Stat 2261, is the availability of public access to tribal codes. It is anticipated that this requirement may serve to stimulate tribal governmental efforts to increase the distribution and accessibility to tribal codes. Tribal economic development initiatives are also serving as a catalyst for improving access to tribal codes.

Chapter 11

Updating Legal Authority with Citators

I. Introduction

Updating the authorities consulted to craft a legal argument is a critical element of every legal research project. Statutes may be renumbered, repealed, or amended. Cases may be reversed on appeal, overturned by subsequent law, followed with approval by other courts, or criticized in subsequent decisions. Constitutions may be amended, and both state and federal regulations are subject to change. In each of these instances, the process of updating will help to determine how, or whether, each piece of legal authority should be used. Not only is updating an important step for determining the current status and value of a piece of legal authority, it is also an excellent method for expanding the scope of relevant research resources when performed toward the beginning of the research process.

The process of updating can be called a number of different things, including validating authorities, KeyCiting, or Shepardizing. Shepardizing is one of the most common terms used for this process because *Shepard's Citations* was the first product developed by a legal publisher to assist in the updating process.[1] All products created for this purpose are generally referred to as citators.

---

1. *Shepard's Citations* began as a print publication in 1875 and is currently available in both print and electronic formats. For more information about the creation of *Shepard's*, see Patti Ogden, *"Mastering the Lawless Science of our Law": A Story of Legal Citation Indexes*, 85 Law Libr. J. 1 (1993).

Regardless of the product used to undertake this critical step in legal research, the basic elements of updating are the same.[2] Updating begins with consultation of a citator to access a comprehensive list of resources that cite to the case, statute, regulation, or other resource you have in hand. This chapter uses the example of a case for simplicity, so the resource being updated is called the *cited case*. Those legal authorities that cite to the cited case are called *citing references*. After retrieving the list of citing references, you should critically examine the references to determine how the cited case has been treated, according to the editors of the citator used. After careful and attentive use of the features of the chosen citator, described in detail in this chapter, the most crucial part of the updating process takes place. You must read and carefully analyze the impact of each citing reference that is relevant to the issues of importance to your case. While citators are extraordinarily valuable research tools, they can never replace the careful analysis of the researcher based on a complete reading of the citing references.

II. When to Use a Citator

For most research projects, it is wise to use a citator at three distinct points in the research process. During the initial collection of

2. This chapter will explore the essential place of updating in the research process, including the timing, functions, and methods for updating legal authorities. However, this chapter will not offer detailed instruction on the use of print citators. Best practices in research dictate that updating should be done using the most current methods and resources available. Print citators, while still effective for finding older citing references, lag behind their online counterparts in delivering the most up-to-date information. Using a print citator may result in missing critically important citing references because they are more recent than the most current update to the print citator. A thorough researcher may begin updating with a print citator, but an online service should always be consulted prior to the completion of any research project. For detailed instructions on the use of print citators, consult Steven M. Barkan, Roy M. Mersky & Donald J. Dunn, *Fundamentals of Legal Research* 301–15 (9th ed. 2009).

relevant authorities, a citator serves two critical functions. First, it can provide validation for the documents already acquired to support a legal argument. Before supporting a legal argument with any case, statute, regulation, or other piece of primary authority, it is essential to determine that the authority is still "good law." "Good law" is the phrase typically used to indicate that the cited reference has not been reversed, overruled, repealed, amended, or otherwise seriously negatively impacted by later precedent. The second purpose for using a citator at the outset of a research project is the expansion of useful authorities. By reviewing the citing references to one relevant case or statute, a number of other primary and secondary sources on point can be discovered.

The next logical opportunity to use a citator comes at the end of gathering research references and the beginning of the writing process. Whether the writing is a brief, memo, paper, or article, the importance of consulting a citator is the same. Because the value of an authority has the potential to be impacted by subsequent authority, and because the initial stages of research may take some time, validation of the resources that are likely to be included in the legal argument is essential. Using a citator at this point in the process is a straightforward matter and typically focuses only on whether each authority is still good law.

The final time to use a citator is at the very end of the project. Depending on the magnitude of the project, a significant amount of time may have passed between the beginning of the writing and its completion. Before submitting any piece of legal writing, a final citator consultation is imperative. Again, the purpose of this final validation is to assure that none of the authorities used to support a legal argument has been negatively impacted by subsequent authority. Only after this final check has been completed is your work ready to submit.

III. KeyCite on WestlawNext

KeyCite on WestlawNext[3] is available for use with all cases in the National Reporter System, a significant number of unpublished cases, federal and state statutes, federal regulations, selected state regulations, selected federal and state administrative decisions, ALR annotations, law review articles, and patents issued by the U.S. Patent and Trademark Office.[4] For clarity, this chapter focuses only on the use of KeyCite for Oklahoma cases and statutes. The basic functionalities of KeyCite for cases and statutes can be applied to the other authorities listed as well.

A. KeyCite for Cases

To begin KeyCiting a case, determine the most appropriate way to access the KeyCite information. The simplest method is to retrieve a case by using a citation or conducting a search. Figure 11-1 illustrates the WestlawNext screen displayed when the *Sicking* case is retrieved. Another method is to enter "KC:" and the case citation in the search box on the main screen.

The first significant piece of information provided is the red KeyCite Status Flag located in the upper left-hand corner of the screen. A summary of the KeyCite Status flags is found in Table 11-1. A red flag indicates that this case is no longer "good law" for at least one of the points of law discussed in the case. It is important to remember that most cases contain multiple points of law and that a single status flag does not express the treatment each point of law has

3. Due to both the strong trend toward adoption of WestlawNext in Oklahoma law schools and firms, and the significant improvements made on this platform to the KeyCite service, this chapter focuses exclusively on the use of KeyCite in WestlawNext. For training and assistance in the use of KeyCite on Westlaw's classic platform, Westlaw offers user guides and tutorials through its online e-learning center.

4. The sources available in KeyCite are likely to expand. Check the coverage by contacting a West representative.

Figure 11-1. KeyCite Status Flag for *Sicking* Case

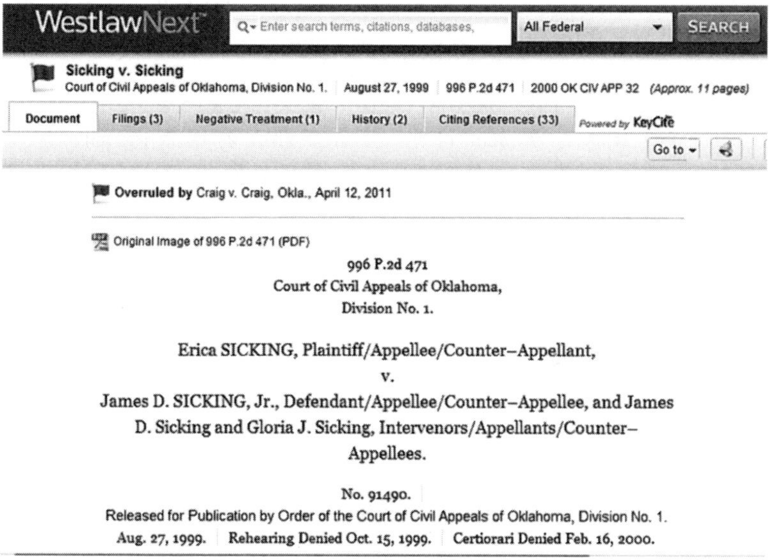

Reprinted with permission of Thomson Reuters.

received. Only a careful reading of the negative citing references to the case can ultimately assist in providing a clear picture of whether the case should be used for your purposes. A red flag is accompanied by a statement about the most negative treatment received. Figure 11-1 shows that at least one point of law in the *Sicking* case was overruled by the *Craig* case.

Table 11-1. KeyCite Status Flags

KeyCite Status Flags	Meaning
Red flag	A decision is no longer good law for at least one of the points of law it contains.
Yellow flag	A decision has some negative history but has not been reversed or overruled.

If the cited case has received some negative treatment but has not been overruled or reversed, a yellow flag may appear in the upper left corner of the screen. As with the red flag, a yellow flag will be accompanied by a summary of the most negative treatment the case has received. It is also possible that there will not be a KeyCite status flag assigned to the cited case. This indicates that in the opinion of the West editors, there were no negative citing references. Again, the only way to determine the significance of the presence or absence of a KeyCite status flag is to carefully read the citing references to the case to discover the precise nature of the negative treatment.

After examining the KeyCite Status flag, if there is one, the next step is to examine the information contained in each of the tabs across the top of the screen. The tabs relevant to validation include "Negative Treatment," "History," and "Citing References." Each of these tabs reveals a different type of information about the cited case, and each must be examined in the updating process.

1. Negative Treatment

The Negative Treatment tab contains both the negative direct history of the case and negative citing references. Negative direct history refers to subsequent proceedings in the same line of litigation that negatively impacted the cited case. If the cited case had been reversed on appeal, you would find that information here. The *Sicking* case in this example has no negative direct history. There is, however, a negative citing reference. According to KeyCite, *the Sicking* case was overruled by the *Craig* case. The citation for the *Craig* case is listed, along with a pinpoint citation to the page on which the *Sicking* case is first cited. Other information provided includes the date of decision of the *Craig* case, the extent to which *Craig* discusses the cited case, and the headnotes from the cited case addressed by *Craig*.[5]

5. Consult Chapters 5 and 6 for a complete discussion of the value of headnotes.

2. History

The next tab containing KeyCite information is the History tab. The material provided here summarizes the direct history of the cited case. This includes prior and subsequent phases of the litigation, and is displayed both with a list of citations and a graphical representation. A request for certiorari was made to the United States Supreme Court in the *Sicking* case and the request was denied. No other subsequent or prior history is available. While *Sicking* shows an extremely simple history, one need only examine the History tab for *Roe v. Wade*, 410 U.S. 113 (1973), to see the value in the dual format of the presentation.

3. Citing References

The final tab is the Citing References tab. This tab provides a list of each document that cites to the cited case, including primary authorities, secondary authorities, briefs, and pleadings. When a case has few citing references, it is always wise to thoroughly read all of the references available to determine precisely how each one impacts the precedential value of the cited case.

However, some cases may have hundreds or even thousands of citing references. In these situations, use the narrowing features provided to assist in prioritizing which of the citing references to read in their entirety. Place primary emphasis on citing references with negative treatment of the cited case. Additional criteria to consider include the type of authority (primary or secondary), the jurisdiction of the citing reference, the level of the court from which the citing cases come, and the points of law from the cited case discussed in the citing references. A case from the highest court in your jurisdiction that criticizes the case in hand for the precise point of law relevant to your research should always be read in its entirety. A case from a lower court in a different jurisdiction that cites your case for a point of law unrelated to the matter for which you are using it may not necessarily be a high priority for review.

Figure 11-2 shows the Citing References tab narrowed to display only citing references that are cases. This narrowing feature can be

Figure 11-2. KeyCite Citing References Tab for Cases

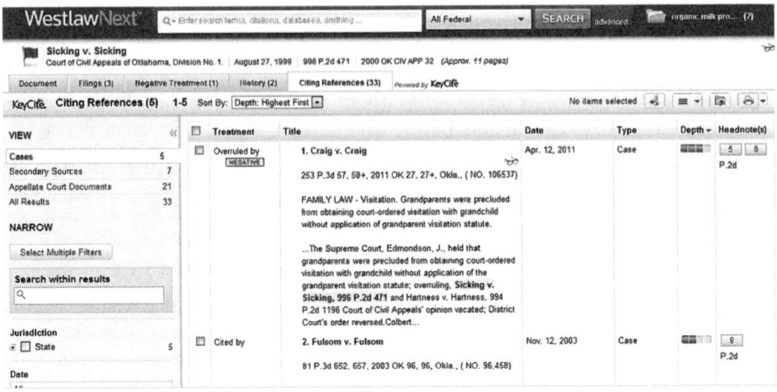

Reprinted with permission of Thomson Reuters.

found on the left side of the screen. Not only can the results be narrowed by type of document, there are also additional filters available depending on the document type chosen. A choice of citing case references allows additional selections for jurisdiction, depth of treatment, headnotes, treatment status, and reported status. If secondary source citing references are selected, additional filters are available for publication type and name. Regardless of the document type chosen, searching within the citing references using keywords is always an option.

Of all the filters available in KeyCite, one of the most valuable is the headnote filter. Because each case contains multiple points of law, it is possible that some of the citing references listed discuss points of law other than the one on which your research is focused. By limiting only to those cases that discuss the same point of law summarized by the relevant headnotes in the cited case, you have a greater chance that the citing references will speak directly to the issues at hand. While this approach may not appear to be a significant advantage for cases that have few citing references, it can be extraordinarily beneficial when KeyCiting cases with thousands of citing references.

B. KeyCite for Statutes

The fundamental principles of KeyCiting a statute are similar to those for KeyCiting a case, yet there are some significant differences in the service worth noting. While both red and yellow flags are used to indicate the status of a statute, they designate different types of negative treatment than they do for cases. The red flag indicates that a statute has been repealed, superseded, held unconstitutional, preempted, or amended by a recent session law. A yellow flag may mean that a statute has been renumbered or transferred, proposed legislation impacting the statute is available, the statute has been limited on constitutional or preemption grounds, its validity has been questioned by case law, or a prior version of a statute has received negative treatment from the courts. As with cases, the flag assigned to a statute will be accompanied by a statement summarizing the most negative treatment the statute has received.

1. History

KeyCite's history information for statutes is arranged slightly differently than it is for cases. The History tab contains several categories of documents: Validity provides citations to proposed legislation, the Editor's and Revisor's Notes summarize changes to the statute since its initial enactment, and Legislative History Materials provide links to available state legislative documents related to the statute.[6] Drafts of bills introduced before the section was enacted would be found here as well.

2. Context and Analysis

The Context and Analysis tab may be extremely useful for the purposes of expanding your research. While the documents provided in

6. Two features found in the History tab for federal statutes and selected state statutes that are not currently available for Oklahoma are the Graphical Statutes and Versions features. For more information about these features, view the WestlawNext Quick Reference Guide available from the Westlaw store at http://store.westlaw.com/.

this tab do not cite to the statute in hand, they are closely related to the legal issues encompassed by the statute and are thus worthy of review, particularly at the beginning of the research process. Moreover, the sources found in this tab may offer a glimpse into the greater context of the statutory scheme that can inform the way the statute is used in legal arguments.

C. *KeyCite Alert*

In the course of many research projects, it may be advantageous to continuously monitor the status of a particular legal authority. WestlawNext offers a service to assist with this task called KeyCite Alert. This alert service is accessed from the main WestlawNext page by clicking on the "Tools" tab. Once in the Tools area, select "Alert Center" from the list provided. A KeyCite Alert can be created from this page by clicking on the word "Create" and entering the citation of the authority to be monitored. You will then be asked to indicate the type of reports you wish to receive and the frequency with which they should be delivered.

IV. Shepard's on Lexis Advance[7]

Though Shepard's first became available electronically in 1980, it did not appear on Lexis until 1997. The Shepard's service on Lexis Advance can be used to validate a wide array of primary and secondary state and federal authorities, including Oklahoma state cases, statutes, court rules, bar association rules, and law reviews. There is, however, one significant omission from the service that bears noting. Shepard's does not provide its service for the Oklahoma Administrative Code. This chapter explains the use of Shepard's for Oklahoma cases and statutes, although the information given also applies to updating other sources.

---

7. Because Shepard's is so similar in form and function on both Lexis and Lexis Advance, this chapter focuses exclusively on the use of Shepard's in Lexis Advance. For training and assistance in the use of Shepard's on the Lexis platform, Lexis offers user guides and tutorials through its learn on-demand center.

Figure 11-3. Shepard's Access from a Case

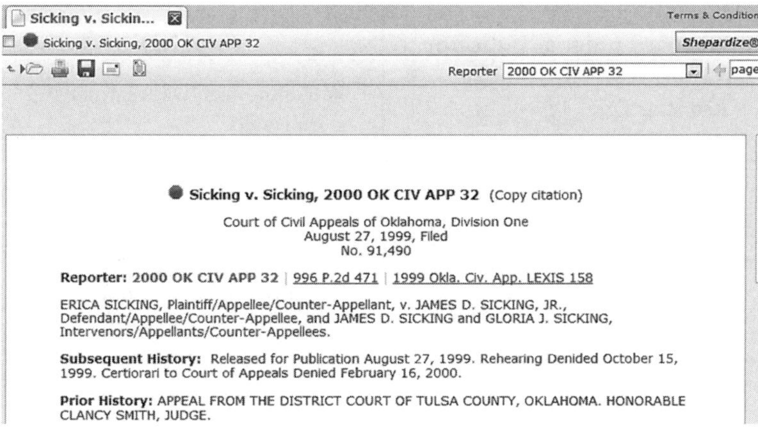

To begin Shepardizing either a case or statute, you must select one of the two basic methods for retrieving a Shepard's summary. One option is to retrieve the cited case or statute, then to use the "Shepardize" button at the top right of the page as shown in Figure 11-3. The other option is to begin at the Lexis main page and select the "Shepard's" tab. After clicking the Shepard's tab, enter the citation of the case or statute to be Shepardized.

A. Shepard's for Cases

Once you have retrieved the report for the cited case, the process of Shepardizing a case is similar to the process described for KeyCite. The first piece of information to consider is the Shepard's Signal Indicator for the case. A list of all available signals can be found by clicking on Legend at the top of the Shepard's citing decisions display; signals relevant to cases are summarized in Table 11-2. The signal assigned by the Lexis editors to the *Sicking* case in this chapter's example is the red stop sign. While the case has clearly received nega-

Table 11-2. Shepard's Signal Indicators

Shepard's Signal Indicator	Meaning
Red stop sign	Warning: negative treatment is indicated
Red exclamation point inside a circle	Warning: negative case treatment is indicated for a statute
Orange "Q"	Questioned: validity questioned by citing references
Yellow triangle	Caution: possible negative treatment
Green diamond	Positive: positive treatment is indicated
Blue "A"	Neutral: citing references with treatment are available
Blue "I"	Cited by: citation information is available

tive treatment, the type of treatment is not presented with the signal as it is in KeyCite. Instead, the Shepard's Report provides additional information about the status of the case.

The Shepard's report, shown in Figure 11-4, provides options for reviewing the treatment received by the cited case. Subsequent appellate history, if there is any, will be noted in the Appellate History display. Citing cases, secondary source references, and a Table of Authorities for the cited case are also included in the Report.

As with KeyCite, the most efficient way to use Shepard's to determine whether or not a case is appropriate for use is to examine the citing references for negative treatment. The basic information given

Figure 11-4. Shepard's Report

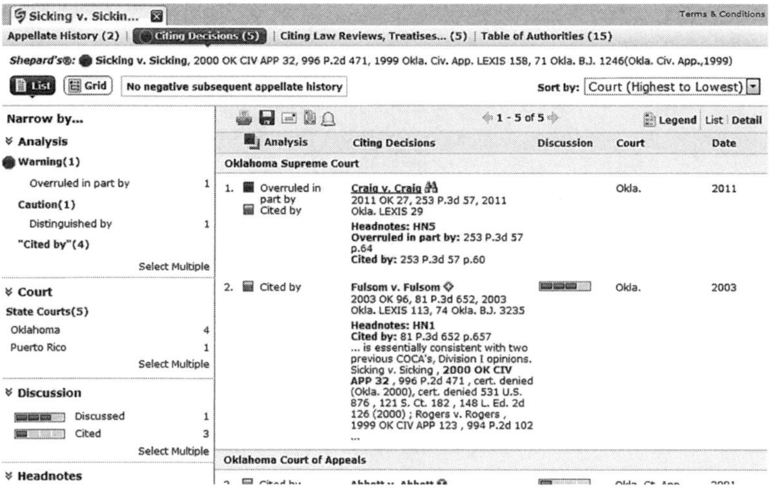

with each citing reference is shown in Figure 11-5. For citing cases, the specific treatment received by the cited case is noted, along with the name and parallel citations for the case. Shepard's also identifies the headnotes from the cited case that are discussed. In this example, headnote 5 from the cited case *Sicking* is discussed in the *Craig* case. By clicking on the link for HN5, you jump directly to the point in the *Craig* case where headnote 5 from the cited case is discussed. Shepard's also gives pinpoint citations for every page on which your case is cited, with hyperlinks that go directly to that section of the citing opinion.

While the sample case has only five citing decisions that can be scrolled through quickly and easily, many cases will have numerous citing references. To assist in narrowing down the number and type of citing references to a manageable and relevant group, Shepard's offers a set of filters that are accessible on the left side of the Shepard's results screen. Like the filtering options available in KeyCite, the filters are dynamic, offering only the filtering options that are available

Figure 11-5. Shepard's Citing Decisions

Analysis	Citing Decisions	Discussion	Court	Date
Oklahoma Supreme Court				
1. Overruled in part by Cited by	**Craig v. Craig** 2011 OK 27, 253 P.3d 57, 2011 Okla. LEXIS 29 **Headnotes: HN5** **Overruled in part by:** 253 P.3d 57 p.64 **Cited by:** 253 P.3d 57 p.60		Okla.	2011

for the case you have Shepardized. Filters include analysis (often referred to as treatment), jurisdiction, Lexis headnotes, and date. A keyword search can also be conducted within the citing references by using the "Terms within results" box provided.

B. Shepard's for Statutes

Although the fundamental principles of Shepardizing a statute are similar to those for Shepardizing a case, some significant differences exist. First, there is a Shepard's Signal Indicator used only for statutes, as seen previously in Table 11-2. Any statute that has received negative case law treatment will be assigned a red exclamation point inside a circle. Second, the Shepard's Report for statutes includes a Legislative History display for the statute, showing its original date of enactment, the session law information, and any subsequent amendments. Third, if current pending legislation would impact the statute, an alert can be found at the top of the Shepard's Report with a link to the list of pending bills.

C. Table of Authorities

One particularly useful service offered by Shepard's is the Table of Authorities report. This service, used primarily when Shepardizing cases, provides a list of all the authorities cited within the cited case.[8] These authorities are the precedential building blocks on which the cited case is founded. The true value in the Table of Authorities feature is the Shepard's signal indicator given for each of the listed cases. You are able to see the signal indicator each case would receive if you were to Shepardize it.

Figure 11-6 shows the Table of Authorities report for the *Sicking* case. The written opinion in *Sicking* relied on fifteen cases to support its holding. Of the first three cases shown, two have received some subsequent negative treatment, while two have received positive treatment. Even if the *Sicking* case itself had received no negative treatment, the Table of Authorities report might caution against using it if the majority of the cases relied upon in *Sicking* had been overturned or otherwise negatively impacted.[9]

D. Shepard's Alert

Like KeyCite, Shepard's offers the opportunity for continuous monitoring of the status of a particular legal authority for purposes of validation. The Shepard's Alert service can be activated from the Shepard's Report itself. While viewing the Shepard's Report, as seen in Figure 11-4, simply click the image of the alarm bell just above the list of citing decisions. The alert template allows you to determine what types of changes you wish to see and the frequency with which you would like to receive the alert reports.

---

8. The Table of Authorities is also available for law review articles and other select sources.

9. Note that WestlawNext does not currently offer the Table of Authorities feature, though it is still part of the Westlaw classic platform. In coming years, the Table of Authorities is likely to be included on WestlawNext.

Figure 11-6. Shepard's Table of Authorities

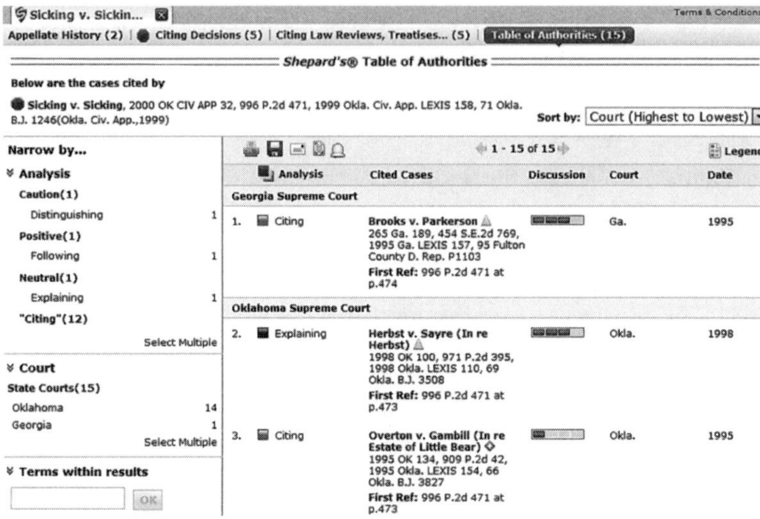

V. OSCN's Citationizer

While KeyCite and Shepard's are the primary online subscription services for updating legal authorities, the Oklahoma State Court Network (discussed more fully in Chapter 2) does provide a limited service within the Legal Research section of its website[10] called "Citationizer." Like KeyCite and Shepard's, the Citationizer provides citations to legal resources that cite to the case or statute you are examining. OSCN describes Citationizing as follows: "Citiationizing is the Oklahoma Supreme Court Network's method of checking citation history to determine if a case is still good law, or if the rule(s) of

10. Oklahoma State Court Network, http://www.oscn.net.

law set forth in the case have been expanded upon or modified."[11] The description focuses only on case law, but OSCN advertises its Oklahoma Statutes as "Citationized" also. Other sources, such as the Oklahoma Constitution and attorney general opinions, do not offer the Citationizer feature.

Although OSCN's Citationizer can be a useful tool, a word of caution is appropriate. The Citationizer is by no means comprehensive and should not be relied on to the exclusion of other citators. One example of a serious omission from the Citationizer service is its failure to include *Neal v. Lee*, 14 P.3d 547 (2000) in the Citationizer summary for 10 O.S. § 5.[12] The application and constitutionality of this statute was the primary focus of the *Neal* case. Such an omission clearly illustrates the reason OSCN's Citationizer should never be the only tool used for updating cases and statutes. However, because OSCN is a free service and does provide a list of the majority of citing references available through OSCN for cases and statutes, it may still be a useful and cost-effective starting point for the updating process.

Figure 11-7 shows the Citationizer summary for this case. According to the display, four cases have cited this case. One case has merely cited it, which indicates there is very little discussion of the cited case, if any. Two cases have discussed the cited case, which means they have given a bit more attention to the cited case in the language of the opinion. Finally, one case has discussed the cited case at length, indicating that there is some extensive discussion of the cited case.

While this display clearly indicates the amount of discussion of the cited case, note the absence of treatment symbols for these citing references. A researcher accustomed to using KeyCite or Shepard's would be surprised to discover that the final case in the list actually

11. *See* http://www.oscn.net/applications/oscn/SimpleHelp.asp?HelpContextID=6.

12. This statute has since been renumbered as 43 O.S. § 109.4, and the *Neal* case is not listed in the Citationizer for the new statute either.

Figure 11-7. Citationizer on OSCN

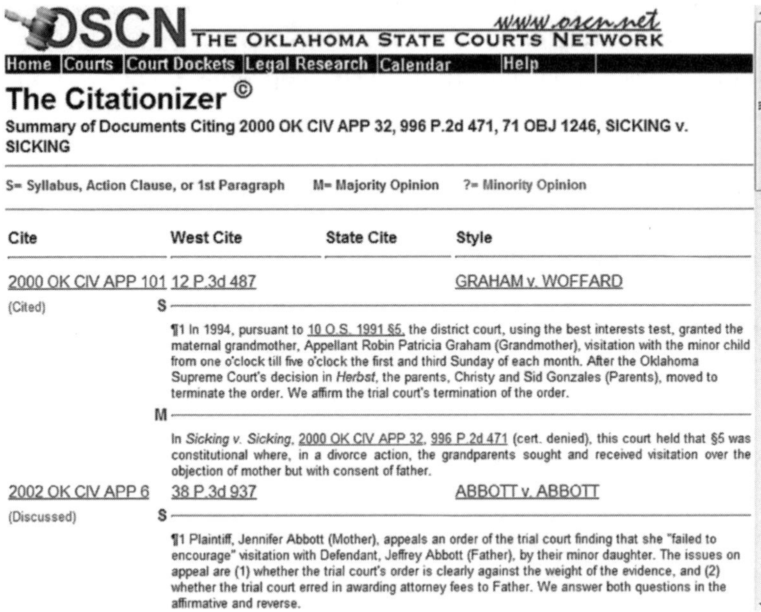

OSCN www.oscn.net THE OKLAHOMA STATE COURTS NETWORK

Home | Courts | Court Dockets | Legal Research | Calendar | Help

The Citationizer ©

Summary of Documents Citing 2000 OK CIV APP 32, 996 P.2d 471, 71 OBJ 1246, SICKING v. SICKING

S= Syllabus, Action Clause, or 1st Paragraph M= Majority Opinion ?= Minority Opinion

Cite	West Cite	State Cite	Style
2000 OK CIV APP 101 (Cited)	12 P.3d 487		GRAHAM v. WOFFARD

S — ¶1 In 1994, pursuant to 10 O.S. 1991 §5, the district court, using the best interests test, granted the maternal grandmother, Appellant Robin Patricia Graham (Grandmother), visitation with the minor child from one o'clock till five o'clock the first and third Sunday of each month. After the Oklahoma Supreme Court's decision in *Herbst*, the parents, Christy and Sid Gonzales (Parents), moved to terminate the order. We affirm the trial court's termination of the order.

M — In *Sicking v. Sicking*, 2000 OK CIV APP 32, 996 P.2d 471 (cert. denied), this court held that §5 was constitutional where, in a divorce action, the grandparents sought and received visitation over the objection of mother but with consent of father.

Cite	West Cite	State Cite	Style
2002 OK CIV APP 6 (Discussed)	38 P.3d 937		ABBOTT v. ABBOTT

S — ¶1 Plaintiff, Jennifer Abbott (Mother), appeals an order of the trial court finding that she "failed to encourage" visitation with Defendant, Jeffrey Abbott (Father), by their minor daughter. The issues on appeal are (1) whether the trial court's order is clearly against the weight of the evidence, and (2) whether the trial court erred in awarding attorney fees to Father. We answer both questions in the affirmative and reverse.

Source: Oklahoma State Court Network, www.oscn.net.

overrules the cited case, a crucial fact not readily apparent from the Citationizer Summary. Though a researcher ought never to rely on treatment symbols alone to determine how a cited case has been affected, the symbols used in other citators may increase efficiency by helping to narrow down the citing cases that should be read in their entirety before relying on the cited case.

Chapter 12

Research Strategies and Organization

The model for the research process outlined in Chapter 1 assumes a project that is undertaken from scratch, with no prior knowledge of the area of law or essential relevant authorities. However, each research project is by nature unique, and thus it requires that a distinctive strategy be applied. This chapter explores the ways in which a savvy researcher can take the essential elements of a fresh search, examine answers to some critical questions related to the issue(s) at hand, develop a strategy for approaching the research process that fits the unique problem, and implement that strategy in a cost-effective and efficient way. It culminates in recommendations for organizing the information gathered so that you may convey your findings in a clear, thoughtful, and useful manner. The chapter concludes with tips on how to know when to end your research.

I. Developing a Research Strategy

A. Review the Research Process

As explained in Chapter 1, the research process has some essential elements that must be completed in order for the work you do to be thorough. These elements include 1) framing the issues and developing search terms; 2) identifying, prioritizing, and consulting relevant sources; 3) expanding and updating your research; 4) making sure your research is responsive to each issue presented; and 5) knowing when to stop. Within each element is a series of discrete tasks that, when conducted carefully and with attention to detail, help to assure a high quality work product.

B. Ask the Critical Questions

Before spending any significant time conducting research on the issues you have identified, always take a moment to consider the critical questions that will define the contours of your research. Thinking about questions such as the ones listed here at the outset of your project will help to more clearly define the best strategy for the work ahead. While this list certainly isn't exhaustive of the questions that should be asked, it should provide an important starting point for developing a solid research strategy.

- How much time do I have to complete the research?

A sound strategic approach for an issue that must be delivered within a few hours will look markedly different from the strategy adopted for a problem you have several days or weeks to address. Moreover, because some of the time spent on research may ultimately be billed back to the client, understanding the time you are expected to put into the work can inform the strategy you adopt.

- What are the budgetary constraints of the project?

Both the amount of time you spend and the types of resources you consult will be determined in great part by the amount of money that should be spent on the case at hand. Large-scale toxic tort litigation may require both significant time and access to detailed and expensive research resources. In contrast, a small claims action arising out of a dispute between neighbors is likely to require less time and probably will not merit the expense associated with accessing a large number of costly resources. While it is true that the scope of a research project may change after you conduct some initial inquiries, it is important to begin with a good sense of the appropriate fiscal resources to devote to the matter.

- What kinds of research resources are available and how are they billed?

Whether you work in a small solo practice, a government office, or a large firm, having a robust knowledge of the research resources available to you and the kinds of costs associated with those resources is critical to developing and implementing your research strategy. The unfettered access to print and electronic resources that most attorneys experienced in law school will likely be a thing of the past in the workplace. A good research strategy will include a plan to review resources that are relevant, are easily accessed, and fit within the time and budgetary constraints of your project.

- What types of authorities are likely to control?

Asking this question forces you to examine the area of law you are working with to decide which authorities are most likely to have a determinative impact on the outcome of the case. If the area of law is heavily regulated, make sure your strategy includes and emphasizes federal, state, or municipal regulations as appropriate and be attentive to them when they are referenced in secondary sources. If common law is more likely to control, make sure you focus some portion of your strategy on efficient and effective case law research. While the goal of every good research strategy is to be thorough in consulting all potentially relevant or determinative authorities, spending a little bit of time thinking about which authorities are likely to be most important can improve both your efficiency and effectiveness.

- What is the appropriate jurisdiction for this problem?

In many instances, it will be fairly clear whether an issue is controlled by state law, federal law, or both. However, you may encounter a problem in which the controlling jurisdiction is not clear. Asking this question at the beginning of the research process can help you recognize whether or not you should spend some of your valuable research time clarifying this matter before spending unnecessary time and money researching your problem in the wrong jurisdiction.

- What information do I already have?

Perhaps the most important question to ask at the outset of the research process is what valuable information you already possess. When you were assigned this project, were you given the name of a relevant case or the citation to a controlling statute or regulation? Do you know the date on which the cause of action arose? Has your law office or firm handled similar cases in the past, and if so are there briefs or filings from earlier cases that might help you quickly identify potentially relevant resources? Identifying pieces of the research puzzle already in place can help you decide how to proceed efficiently.

Recognize that you may not initially have the answers to these and other critical questions. If that is the case, write the outstanding questions in your research notes (which will be discussed later in this chapter) and make sure to pursue the answers before you start researching in earnest. Because these types of questions can have a significant impact on your overall research strategy, answering them up front will save you time and energy.

C. Take Notes That Make a Difference

One of the simplest and most effective tools for developing and implementing a solid research strategy is the act of keeping quality research notes. Good notes provide a visual reminder of your research plan, help track the steps already taken, reflect both the fruitful inquiries and the dead ends you have encountered, and allow space for both process-oriented notes and analytical connections between the concepts and resources explored. It does not matter whether you prefer to use a pencil and paper, a computer, a tablet, or a smart phone to record your research notes. The most important part of note taking is giving yourself a space to keep track of your work and make important connections between the concepts and ideas you discover along the way.

Table 12-1 shows one example of a framework for taking research notes. The first four of the five essential elements of the research process are clearly reflected in the template. It includes space to note relevant facts and flesh out a clear issue statement. An area for reflecting on important considerations from the critical questions asked at the outset of the research process is also provided. Chapter 1 of this book contains a detailed discussion of choosing search terms for your work, and the template offers a section in which each of these search terms can be recorded. Another valuable feature of this particular framework is the dedicated space for recording both the resources al-

Table 12-1. Template for Research Notes

<table>
<tr><td colspan="4">Facts:

Issue Statement/Questions Presented:</td></tr>
<tr><td colspan="4">Critical Questions:
Time:
Money:
Controlling Authority:
Jurisdiction:
What is Known:</td></tr>
<tr><td colspan="4">Search Terms:</td></tr>
<tr><td><u>Things</u></td><td><u>Actions</u></td><td><u>Relief</u></td><td><u>Persons</u></td></tr>
<tr><td colspan="2"><u>Sources Consulted</u></td><td colspan="2"><u>Secondary References</u></td></tr>
<tr><td colspan="2"><u>Statutes and/or Regulations</u></td><td colspan="2"><u>Case Citations and Digest Topic & Key Numbers</u></td></tr>
<tr><td colspan="4">Follow-up Questions and Connections:</td></tr>
</table>

ready consulted as well as the references to additional authorities encountered along the way. Equally important is the section at the bottom of the template reserved for analytical notes dealing with the connections between concepts and the questions that remain unanswered. Finally, useful research notes will include both the date on which the research was conducted as well as clear citation information for the sources consulted. Knowing precisely what you reviewed and when you reviewed it is one way to maximize efficiency by reducing the likelihood that you will have to re-trace your steps.

By committing to taking research notes, you avoid the tempting habit of printing resources and highlighting relevant sections without really digesting the material you are reading. Putting concepts and connections in your own words and writing them down helps to more firmly situate them in your mind. Note taking is a more active approach to research that encourages you to become genuinely engaged with the material rather than skimming or scanning it. This kind of active engagement is critical to making the kinds of connections required to really understand the research problem at hand.

D. Choose a Strategy That Fits

Once you have asked the critical questions and prepared yourself to take good notes, it is time to begin shaping the fundamental elements of the research process into a unique strategy for your problem. A good strategy will lay out the steps you plan to take in the research process while being flexible enough to allow for change if new information comes to light.

1. The Fresh Search

Chapter 1 provides an overview of the research process that assumes you have no prior familiarity with the area of law or resources best suited to answer the issues posed. When undertaking a fresh search, the best strategy is typically to work through the research process in the order described in that chapter.

Begin by framing your research issue and developing useful search terms. Ask the critical questions described above and then create a foundational understanding of the issues involved by consulting secondary sources. Let the secondary sources inform your understanding of the legal context of the problem and search them for citations to relevant primary authorities. As you examine the primary authorities, make sure to KeyCite or Shepardize each one before relying on it for your analysis.

Once you have immersed yourself in the sources you have located, review your issues presented to ensure that each point is addressed by the research you have done. When the issues presented have been satisfactorily answered, or alternatively there is an absence of mandatory authority on point despite exhaustive searching, turn your attention to organizing your findings and delivering the results.

2. Starting with a Case, Statute, or Regulation on Point

Occasionally, the issue you must explore is given to you along with a citation to a relevant primary authority. You may be aware of a case that discusses the matter, the interpretation or application of a given statute may be at issue, or a regulation could be the subject of the dispute. In one of these circumstances, you may choose to alter your strategy to take advantage of the information you already know.

Rather than immediately searching for secondary sources to help build a foundational understanding of the problem, first consult the primary authority in hand. Think about the language used and make sure your search terms list includes the important words, phrases, and concepts found there. Take time to KeyCite or Shepardize the source you have. Use these validation tools not just to verify that the authority is "good law," but also to help you expand your research. A thorough discussion of both functions of a citator can be found in Chapter 11.

If the primary authority in hand is a case, use the editorial features of Westlaw or Lexis to help you find other, similar case law in your jurisdiction. Chapter 6 covers researching judicial opinions and can provide an overview of the methods for using a single good case to find other cases. If you are working with a statute, consult an annotated code to find cases that interpret or construe the statute and secondary sources that deal with the same area of law, as discussed in Chapter 7. Should you find yourself with a regulation in hand, review and follow the recommendations set out in Chapter 9 to help develop your foundation and locate additional authorities.

3. *Use an Iterative Approach*

In developing your strategy, remember that research is not necessarily a linear process. Rather, it is an iterative process in which the primary objective is a thorough exploration of your issue. Rather than focusing on completing each element of the research process in a particular order, focus instead on making sure you have been appropriately attentive to each step. You need not complete all the steps in a particular order, so long as you are careful to complete them.

4. *Research with Time Constraints*

Time limitations provide another important reason to carefully consider adjusting your research strategy. When pressed for time, the most valuable action to take is to carefully define the issue or question presented. Being very specific about the information you need to gather is the best way to save time and energy and to avoid chasing leads for peripheral issues. Once you have honed in on the precise information you need, then focus on what you already know. If you have been presented with a problem that requires a fresh search, follow the recommendations in Section D.1. above with an eye toward using the most quickly and easily accessed resources. If you have some authorities already in hand, get the maximum benefit from them by following the guidelines in Section D.2. above.

E. Cost-Effective Research Methods

Though this chapter has already touched on some of the elements of cost-effective legal research, you should apply a few basic principles to each project you undertake to maximize your effectiveness for the research dollars you spend.

1. *Consider the Format*

First, think about the cost of accessing a resource in print versus online. The simple act of considering a resource's format has the potential to have a significant impact on the amount of money and time you spend researching an issue.

This is particularly true in the early stages of research. When developing a foundational knowledge of the area of law with which you are working, the ability to browse a greater number of secondary sources in an inexpensive context is key. Print sources do not have an hourly or transactional cost associated with them, so you can browse as many of them as you like for as long as you need to without incurring any expense beyond the initial purchase. If you are fortunate enough to have access to a law firm library, find out what kinds of secondary sources are available in print. Consider access to a nearby state or county court library or an academic library in the area where you can obtain low-cost access. The less focused you are in your research process, the more valuable browsing a wide variety of low-cost resources can be.

While print research certainly has cost-based advantages, remember also that there is a monetary value for the time spent researching. Though print research can often be conducted just as quickly, if not more quickly, than electronic research, there may be times when print research would take much longer than a comparable search in a fee-based electronic resource. As you become a more experienced researcher, you will learn to identify these instances. Shepardizing is one task that is faster and far more comprehensive when done electronically. Ultimately, you will have to engage in a cost-benefit analysis to determine if it is better to spend a greater amount of time or money on a given task, and format will certainly be part of that evaluation.

2. Consider Free Sources

The ubiquity of fee-based database access during law school leaves many novice researchers with the mistaken impression that a fee-based platform is essential to get access to trustworthy, current, or editorially enhanced legal information. In fact, there are a number of government, non-profit, and other online resources that provide easy access to high quality, trustworthy, and even official or authenticated material. Many state bar associations have relationships with vendors such as Fastcase or Casemaker that allow free access to those who are members of the bar. At the date of writing, the Oklahoma

Bar Association provides free access to Fastcase for its members. Additionally, resources such as the Oklahoma State Court Network,[1] Cornell's Legal Information Institute,[2] and the Government Printing Office's Federal Digital System[3] (FDsys) offer free access to valuable research resources. For a thorough discussion of online legal research, including more information about free online sources, consult Chapter 2.

F. Sample Strategy

To make the recommendations offered in this chapter more concrete, consider the following hypothetical, first introduced in Chapter 1, and sample research strategy. Your client is a recently widowed woman in Tulsa, Oklahoma. Prior to his death, her husband consulted with a local attorney who re-drafted his will. The new will provides that a considerable portion of his estate be left to a non-profit organization on whose governing board the drafting attorney currently sits. Your client does not want this new will to be honored and asks if there are grounds for invalidating the will. You have been given one week in which to research the issue and draft a memorandum to your supervising attorney. You have been told to keep the costs "reasonable" and have not been offered any authorities on point to start your research. Table 12-21 lists the strategic steps you might take to complete the assignment.

II. Organization

While much of this chapter emphasizes the organization of your research for maximum efficiency and effectiveness, also consider or-

1. Oklahoma State Court Network, http://www.oscn.net.
2. Cornell's Legal Information Institute, http://www.law.cornell.edu/.
3. FDsys, http://www.gpo.gov/fdsys/.

Table 12-2. Sample Research Strategy

1.	Frame the issues presented to the best of your ability and write what you develop at the top of your research notes.
2.	Review critical questions, such as your time and cost limitations, the research resources readily available to you, the jurisdiction for your problem, and the authorities that are likely to control. Be sure to make note of information already in your possession that may help you answer the question.
3.	Generate search terms, as described in Chapter 1.
4.	Choose appropriate secondary authorities to help you develop a foundational knowledge of the area of law. There is an excellent ALR annotation on undue influence in will drafting, and AmJur contains a significant amount of valuable information as well.
5.	Note the primary authorities you found in both the discussion and footnotes of the secondary sources consulted. In this instance, most of those authorities will be cases.
6.	Skim the cases, and note important concepts, rules, or additional primary authorities such as statutes. Then go back and carefully read and consider the authorities that are most relevant to your problem.
7.	KeyCite or Shepardize those primary authorities on which you intend to rely both to assure that they are "good law" and to expand your research.
8.	Note follow-up questions and summarize the connections you have made.
9.	Follow up on any outstanding questions, organize your findings, and prepare to draft your memo.

ganizing the results of your research to help you develop your analysis. This includes organizing the secondary sources and primary authorities on which you will base your assessment of the legal situation, as well as organizing the ultimate analysis of the problem.

A. Organizing Authorities

In organizing the authorities themselves, consider making a print copy of every primary authority on which you intend to rely in your analysis. It is often helpful to make notes on each source indicating why it is important. Rather than simply highlighting critical passages in the text, either make analytical notes in the margins or cross-reference your research notes in a way that is clear and meaningful to you.

It is much less important to retain print copies of secondary authorities you reviewed in your research, but you may wish to keep selected secondary sources that significantly contributed to your understanding of the legal context or provided a particularly useful list of references to relevant primary authorities. When in doubt, err on the side of retaining more material in print rather than less, as it is much easier to recycle extra materials at the end of your work than to retrieve the authorities again later.

You may choose to organize the print copies of authorities by the type of authority, by the subject matter addressed, or by chronology. Any of these organizational schemes may be a good choice, depending on the problem you are researching.

B. Organizing Analysis

As with research notes, there are a number of ways to organize the analysis of a research problem so that the work you have done can be easily reviewed and summarized. The format you choose is not nearly as important as the fact that you create some kind of document reflecting your work. One method for organizing your findings is offered in Table 12-2. Again, the client is the widow and the issue is the undue influence of the attorney who drafted her husband's will, described as an example earlier in this chapter.

An analysis chart such as the one in Table 12-2 helps to identify the authorities that relate both to the overarching questions in your research as well as to the more specific sub-issues that must be addressed. A chart with this level of detail may seem unnecessary when you are working with a fairly straightforward question or very few primary authorities. However, as you research subjects that are more complicated, have a greater number of sub-issues, or involve more complex primary authorities, this type of organizational structure can help bring clarity to each aspect of your research. This type of chart is also incredibly helpful if you are conducting research at the request of a supervisor and will ultimately need to turn your results over to that individual.

Table 12-3. Organizing Research Results

Issue presented: *Are there grounds to contest a will where the will designates as a beneficiary a non-profit organization on which the will's drafter (who was also the decedent's attorney) sits as a board member?*			
Sub-issue #1: *What are the possible grounds for a will contest in Oklahoma?*			
Relevant authority	**Summary of authority**	**Client facts**	**Assessment**
58 O.S. §61	Sets out the method and grounds for a will contest. Grounds include testator's lack of competence, as well as external duress, menace, fraud, or undue influence.	Client wishes for the will to be denied probate.	Assuming undue influence by the drafting attorney can be demonstrated, our client may be able to move forward with a will contest.
84 O.S. §43	Affirms that a will procured by undue influence may be denied probate and that the revocation of a prior will through undue influence can be declared void.	Decedent had an earlier will that was revoked when the new will was drafted.	Revocation of earlier will upon the recent redrafting of the will in question may be declared void if undue influence is shown.

Table 12-3. Organizing Research Results (*continued*)

Sub-issue #2: *What constitutes undue influence in the procurement of a will?*			
White v. Palmer 498 P.2d 1401	Undue influence can be shown either by direct testimony or by review of all the circumstances surrounding the procurement of the will. Circumstantial evidence includes the relationship of the parties, opportunity for influence, and the favorable terms of the will, among others.	Drafter of the will may benefit from the disposition of the new will. Drafter had opportunity and relationship to influence decedent.	While the facts do not indicate whether there is direct evidence of the exercise of undue influence, it is possible to show undue influence sufficient to deny probate by reference to circumstantial evidence.

III. Ending Research

As noted in Chapter 1, knowing when to end a project is one of the greatest challenges novice researchers face. While some legal questions have clear answers stated definitively in relevant primary authorities, most research projects will not have an obvious and natural stopping point. For questions of first impression, no binding authority exists in your jurisdiction on which you may rely. Other issues can be resolved in part, but some sub-questions may remain unanswered. While the art of ending the research process is one you must develop through experience, the following strategies may help you identify an appropriate stopping point.

Ask yourself if the resources you have discovered are responsive to the questions you are attempting to answer or the issues you are working to address. The analysis chart in Table 12-3 may help you determine when you have sufficient answers to the relevant questions, assuming you have developed the chart in a detailed and thoughtful way. If issues remain unaddressed, review the basic steps in the research process again and consider whether you have neglected to work through any steps. If there is no binding authority in your jurisdiction on a particular issue, have you considered persuasive or analogous authority? Has your research put you in a position to make a persuasive argument, even if there is no dispositive authority for your issue? Finally, be attentive to the point in your research when you cease to find new authorities on point. When continued work fails to yield new results, you have likely reached an appropriate stopping point.

Appendix A

Legal Citation

I. Introduction

American life is governed by legal rules. There are rules against crimes, rules about roads and cars, and rules governing marriage. Citation rules allow attorneys and citizens alike to efficiently identify and locate the legal rules that impact them.

Legal citation rules are also important for another reason—precedent. In the American legal system, every statement of law must be established by referring to a court opinion, statute, regulation, or other primary law source. In fact, several Oklahoma courts have stated that "[a] proposition unsupported by argument or citation of authority will not be considered on appeal."[1] Moreover, as an individual court applies legal rules to the particular case before it, the court must take into account not only the text of any relevant statute or regulation, but also the rules established by higher courts as they interpreted the statute or regulation. In other words, lower courts must know what higher courts have said about a particular legal rule and how they have interpreted it. Legal citation rules allow judges and attorneys to clearly and efficiently identify earlier court opinions, statutes, regulations, and other types of legal publications.

Table A-1 describes the four major purposes for legal citation rules.

---

1. *See Mid-Continent Cas. Co. v. Jenkins*, 1967 OK 54, ¶ 14, 431 P.2d 349 (Okla. 1967); *Hough v. Hough*, 2004 OK 45, ¶ 16, 92 P.3d 695 (Okla. 2004).

Table A-1. Purposes of Legal Citation Rules*

1.Tells the reader where to find the cited source and the page(s) of any specific references.
2.Indicates the weight and persuasiveness of the cited source, such as the level of court or the jurisdiction of the law being discussed.
3.Conveys the type and degree of support, such as when a case contradicts or supports a particular statement.
4.Demonstrates that a position is well researched and well supported, and gives credit to others their original ideas appearing in the document.

*Adapted from *AWLD Citation Manual: A Professional System of Citation* (4th ed. 2010).

Legal citation is truly an exercise in precision and detail. Both of the major citation manuals contain dozens of rules with dozens more variations within each rule. Citation rules specify everything from typeface to spacing to abbreviations to capitalization. If you are off by one number or if you mistype an abbreviation, you might lead the reader (often the judge in your case!) on a wild goose chase looking for the cited case, statute, or other publication.

II. Sources of Legal Citation Rules

There are two major sources for legal citation rules: local court rules and citation manuals. Courts often have citation requirements included within their local court rules. These rules may be published as part of the state statutes, in an annual print publication, or separately on the court's website. Before filing any documentation with a court, check the citation (and other formatting) rules for the court in question.

There are also two national citation manuals used by the legal profession: *The Bluebook: A Uniform System of Citation* and the *ALWD Citation Manual: A Professional System of Citation.* Both of these citation manuals provide exhaustive and highly detailed rules for every type of legal publication. This chapter will explore Oklahoma citation rules and the two national legal citation manuals, but it will first begin with some general legal citation principles and examples.

III. Legal Citation Basics

Although each court can establish its own citation rules, there are some general citation principles that are commonly used in every jurisdiction in the United States. This section will describe a few basic concepts and provide a few examples that will allow novice researchers to locate court opinions, statutes, and law journal articles.

A. Court Opinions

Citations to court opinions are composed of six parts: (1) the case name (which includes the names of the parties), (2) the reporter volume, (3) the abbreviated reporter name, (4) the beginning page number of the case, (5) the date the case was decided, and (6) an indication of the court that decided the case. Citations to court opinions often also include a pinpoint cite page number. Figure A-1 illustrates a typical citation to a U.S. Supreme Court opinion. In this citation, the case name is "*Roe v. Wade*." The case can be found in volume 410 of the *United States Reports*, which is abbreviated "U.S.," and it begins on page 113 of that volume. Finally, the case was decided in 1973. This citation does not need a special indicator of the court that decided the case because only decisions of the U.S. Supreme Court are included in *United States Reports*. For cases published in a regional reporter, like the *Pacific Reporter*, an abbreviation is included in the date parenthetical to indicate which state court decided the case. See Tables A-2 through A-5 later in this chapter for additional examples.

Figure A-1. Components of a Case Citation

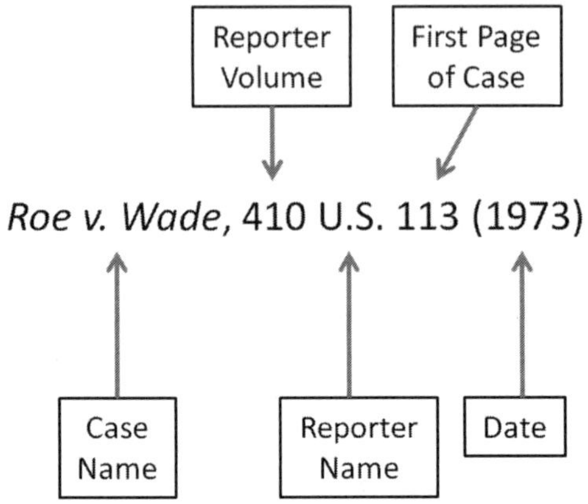

The citation format is based on how cases have historically been published in print reporters. In other words, the citation provides the reporter name, the volume number, and the first page because that is the information a researcher would need to locate the case in a print reporter. However, the same citation will work in all online legal research systems, such as Westlaw, Lexis, or Bloomberg Law, to retrieve the case. Figure A-2 shows how the first page of the decision looks, as it was reported in the *Supreme Court Reporter*, which is published by West. The citation to *Roe v. Wade* in that reporter is 93 S. Ct. 705 (1973).

Some jurisdictions, including Oklahoma, have an official vendor neutral citation format, which is usually based on paragraph numbering. For example, in Oklahoma, you might encounter a citation that looks like this: *Skinner v. Braum's Ice Cream Store*, 1995 OK 11, 890 P.2d 922. In this instance, the first citation shown—1995 OK 11—is the required Oklahoma paragraph citation format. "1995" refers to the year the case was decided. "OK" is the abbreviation for

Figure A-2. Excerpt of a Sample Case in a Print Reporter

410 U.S. 113 **ROE v. WADE** **705**

Cite as 93 S.Ct. 705 (1973)

410 U.S. 113, 35 L.Ed.2d 147

Jane ROE, et al., Appellants,

v.

Henry WADE.

No. 70-18.

Argued Dec. 13, 1971.

Reargued Oct. 11, 1972.

Decided Jan. 22, 1973.

Rehearing Denied Feb. 26, 1973.

See 410 U.S. 959, 93 S.Ct. 1409.

Action was brought for a declaratory and injunctive relief respecting Texas criminal abortion laws which were claimed to be unconstitutional. A

declaratory aspects of case attacking constitutionality of Texas criminal abortion statutes where case was properly before Supreme Court on direct appeal from decision of three-judge district court specifically denying injunctive relief and the arguments as to both aspects were necessarily identical. 28 U.S.C.A. § 1253.

2. Constitutional Law ⚿42.1(3), 46(1)

With respect to single, pregnant female who alleged that she was unable to obtain a legal abortion in Texas, when viewed as of the time of filing of case and for several months thereafter, she had standing to challenge constitution-

the Oklahoma Supreme Court, and "11" indicates that the *Skinner* opinion is the eleventh opinion issued by the Court in 1995. Note that this format is primarily used to locate court opinions online in Oklahoma via the Oklahoma State Court Network.[2] There is no dedicated print source that uses the paragraph citation format in Oklahoma. In print, Oklahoma cases are published by West in the *Pacific Reporter* (first, second, and third series), and that is the designated "official reporter" in Oklahoma.[3] Paragraph numbering of Oklahoma cases does appear in cases reported in the *Pacific Reporter*.

---

2. Oklahoma State Court Network, http://www.oscn.net.

3. Okla.Sup.Ct.R. 1.200(c).

4. Some statutory codes have titles that are topics rather than numbers. For example, California's statutes have titles such as "Civil Procedure," "Labor," and "Probate."

B. Statutes

Citation rules for statues are more varied than citation rules for court opinions, but again, there are some general concepts that apply to all jurisdictions. A typical statutory citation is composed of four parts: (1) the title of the statutory code,[4] (1) the name of statutory code, (3) the section of the code, and (4) the year the code was published. The federal statute cited in Figure A-3 specifies when stars are added to the United States flag.

To locate the statute in Figure A-3 using a print source, you would first locate the *United States Code Annotated* (USCA), published by West. You would next look for a volume that contains title 4. In print, the title number of each volume will be printed on the spine. Finally,

Figure A-3. Components of a Statutory Citation

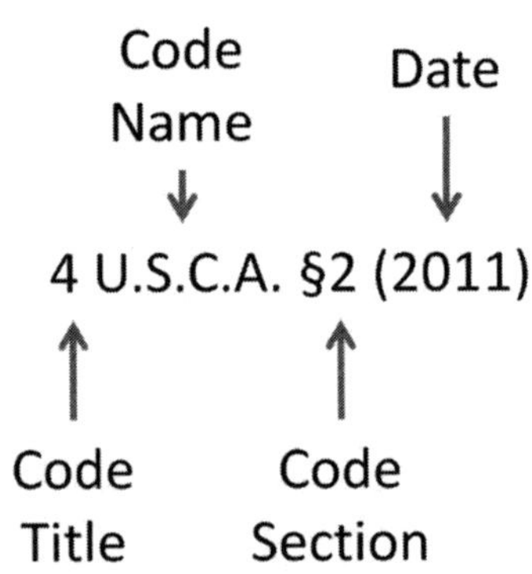

you would look for section 2. Section ranges are typically printed on the spine of each volume, and the top corner of each page indicates the section numbers found on that particular page. When researching online, you need only enter the citation into the Westlaw, Lexis, Bloomberg Law, or another service, and the statutory section will be retrieved automatically.

Figure A-4. Components of a Law Journal Citation

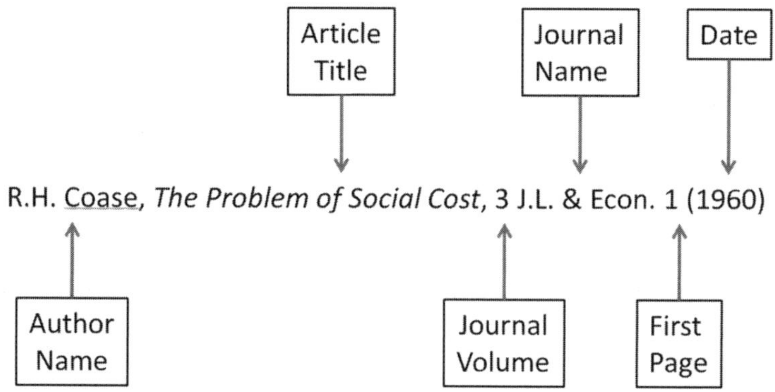

C. Law Journals and Law Reviews

Citations for law journals are written in a similar fashion to court opinions because law journals are published chronologically, in much the same way as court opinions. Each issue of a law journal is published in chronological order, and one or more issues make up a volume for each journal. A typical law journal citation is composed of six parts: (1) the author of the article, (2) the article title, (3) the volume of the journal, (4) the abbreviated journal name, (5) the beginning page number, and (6) the date. In the example shown in Figure A-4, the author of the article is "R.H. Coase." The title of the article is "*The Problem of Social Cost.*" The article was published in volume 3 of the *Journal of Law and Economics*, and it began on page 1 of that volume. Finally, it was published in 1960.

D. Abbreviations

In order to understand a legal citation, you must be able to interpret the abbreviations that are used. Abbreviations are used for everything from court names to journal titles to geographic designations. The reason so many abbreviations are used has to do with the way legal documents and court opinions are written. The legal profession has a tradition of placing citations right in the text of the memo, brief, or court opinion. Abbreviations minimize the space taken by citations while still providing enough information for the reader to located the cited source.

In the citation example in Figure A-1, A-3, and A-4, you must be able to determine that "U.S.." stands for *United States Reports*, that U.S.C.A. refers to the *United States Code Annotated*, and that "J.L. & Econ." stands for the *Journal of Law and Economics* in order to find the *Roe v. Wade* case, the statute, and journal article in question. Thankfully, the major online research services are able to interpret the abbreviations of most legal publications automatically. So, simply by entering the citation "410 U.S. 113," the online research service will retrieve the desired case. However, when using print resources, you may need to consult one of the major citation manuals to interpret an abbreviation.

The Bluebook and the *ALWD Citation Manual* (which are discussed in more detail later in this chapter) contain tables that allow researchers to interpret abbreviations. Abbreviations are broken down by jurisdiction and publication type. So, for instance, in *The Bluebook*, a researcher can look in the Oklahoma section of Table 1 to find the abbreviations for Oklahoma case reporters, statutes, and regulations. Abbreviations for law journals can be found in Table 13.

E. Pinpoint Citations

Pinpoint citations are citations to a specific page of a court opinion or law journal article. Keep in mind that court opinions are often 50, 100, or even 150 pages long, and each opinion can discuss dozens of issues and make many statements of law. When citing to a prior case to support your client's position, you must use pinpoint cites to direct the reader to the exact page or paragraph of the case that supports your position and states the law that is at issue. This saves the reader the trouble of having to read the entire case to locate the quotation or statement of law to which you are referring.

A pinpoint citation is simply another number, following the first page in the citation, referring the reader to a specific page in the case where a particular statement of law or quotation occurs. For example, assume that you want to cite to a statement of law on page 116 of the *Roe v. Wade* case. You would write the citation in the following way:

> Our task, of course, is to resolve the issue by constitutional measurement, free of emotion and of predilection. *Roe v. Wade*, 410 U.S. 113, 116 (1973).

Placing "116" in the citation indicates to the reader that the *Roe* case begins on page 113, but the statement to which you are referring is located on page 116 of the *Roe* case as it appears in the *United States Reports*.

In jurisdictions that use a paragraph citation form, such as Oklahoma, pinpoint citations are written using paragraph numbers. For instance, to direct the reader to paragraph 9 of the Oklahoma case *Christian v. Gray*, the pinpoint citation would be written in the following way: *Christian v. Gray*, 2003 OK 10, ¶ 9, 65 P.3d 591.

F. Parallel Citations

Court opinions are often published in more than one reporter. In addition to West's National Reporter System, there are a variety of other specialty reporters and reporters published by other vendors. For example, U.S. Supreme Court opinions are published in three major reporters: the *United States Reports* (U.S.), the *Supreme Court Reporter* (S. Ct.), and the *United States Supreme Court Reports, Lawyers' Edition* (L. Ed.). The *Roe v. Wade* case discussed earlier in this chapter is an example of case with parallel citation to all three Supreme Court reporters: *Roe v. Wade*, 410 U.S. 113, 93 S. Ct. 705, 35 L. Ed. 2d 147 (1973).

Some citation rules will require parallel citations to multiple reporters. For instance, Oklahoma Court of Criminal Appeals Rule 3.5 (discussed below) requires that all citations to U.S. Supreme Court opinions include parallel citations to all three Supreme Court reporters.

IV. Oklahoma Citation Rules

Oklahoma has specific rules that govern citations to Oklahoma court opinions, Oklahoma statutes, and Oklahoma regulations. Rules for citing to court opinions can be found in the court rules of the Oklahoma Supreme Court and the Oklahoma Court of Criminal Appeals. Statutory citation rules can be found in the print volumes of the *Oklahoma Statutes* and its supplements. Rules for citing to regulations can be found at the beginning of the print volumes of the *Oklahoma Administrative Code* and the *Oklahoma Register*. Oklahoma has not expressly adopted either of the national citation manuals as the official style guide for legal citations. In practice, *The Bluebook* is used in Oklahoma as the citation manual of choice unless a specific court rule exists.

A. Rules for Citing to Oklahoma Court Opinions

The Oklahoma Supreme Court has established two key rules for citing to court opinions in documents filed with the Oklahoma courts: Rule 1.11 and Rule 1.200.[5] Rule 1.11(l) has three specific requirements. First, it requires that citations to all opinions of the Oklahoma Supreme Court and the Oklahoma Court of Civil Appeals shall be in accordance with Rule 1.200 (discussed below). Second, it requires that all other citations to court opinions shall be to West's National Reporter System, which includes the regional reporters, the *Federal Supplement*, the *Federal Reporter*, and the *Supreme Court Reporter*. The third requirement of this rule states that U.S. Supreme Court opinions shall be cited to the official reporter, the *United States Reports*, though parallel citations to the other Supreme Court reporters may also be included.

Rule 1.200 establishes a vendor neutral, paragraph citation form for citing to Oklahoma court opinions. Oklahoma Supreme Court and Oklahoma Court of Civil Appeals opinions published after May 1, 1997, must be cited using the official paragraph citation form, and they must also include a citation to the official reporter, the *Pacific*

5. Okla.Sup.Ct.R. 1.200 (2012).

Table A-2. Oklahoma Citation Forms After May 1, 1997

Skinner v. Braum's Ice Cream Store, 1995 OK 11, 890 P.2d 922.
Skinner v. Braum's Ice Cream Store, 1995 OK 11, ¶9, 890 P.2d 922.
Skinner v. Braum's Ice Cream Store, 1995 OK 11, ¶9, 890 P.2d 922, 925.
Skinner v. Braum's Ice Cream Store, 1995 OK 11, n. 10, 890 P.2d 922.

Reporter. Court opinions published prior to May 1, 1997, must include a citation to the *Pacific Reporter* (including the more recent second and third series). For these older cases, a parallel citation to the official paragraph citation form is permitted but not required.

Table A-2 shows permissible examples of citations to Oklahoma Supreme Court and Oklahoma Court of Civil Appeals opinions decided after May 1, 1997. Notice how the citation includes both the Oklahoma paragraph citation form (1995 OK 11) and the citation to the official *Pacific Reporter* (890 P.2d 922).

Table A-3 shows permissible examples of citations to an Oklahoma court opinion published prior May 1, 1997. Notice that a citation to the Oklahoma paragraph citation form is not to be included as a parallel citation. Here, either citation may include any pinpoint pagination. Note that either "Okla." or "Okl." may be used as an abbreviation for Oklahoma. When citing only to the *Pacific Reporter*, a state abbreviation is needed to notify the reader that the case is an Oklahoma case. The *Pacific Reporter* includes court opinions from a dozen western states.

The Oklahoma Court of Criminal Appeals (OCCA) also has rules that govern citation to its own opinions. Rule 3.5(c) of the OCCA has several requirements.[6] First, Rule 3.5(C)(2)(a) requires that all citations to OCCA opinions must include citations to the *Pacific*, *Pacific*

6. Oklahoma Court of Criminal Appeals, *Rules of the Oklahoma Court of Criminal Appeals*, http://www.okcca.net/online/rules/rulesrvr.jsp?r=26.

Table A-3. Oklahoma Citation Forms Before May 1, 1997

Skinner v. Braum's Ice Cream Store, 1995 OK 11, 890 P.2d 922.
Skinner v. Braum's Ice Cream Store, 1995 OK 11, ¶ 9, 890 P.2d 922.
Skinner v. Braum's Ice Cream Store, 1995 OK 11, 890 P.2d 922, 925.
Skinner v. Braum's Ice Cream Store, 890 P.2d 922 (Okla. 1995)
Skinner v. Braum's Ice Cream Store, 890 P.2d 922, 925 (Okla. 1995).
Skinner v. Braum's Ice Cream Store, 890 P.2d 922 (Okl. 1995).
Skinner v. Braum's Ice Cream Store, 890 P.2d 922, 925 (Okl. 1995).
Skinner v. Braum's Ice Cream Store, Okl., 890 P.2d 922 (1995).
Skinner v. Braum's Ice Cream Store, Okl., 890 P.2d 922, 925 (1995).

2d, and *Pacific 3d* reporters. Citations to Oklahoma's paragraph citation form are permitted but not required.

Effective January 1, 1998, the following citation rules also apply. For OCCA opinions issued prior to January 1, 1954, citation to the *Pacific Reporter* and *Pacific 2d* is required. Parallel citations to the *Oklahoma Criminal Reports* are strongly encouraged, but not required. Table A-4 has examples of permissible citations forms, as provided in the OCCA rules.

For OCCA opinions issued after January 1, 1954, citations to the *Pacific, Pacific 2d, and Pacific 3d* are required. Parallel citations to the

Table A-4. OCCA Citation Examples Prior to 1954

Hunter v. State, 97 Okl.Cr. 402, 264 P.2d 997 (1953).
Hunter v. State, 97 Okl.Cr. 402, 264 P.2d 997, 998 (1953).
Hunter v. State, 97 Okl.Cr. 402, 403, 264 P.2d 997, 998 (1953).
Hunter v. State, 264 P.2d 997 (Okl.Cr.1953).
Hunter v. State, 264 P.2d 997, 998 (Okl.Cr.1953).

Table A-5. OCCA Citation Examples After January 1, 1954

Burns v. State, 1955 OK CR 46, 282 P.2d 258.
Burns v. State, 1955 OK CR 46, 282 P.2d 258, 259.
Burns v. State, 1955 OK CR 46, ¶ 9, 282 P.2d 258, 259.
Burns v. State, 282 P.2d 258 (Okl.Cr.1955).
Burns v. State, 282 P.2d 258, 259 (Okl.Cr.1955).

official Oklahoma paragraph citation form are strongly encouraged. See Table A-5 for examples of permissible citation forms, as provided in the OCCA rules.

With regard to U.S. Supreme Court opinions, Rule 3.5(C)(4) requires citation to all three of the Supreme Court reporters: *United States Reports* (U.S.), the *Supreme Court Reporter* (S. Ct.), and the *United States Supreme Court Reports, Lawyers' Edition* (L. Ed.).

Rule 3.5(C)(6) states that "[f]ailure to present relevant authority in compliance with these requirements will result in the issue being forfeited on appeal."[7] It is critical for attorneys and anyone filing documents with the court to provide the supporting authority with appropriate legal citations.

B. Rules for Citing to Oklahoma Statutes

Citations to the *Oklahoma Statutes* are governed by a rule found at the beginning of the first volume of the statutes themselves. The rule states: "This Edition shall be cited as "O.S.2011" including Title and Section, namely: 4 O.S.2011, §42.1."[8] There is one additional rule regarding proper statute citation form used in Oklahoma, and it is based on the way that the official Oklahoma statutes are published. The official statutes are published in full every 10 years. Annual sup-

7. Oklahoma Court of Criminal Appeals, Rule 3.5(C)(6), http://www.okcca.net/online/rules/rulesrvr.jsp?r=26.

8. *Oklahoma Statutes 2011*, at IX.

plements, in the form of separate hardbound volumes, are published every year. As a result, if a new version of a statute has been published since the last full compilation of the statutes, the abbreviation "Supp." is inserted into the citation. Instructions on citing to statutes found in the supplement can be found at the beginning of the first volume of *Oklahoma Statutes*. The rule states: "Cite this supplement by Title and Section thus: ___ O.S.Supp, § ___."[9] For example, assume the year is 2012. The 2012 supplement to the Oklahoma Statutes contained the most recent additions to the *Oklahoma Statutes* because the last full compilation of the statutes occurred in 2001. A citation to a new statute in the 2012 supplement would look like this: 12 O.S.Supp.2012 § 551. Note that court opinions more frequently put a space just before the "Supp." part of the citation, although no space is shown in rule as stated in the statutes.[10]

Regarding annotated statutes, the preface to the *Oklahoma Statutes Annotated*, published by West, states that citations to the annotated statutes shall be in the following format: ___ Okl. St. Ann. § ___. However, this format is rarely seen in Oklahoma court opinions. Practitioners, as described above, more frequently use citations to the official Oklahoma Statutes.

C. Rules for Citing Oklahoma Court Rules

Rule 1.1(a) of the Oklahoma Supreme Court states that citations to its rules shall be in the following format: Okla.Sup.Ct.R. [Rule Number]. Rule 1.0(D) of the Oklahoma Court of Criminal Appeals states that citations to the rules of that court shall use the following format: Rule ___, *Rules of the Oklahoma Court of Criminal Appeals*, Title 22, Ch 18, App. (year).

---

9. *2010 Supplement, Oklahoma Statutes*, at XI.

10. As of July 15, 2012, approximately 6,300 court opinions did not place a space before "Supp." and approximately 1,300 did use a space.

11. *Oklahoma Administrative Code: 2011 Edition*, at xi.

D. Rules for Citing to Oklahoma Regulations

Oklahoma regulations are first published in the *Oklahoma Register* and later compiled in subject arrangement in the *Oklahoma Administrative Code.* Rules for citing to regulations can be found at the front of each of these publications. Citations to a regulation in the *Oklahoma Administrative Code* should follow this format: OAC 165:56-5-3.[11] In this example, the number 165 refers to the title of code, which is "Corporation Commission." The number 56 refers to a chapter within title 165. Chapter 56 relates to "Resellers of Interexchange Telecommunications Services." The number 5 refers to a subchapter within chapter 56, and finally, the number 3 refers to the section number within that subchapter.

New regulations appearing in the *Oklahoma Register* should be cited "by the volume and the beginning page number of the document in the *Register. For example: 28 OK Reg 256.*"[12] The number 28 refers to the volume of the *Oklahoma Register*, and the number 256 refers to the beginning page number of that volume where the cited regulation appears.

V. The Bluebook

The Bluebook: A Uniform System of Citation is the most widely used and longest running citation manual in the legal profession.[13] Currently in its nineteenth edition, *The Bluebook* is compiled by the editors of the Columbia Law Review, the Harvard Law Review, the University of Pennsylvania Law Review, and the Yale Law Journal. It was first published in 1926 as an internal style guide for the Harvard Law Review.[14]

---

12. See the inside front cover of every *Oklahoma Register* edition.

13. According to a recent survey of legal writing directors at law schools, *The Bluebook* is taught at the sole citation manual by approximately 70% of U.S. law schools. Association of Legal Writing Directors, *Report of the Annual Legal Writing Survey 2011*, http://www.alwd.org/surveys/survey_results/2011_LWI_ALWD_Survey.pdf, at page vi. Another 7% teach both *The Bluebook* and the *ALWD Citation Manual*, and 6% leave the choice of which citation manual to use up to the individual writing faculty. *Id.*

14. Darby Dickerson, *An Un-Uniform System of Citation: Surviving with the New Bluebook*, 26 Stet L. Rev. 53, 61 (1996).

The first edition was a mere twenty-six pages long. The nineteenth edition has grown to a whopping 512 pages of citation rules covering U.S. federal and state primary law publications, print and online publications, secondary sources, and foreign and international publications.

The Bluebook contains three separate parts. The first part, called the "blue pages" because they are printed on blue paper, is a "how-to-guide created primarily for practitioners and law clerks to use when citing authority within non-academic legal documents."[15] At the end of the blue pages is a table that lists jurisdiction-specific citation rules. This table is extremely important for practitioners because it tells them when local rules may override the rules found in *The Bluebook.*

The second part of *The Bluebook* contains the detailed citation rules themselves. There are twenty-one rules in all covering everything from citing cases and statutes to citing Internet sources and web pages to citing foreign and international sources. The first eight rules cover topics like introductory signals (for example, *See, E.g., Cf.*), typefaces conventions, short citation forms (for example, *Id., Supra*), quotations, abbreviations, and capitalization. The remaining rules cover each type of legal publication, such as cases, statutes, regulations, books, periodicals, online sources, and foreign and international sources. It is important to remember that the instructions and examples in this part of *The Bluebook* are aimed at academic writing. While practitioners will need to refer to the rules in this part of *The Bluebook*, reference to the blue pages in part one will show what citations look like in practice documents.

The final part of *The Bluebook* contains tables showing abbreviations and sample citations. Table 1 provides examples of common citations for every jurisdiction in the U.S. For instance, the Oklahoma section of Table 1 provides examples of citations to all of the opinions of Oklahoma courts, Oklahoma statutes and session laws, and Oklahoma regulations and administrative decisions. Again, this part of *The Bluebook* is intended for academic publications.

15. *The Bluebook: A Uniform System of Citation* 3 (19th ed. 2010).

Probably the two most heavily used pages of *The Bluebook* are the inside of the front and back covers. The inside of the front cover is a quick reference guide for law review authors and editors that gives examples of commonly used citation forms printed in the typefaces used in law review footnotes. The back cover is a quick reference guide for attorneys and other legal professionals; it gives examples of commonly used citation forms printed in the typefaces used in briefs and legal memoranda.

VI. ALWD Citation Manual

The *ALWD Citation Manual: A Professional System of Citation* is an alternative citation manual to *The Bluebook*. It is prepared by the Association of Legal Writing Directors (ALWD). The first edition was first published in 2000, and it is currently in its fourth edition. It is primarily a guide for teaching legal citation,[16] and only a few courts have formally adopted it as their official citation manual.

The *ALWD Citation Manual* distinguishes itself from *The Bluebook* through its clear explanations and abundant examples.[17] It has many of the same features as *The Bluebook*. It presents the main body of citation rules in forty-nine separate rules, and it includes appendices at the end, similar to *The Bluebook's* tables, which provide jurisdiction-

---

16. According to a 2011 survey of legal writing professionals at U.S. law schools, the *ALWD Citation Manual* has been adopted as the sole citation manual by 14.4% of law schools. Association of Legal Writing Directors, *Report of the Annual Legal Writing Survey 2011*, http://www.alwd.org/surveys/survey_results/2011_LWI_ALWD_Survey.pdf, at page vi. As noted earlier, 7% of law schools teach both *The Bluebook* and the *ALWD Citation Manual*, while another 6% vary as to which citation manual writing faculty use. *Id.*

17. The *ALWD Citation Manual* was created because the ALWD saw a need for a "citation manual that is easy to use, easy to teach from, and easy to learn from." Preface, *ALWD Citation Manual: A Professional System of Citation,* at xxiii.

specific citation rules and examples and tables of abbreviations for law journals, courts, and other bodies.

Citations in briefs and legal memoranda under the two manuals—*The Bluebook* and the *ALWD Citation Manual*—are often identical.

About the Authors

Darin K. Fox is Director of the Law Library and Professor of Law at the Donald E. Pray Law Library at the University of Oklahoma College of Law. He received his law degree from the University of Oklahoma and his masters degree in Library and Information Science from the University of Illinois. He was previously Associate Dean for Information Technology and Law Library at the University of Southern California Law School in Los Angeles before returning to Oklahoma.

Darla Jackson is Director of the McKusick Law Library at the University of South Dakota. Until 2012, she was the Associate Law Library Director at Oklahoma City University School of Law. She received her law degree and a masters degree in Library and Information Studies from the University of Oklahoma and holds an LL.M. and another masters degree from other institutions. She has taught at the University of Oklahoma School of Library and Information Studies, the Oklahoma City University Meinders School of Business and School of Law, and the United States Air Force Academy.

Courtney L. Selby is the Associate Dean for Information Services, Director of the Law Library, and Associate Professor of Law at the Maurice A. Deane School of Law at Hofstra University. Previously, she was the Collection Development and Instructional Services Law Librarian at the University of Tulsa College of Law Mabee Legal Information Center. She is a graduate of the University of Tulsa College of Law and holds a masters degree in Library and Information Studies from the University of Oklahoma.

Index